TRANSITIONS

AMERICAN VALUES OF DEMOCRACY AND FREE MARKETS IN THE POST-COLD WAR WORLD

A Memoir

by

Ted Weihe

Other Books by the Author

Saving Fine Chocolate: Equity, Productivity and Quality in Cocoa Co-ops

Chocolate & Cooperative Equity: Reforming Small Farmer Co-ops So They Can Prosper

Elizabeth Weihe: A Centennial Life

Vernon I. Weihe: Avionics Pioneer

Model Boats from Around the World

Falling in Love with MC Scows & Racing Tips I Need to Learn

Built for the Bay: The Chesapeake 20

Preface

This book is about transitions. At the end of the Cold War, the United States tried to export its vision of free markets and democracy. There was euphoria as we thought we would usher in a new world order consistent with U.S. values.

On November 9, 1989, jubilant Germans brought down the most visible symbol of division at the heart of Europe—the Berlin Wall. For two generations, the Wall was the physical representation of the Iron Curtain. Its fall symbolized the end of the Cold War.

The peaceful collapse of the former Soviet bloc regimes was not pre-ordained. Soviet tanks crushed demonstrators in East Berlin in June 1953, Hungary in 1956, and Czechoslovakia in 1968.

As the Wall came down and the fears of a Soviet reaction receded, the dominoes started falling quickly.

Mikhail Gorbachev's policies of perestroika (restructuring) and glasnost (transparency) legitimized popular calls for reform in Eastern and Central socialist countries. The Soviet Union abandoned its policy of military intervention.

On February 6, 1989, negotiations between the Polish government and members of Solidarity opened in Warsaw. By August 24, 1989, ten years after Solidarity emerged, Tadeusz Mazowiecki won a crushing electoral victory to become the first non-communist prime minister in Eastern Europe.

In Hungary, drastic changes were under way. The government, already the most liberal of the communist governments, allowed free association and assembly and ordered the opening of the country's border with the West.

In October 1989, riot police arrested hundreds of demonstrators in Prague and weeks later, many thousands protested the government. A new, non-communist government took the country's reins on December 29, 1989 as Vaclav Havel, the famed playwright and dissident, was elected president.

In Bulgaria, protests led to the removal of Todor Zhivkov, the long-time leader of the Bulgarian Communist Party, and his replacement with reformist communist, Petar Mlaenov. The new government quickly announced that the government would hold free elections in 1990.

Only in Romania did these momentous events turn violent. Nicolae Ceausescu, an increasingly idiosyncratic relic of Stalinist times, refused any reforms. On December 17, 1989 in Timisoara, the army and police fired into crowds protesting government policies, killing dozens. Protests and violence spread to other cities. Ceausescu fled to Bucharest, was arrested and along with his wife was executed on December 25, 1989. The interim government, led by a reformist communist Ion Iliescu, came to power.

The former communist regimes of Poland, Hungary, East Germany and Czechoslovakia were governed by newly formed center-right parties for the first time since the end of World War II.

In the early 1990s, Yugoslavia broke into separate republics: Slovenia, Croatia, Bosnia and Herzegovina, Serbia, Montenegro and Macedonia. Civil and ethnic wars broke out in Bosnia, Croatia and the semi-autonomous Kosovo.

In 1990, Milošević began to lose power in the first multi-party elections held. War broke out across the republics with the Dayton Accords ending the Bosnian war. In 2000, Milošević was overthrown. On May 21, 2006, Montenegro held an independence referendum and separated from Serbia.

The last Soviet bloc country to topple was Albania. Enver Hoxha and his successors governed the most repressive and isolated country in Europe. In 1991, the socialist republic dissolved and the Republic of Albania was established.

On June 12, 1991, Boris Yeltsin was elected by popular vote to the newly created post of president of the Russian Soviet Federative Socialist Republic (RSFSR). With the forced resignation of Mikhail Gorbachev, Yeltsin's election led to the dissolution of the Soviet Union.

With the end of the Cold War, the course was set for a reintegrated Eastern and Central Europe into Western economic, political, and security frameworks. A new era was expected in U.S. relationships with the former Soviet republics.

These transitions did not take place only in Europe.

In the Philippines, Cory Aquino was the most prominent figure of the 1986 People Power Revolution. She ended the 20-year authoritarian rule of President Ferdinand E. Marcos and restored democracy. In 1988, Chile undertook a national plebiscite which General Pinochet lost, and in October 1989, Christian Democrat Patricio Aylwin won the democratic election with 55% of the vote.

The Farabundo Martí National Liberation Front (FMLN) was winning the Salvadoran Civil War until the Soviet Union collapsed along with its support. After peace accords signed in 1992, armed FMLN units were demobilized, and their organization became a legal left-wing political party in El Salvador. On March 15, 2009, the FMLN won the presidential elections with former journalist Mauricio Funes as its candidate.

In Ecuador, elections were held on April 29, 1979 after nearly a decade of civilian and military dictatorships. In 2006, Rafael Correa gained the presidency as a socialist and first Indian to rule the country.

In 1995, the Oslo Accords marked the start of a peace process between Israel and the PLO. Its goal was to fulfill the "right of the Palestinian people to self-determination." The Palestinian Authority took control over the West Bank from Jordan though a heavy Israeli military presence continues.

Transition projects began

The U.S. Agency for International Development (USAID) immediately began programs in each of these countries. It supported political reformers, private businesses and organizations that espoused democratic and free market values.

I was present at the beginning of all of these transformations: Albania, Bosnia, Bulgaria, Chile, Croatia, El Salvador, Estonia, Georgia, Montenegro, Palestine/West Bank, Philippines, Poland, Romania, Russia, South Sudan and Ukraine. In many cases, I flew into the countries within weeks of the formation of democratic governments.

It was a magical moment with much hope and new opportunities. As a student and in the military, I was a Cold Warrior in thought and service. The sudden transformations turned me into a democratic reformer.

Globalization, reintegration with Western markets and dissolution of state companies fueled private sector entrepreneurship. Democratic reformers toppled dictatorships. They mobilized people's movements through Internet and social media.

In each country, family-owned companies and nascent cooperatives emerged to compete with failing state enterprises and collective farms. Successful projects relied on the simplest but profound premise of people-to-people assistance by Americans who held deep beliefs in democracy and lifelong experiences in running successful businesses and farms.

Newly democratic countries faced daunting challenges in the transition to market economies with displaced state workers, weak political institutions, rapid privatization and dismantling of state companies and farm collectives.

Deep corruption remained pervasive. The hope was that a new class of democrats and private business leaders would win the battle of ideas and political power. At the same time, hardships were devastating for former state employees and pensioners who experienced hyperinflation, loss of personal security, and anguish in trying to shift their mind sets from socialism to market economics.

Authoritarian leaders learned how to regain or consolidate power and oppress individuals, democratic parties and press freedoms, especially human rights organizations. This backlash cut off donor funding for non-governmental organizations in Egypt, Russia, Ecuador and other countries.

These unscrupulous leaders successfully used ethnic differences and loss of national pride to divide and usher in counter-revolutions.

Former apparatchik and oligarchs took over the large and even small enterprises in the former Soviet republics and stifled the emergence of an entrepreneurial class.

Despite these newly repressive regimes, a ground swell of entrepreneurs and democratic advocates achieved immediate results. Much progress took place on market reforms. The bi-polar conflict between communism and free enterprise systems no longer existed.

Today, the ingrained values of private enterprise and democratic forces in these societies remain hopeful despite the rise of terrorism, ethnic and religious conflicts and failed states.

Facing a changed world

No experience changed me more than the Spartan conditions and moral dilemma as an Air Force ICBM launch officer; I was an opponent of the Vietnam war while I was in college, disillusioned with authority and could not imagine that I would be responsible for killing millions of people.

In a Congressional trip to Israel immediately after the signing of the Camp David Accords, we failed to slow Israeli settlements on the West Bank. The seeds of violence in Palestine were planted with military occupation and two Intifada uprisings.

Through an unprecedented emergency food aid amendment, a million refugees in Pakistan, Thailand and Ethiopia, and many starving Africans were saved. Mental images of pervasive hunger in Haiti and South Sudan remind me how difficult it is to end extreme poverty.

In Chile, the most effective and largest voter education program resulted in its return to democracy. The human rights leader who led this effort prevented a military coup by General Augusto Pinochet to nullify the plebiscite, which ended his 17-year dictatorship.

Coalitions for foreign aid led shifts in U.S. resources from Cold War security programs to people-centered humanitarian assistance: The Floating Crap Game at the Methodist building across from the Supreme Court with mostly religious groups, Action for World Development at the Chamber of Commerce with international businesses, and Private Agencies in Development, now InterAction, a lobby for 180 humanitarian organizations.

The ultimate coalition for international funding, the U.S. Global Leadership Coalition (GLC), is led by all living former Secretaries of State, National Security Advisors and over 140 retired Four-Star Generals and Admirals. It placed humanitarian assistance next to diplomacy and the military as critical post-Cold War assets to address international crises.

Role of cooperatives

At its core, this book talks about how cooperatives lift economic and social lives of the disadvantaged in diverse fields of telecommunications, agriculture, insurance, rural electrification, and health.

These cooperatives demonstrate the power of self-help to improve lives and communities. Over 23 years from 1980 to 2003, the coalition of U.S. cooperative development organizations gained a 16-fold increase in USAID funding from $25 million to $400 million, made possible with a new Congressional mandate, earmarks, and directive report language. They remain at the forefront of people-to-people assistance.

American cooperative advisors helped local mayors of Rural Solidarity in Poland gain access to telephones where few existed during communist rule. They hastened agricultural reforms in Bulgaria, Estonia, Macedonia, and Romania in dairy and meat sectors as they began to compete with European imports.

Thousands of dairy women of Albania learned to milk properly, care for their animals and create soft cheeses to feed their families in the poorest country in Europe. They became the backbone of a modern dairy industry.

Cooperatives brought reconciliation to ancient and emerging ethnic conflicts in Macedonia and Bosnia but could not address more ingrained hostilities.

U.S. agricultural volunteers assisted emerging independent farmers and groups in the market transitions of Russia in privatizing collectives, in Georgia in restarting wheat production, and in Ukraine in fruits and vegetables delivered to new Costco-type grocery chains.

Insurance brought peace of mind to credit union members in Barbados and strengthened micro-enterprises in Bolivia, Colombia, and Guatemala. Child survival help babies under five prevent or recover from malaria and other crippling diseases through pre-paid health insurance plans in southern Uganda.

Rural electric coops became *peace dividends* and brought lights to former guerrilla towns in El Salvador and South Sudan as these countries emerged from armed conflict that seems to recur constantly in new forms: youth gangs and tribal warfare.

Fair Trade built direct linkages between small cocoa cooperatives in Ecuador, the Dominican Republic and Peru with U.S. natural food cooperatives, church congregations and American consumers. Quality and productivity improvements at these cooperatives resulted in premiums for the fast-growing dark chocolate market and more money in the pockets of small farmers. Farmers investing in these pioneering cooperatives were able to build capital for their expansion and sustainability

All of these cooperatives in diverse fields and different countries demonstrate that democratic values and changed minds, along with entrepreneurship and group-based businesses, make a more peaceful and hopeful world.

TFW – July 2017 and revised May 2018

Table of Contents

Preface 3

Introduction 14

Chapter 1: Values That Shaped Me.......................25

Chapter 2: Life in the Air Force 39

Chapter 3: Moral Dilemma of a Missileer 59

Chapter 4: An International Career.......................80

Chapter 5: Undercover Trip to Haiti......................91

Chapter 6: Saving a Million Lives 98

Chapter 7: Palestine: The Seeds of Violence............116

Chapter 8: Mr. Cooperative 142

Chapter 9: Advocate for Cooperatives...................156

Chapter 10: Farmer-to-Farmer Volunteers..............190

Chapter 11: Untold Story of Chile's Return to Democracy 203

Chapter 12: Micro-Insurance for the Poor...............253

Chapter 13: Electricity for Peace & Prosperity...........276

Charter 14: Sudan & Yei Electric Coop....................294

Chapter 15: Telephone Coops in Poland...................306

Chapter 16: Market Reforms in Eastern Europe 327

Chapter 17: Seal of Quality in Macedonia 348

Chapter 18: Dairy Farmers of Albania......................358

Chapter 19: Coops in Montenegro & Bosnia 373

Chapter 20: Agricultural Reforms in Russia 387

Chapter 21: Farming Reforms in Georgia 412

Chapter 22: Market Reforms in Ukraine 419

Chapter 23: Sweet Retirement 428

Conclusions 451

Sources...459

Acknowledgements 478

Introduction

Within complex systems, values can be change agents within Congress, U.S. Agency for International Development (USAID), economic assistance, advocacy coalitions and cooperatives.

Systems are conceptual descriptions of how people and institutions are organized. In and of themselves, they are neutral. To bring about change, you must understand complex systems and bring values into play.

Values are defined as broad preferences concerning appropriate courses of action or outcomes. They reflect what "ought" to be. There are ethical and moral values that need to be understood within groups, and values that you bring or align with the group for initiating and influencing behaviors.

The ability to understand, manipulate, and work within these complex systems enables one to achieve innovations and positive results since the systems are inter-related and can be brought together into a coherent whole when needed or desired.

Public or private interest

Congress is difficult to comprehend and is deeply partisan. It does not function as taught in high school classes on "how laws are made." It almost never works that way—bills upward from subcommittee, full committee, floor, conference, etc. Foreign aid legislation is upside down.

"Regular Order" means legislation is authorized with policies set and then funded with appropriations. The reverse occurs with foreign aid legislation which originates in the appropriations

14

committees. Foreign assistance authorization committees have little say, and few foreign aid bills reach the floor. Authorization and appropriations on foreign aid are put into omnibus bills, seldom considered separately on the floor of either the Senate or the House.

The point is that you must work closely with appropriations committees, especially chairmen and staff. You can align your objectives with their support for cooperatives in their own districts. It is an easy stretch to suggest sharing these values and experiences overseas.

There are two types of lobbyists: those who represent the public and those who represent special interests. Public interest lobbyists advocate change with support from broad constituencies whereas the private interest lobbyists benefit a few, those with power, influence and money.

The difference is illustrated by my experience in the natural gas industry. In the 1970s, wellhead gas prices were regulated. The industry created a Committee on Gas Supplies, and it put out a report that natural gas would run out in 20 years if not deregulated – that was 45 years ago. Natural gas supply figures were fabricated. The huge windfall of de-regulation went to the petroleum industry, not natural gas consumers, whose costs went up by billions each year.

In contrast, environmental lobbyists worked for passage of the historic 1974 Clean Air and Water Acts that protect air quality and maintain wetlands as natural purifiers of run off. The American public is a much better, healthier, and the environment cleaner as a result.

As a leader of the Clean Air Coalition, we helped enact health standards based on the levels of air pollution that do not adversely affect children and the elderly. From 1970 to 2010, the Clean Air Act prevented 205,000 early deaths and protected millions of people from illnesses.

The Clean Air Act forced technological changes to meet ever higher standards. As a result, catalytic converters and smoke stack scrubbers dramatically reduced smog in cities and over the Grand Canyon.

The electric utilities and other industries and their private interest lobbyists fought hard to undercut the clean air standards by requiring cost-benefit analysis, rather than health-based standards. They often fabricated the costs, yet retrospective studies in 2011 showed benefits outweighed costs, 30 to 1.

In 2016, President Obama tried to use the Clean Air Act to address global warming by curbing greenhouse gasses under the Paris Accords on global warming. With the 2016 election, the fossil fuel industry and the new administration is reversing these presidential directives through climate change denial, dishonest analysis and moneyed industry lobbyists.

Public interest lobbyists represent public voices of conscience and moral values, not narrow interests. It is a choice that I made in my career.

There are two types of coalitions: broad-based ones that represent large constituencies, and narrow ones that promote private interests. For example, the American public thinks foreign aid is a big part of the budget though it is less than 1%. To educate a skeptical public and Congress, the U.S. Global Leadership Coalition

(GLC) was formed to support the international affairs budget. From modest beginnings in 1994, GLC has grown into a coalition with 21 State-affiliated committees and a staff of 45 as of 2016. GLC brings together Fortune 100 companies, major non-governmental humanitarian, and development organizations and networks of supporters in 50 states who advocate for smart power: military, diplomatic, and development.

GLC advocates historic American values of engagement and peaceful change, not military interventions. It epitomizes U.S. public interest lobbying as well as my views and perspective.

Government-to-government vs grassroots

USAID is another complex bureaucracy. Nominally under the State Department, priorities and programs are often initiated by Congress: micro-finance, child survival, basic education, cooperative development, and biodiversity, among others. Many programs are earmarked.

You cannot understand how USAID works unless you know how it interacts between Congress and the White House.

Initiatives by the White House include Carter's Camp David Accords, Reagan's National Endowment for Democracy and Bush's AIDs program (PEPFAR). The window to understanding USAID and how it functions is to work in its legislative office, the crossroads between executive and legislative branches.

In successfully navigating the USAID bureaucracy, you need to understand how and where decisions are made, and by whom. If there is resistance to programs that you advocate internally, Congress can mandate them.

In USAID, there are different interests: The State Department and USAID missions that mostly advocate strengthening governments and national policies, rather than indigenous, non-governmental organizations.

Which side you choose is a value judgment: capacity building for often corrupt regimes, or support for U.S. and local NGOs that are motivated by humanitarian values. Focusing at the governmental or local level is another choice.

USAID wasted funds on promoting governmental agricultural reforms in Ukraine rather than continue a successful project for fruit and vegetable groups that were flourishing with the growth of the rapidly emerging grocery chains in search of fresh goods.

In Poland, USAID unsuccessfully tried to reform the top-down telecommunications monopoly while reform mayors created two successful telecommunications cooperatives to directly reach unserved rural folks. The mayors generated bottom up reforms that allowed for the first independent telephone companies in Poland.

Many U.S. non-government organizations (NGOs) grew out of our own grassroots movements such as farm cooperatives and credit unions, family planning, women's rights, civil rights, and environmental consciousness and protection.

Overseas, these U.S. organizations promote the same values and strengthen similar movements through their affiliates or counterparts. Land O'Lakes reform efforts for cooperative dairies throughout Eastern Europe were based on its own experience from the 1920's farmers' movement, and the rapid growth of U.S. style credit unions in Poland under Lech Wałęsa was based on a similar U.S. movement in the 1930s.

U.S. NGOs and cooperatives promoted independent advocacy groups as socialist or government-mandated organizations were dismantled in former Soviet bloc countries. The 8,000 strong, woman's dairy network in Albania became an effective voice and coalition for rural women's economic empowerment and rights.

Building broad-based coalitions for change is a difficult and complex endeavor in which emerging leaders must be identified and provided with the organizational tools to mobilize their public. Reforming cooperative laws in the Philippines was achieved through selecting the right leaders and sharing U.S. lobbying techniques and teaching them at regional workshops.

Independent sector

People-to-people and U.S. NGO-to-indigenous NGO programs help create independent sectors, which are neither government nor private enterprise. While not alone as a participatory culture, the U.S. is unmatched in the number of people and nonprofit organizations that impact society through giving, volunteering, and participation. Thus, it is no accident that the U.S. wants to share this experience abroad.

Most of the great movements of our society have origins in the independent sector, for example, abolition of slavery, civil rights, public education, public libraries, women's rights, care and opportunities for the handicapped. The massive voter education program in Chile was based on effective grassroots organizing techniques used by the League of Women Voters that, in turn, grew out of the Suffragette movement.

When individuals and their organizations make the effort not only for causes and helping the poor, something special happens to the giver: a spirit of compassion, comradeship and human connectedness. Giving is an aspect of our lives that is too often taken for granted, and mostly absent in developing countries. Participating in U.S. voluntary technical assistance is life changing through sharing one's expertise. The volunteers learn about other cultures, share ingrained values and build personal and often lasting friendships.

U.S. NGOs are a major component of our independent sector that promote similar "civic space" overseas. They are foundations for free enterprise and democracy; and represent the conscience of society, foster leadership and reform movements.

In my opinion, there is no greater danger to liberty than allowing those in power to have control over their potential reformers. Sufficient political room is necessary for citizen-driven, independent movements to grow and affect political and societal changes. The backlash against U.S. supported NGOs by authoritarian leaders and governments is regrettable but an indicator of their effectiveness in generating reform movements.

Understanding and promoting the role of the independent, nongovernment, nonbusiness sector and its functions has been one of my primary goals in promoting people-to-people assistance.

Cooperatives, value-driven

Economic development projects are complex as well. Bilateral assistance includes USAID, Peace Corps, Inter-American Foundation, and National Endowment for Democracy. Multilateral assistance is provided through the U.N. agencies, World Bank and Inter-American Development Bank, among others, and focuses on government programs.

Bilateral USAID addresses poverty more directly at the grassroots often managed by faith-based organizations. There is a higher value inherent with direct interventions to alleviate poverty such as member-owned credit unions compared to government-based national banks.

Successful economic development is premised on the "development of the mind." If those you are trying to help want to prosper as individuals or businesses, they must change their way of thinking. Self-help and new attitudes are far more powerful than donor-funded physical infrastructure. Individuals associated with NGOs or cooperatives are more likely to change their thinking than those who work in government.

Cooperatives are not simple enterprises. They combine group dynamics, social advancement, business acumen, and sound management. Cooperatives can be organized to oppose oligarchic and exploitative companies. They straddle social and business objectives.

Since cooperatives exist widely in the U.S., sharing their experience overseas represents the best that America has to offer – especially where market failures or private businesses take advantage of the poor, rather than lift them up.

Cooperatives are proven change agents and value driven. They are self-help organizations, not charities. They achieve many goals: promote grassroots democracy and decision-making, benefit low income and disadvantaged people, and build trust among members, especially women and minorities.

Cooperatives simultaneously advance economic and human development. They can bridge ethnic conflicts and build reconciliation as in Bosnia, Macedonia and Montenegro. They can integrate women into the marketplace as in Albania. They brought lights to conflict-ridden towns in El Salvador and South Sudan and, after hurricanes and earthquakes in the Dominican Republic and Haiti.

NGOs and cooperatives promote human values and interpersonal relationships between cultures, especially when deploying U.S. technical volunteers who are motivated by sharing their expertise, not earning consulting fees.

Project design

Writing is an acquired skill and proposal writing, more specialized. Writing is a way to articulate and view complex systems. Effective written words are essential in building coalitions through advocacy in newsletters, speeches, and testimony and by disseminating learning through explanatory documents.

The best proposals are conceptual pathways and guides on how to view development and institute change strategies. Evaluations should expand and share learning on how project interventions work and don't work. They should include vignettes that tell a story, not merely quantifying results, and contain personal reflections so organizations and managers see how best to refocus their projects.

In writing proposals, there is a logical hierarchy: goal, purpose, outputs, inputs, strategy, methodologies, implementation, management, evaluation and lessons-learned which need to be woven together into a comprehensive approach. Projects can strengthen local partners through shared visions, values, mutual interests, and long-term relationships.

Proposals should focus on intellectual appeals to the head (project rationale), ideological ones to the heart (intrinsic values), and financial appeals to the pocket book (economic values).

Without a doubt, observation, personal insight, and discussions with local leaders help conceptualize effective project designs. In my opinion, it is essential to bring imagination and extrapolated experiences to these designs. Success is empowering and inspiring others who want to change their organizations, societies or countries.

Leadership

The most critical aspect of a proposal is the selection of the Chief of Party who must not only manage well but inspire with a vision and set of values. I have been lucky to find these great leaders.

Leadership to bring about change derives from an ethical view of the world – what can we do to change the current status to a more rational and ideal one. It looks at a problem and imagines a way to address it. The goal is to conceptualize and develop the most targeted way to change the system with limited funds, interventions, and time frames.

Critical leadership qualities appear to be decisiveness, self-direction, and independent thinking, an ability to communicate ideas and concepts and to maintain integrity and honesty in these efforts.

Underlying these leadership abilities are moral values of what is right, or what one might call virtue. Change is brought about through the application of virtue within different countries, circumstances, and challenges. It is understanding complex systems and applying one's values and the cultural values of those with whom you work that can help bring about a better world.

Chapter 1: Values That Shaped Me

What makes us who we are? Where do our values come from? I agree with most people, who believe that we are formed not only by our genetic predilections or traits, but also by what we are taught by our parents and what we observe in them, as well as other experiences growing up in school and society, which I see as both formal and informal education. The right combination of these values can lead to a successful life and career. Some lucky opportunities and finding the right spouse can, I believe, lead to a fulfilling life.

I believe that I entered this world with an even balance of both my parents' attributes. My father possessed an inquirer's mind with a honed sense of rationale and dedication to inanimate sciences. My mother was a humanist who understood how people can work together to achieve effective action. Essentially, I have the mind of my father and the heart of my mother. My concerns with human problems derive from my mother, but the approach comes from my father.

My Father, the inventor

I got to know my father, Vernon, very well. He hated to drive, so, as soon as I got my learner's permit at 15, I drove him to and from the airport weekly while in high school and nearly daily to work while attending Georgetown University. On each of these drives, I would ask him about his career, and he loved to tell me his stories.

My father was a system engineer and an inventor. While the head of Army Air Corps navigation and electronics labs at Wright Field (now Wright-Patterson Air Force Base) during the war, he invented the loop antenna, which he patented in 1942 and which was subsequently installed on all U.S. warplanes. We had a model of it in our basement. It allows airplanes to navigate by using radio beams, fly at night with instruments, and land using it. Once, while visiting the World War II museum in New Orleans, I pointed out the antenna to a docent and said, "My father invented that." He replied, "That is why I love this job."

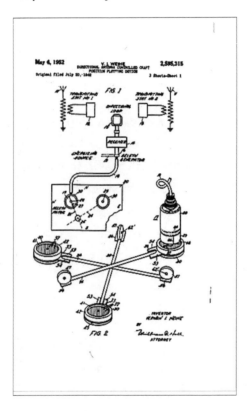

Loop antenna

My father told me about how our troops were seasick in their Higgins landing crafts as they waited all night until daylight in churning seas and got lost before landing on the African beaches. He approached the Army general at a Caribbean test site for his practical navigation system and asked him, "Where are you going to be on the beach in the morning?" The General responded, "Under that large palm tree." At dawn, the lead landing craft in the flotilla landed right in front of him.

Father was very practical. His navigational breakthroughs helped facilitate the long-range retaliatory air raids on the Japanese after Pearl Harbor in 1942 known as the "Doolittle Raid" or the "Raid Over Tokyo." He had a pass from Jimmy Doolittle, the commander of the force, and took each of the navigators to the long range fitted airplanes to practice shooting stars with a sextant.

When Ed Link showed up at my father's lab, he helped him add navigational aids to the Link trainer, a flight simulator for pilots. The Link Trainer improved safety and shortened training time for 500,000 pilots during World War II. Ed Link was a life-long family friend. Father navigated Ed's research vessel, *Sea Diver*, from Gibraltar to the Caribbean where they almost ran up on a reef because Ed made a navigational error. So, father designed a simple navigational device, The Dot Reckoner, that plotted depth readings so that even a seasick sailor could use it.

Probably his most interesting invention was a direction finder that could be dropped as a guide for bombers headed toward targets in Japan. The challenge was that the antenna must be able to be activated and later retracted so Japanese Zeros could not use it to attack the aircraft carriers. He used a salt tab that would slowly dissolve to lower the antenna after a few hours.

When he went to Los Alamos in New Mexico, he noticed the bevy of generals and admirals closely observing the airplane's drop with his device. Only at the close of the war did he learn that the parachute for his direction finder was the same as that of "Little Boy" (the atomic bomb dropped on Hiroshima). His invention, never used, was a cover for the design of the Little Boy parachute so that the nuclear bomb detonated 5,000 feet above Hiroshima.

After the war, he knew that civilian aviation would take off and the family moved to Arlington, Virginia. On behalf of the U.S. Air Transport Association, he traveled the world to international aviation conferences to secure large blocks of the radio wave spectrum that would be needed, and necessary for commercial aircraft communication. My father could see and respond to the future. Many of his patents ran out before they could be used.

The highest award in aviation is the Collier Trophy. The Radio Technical Commission, which my father led, was awarded it in 1948 for the invention of the transponder, which provides for safe operations of aircraft in all weather.

In the 50s, he was approached by a group of engineers who wanted to create an instrument landing system. Their system would have cost $50,000 each, and he asked, "How many general aviation airports do you think there are in the U.S.? Can they afford it?" He decided to create a low-cost alternative using standard available equipment. As a kid, I remember the plywood box he built in our backyard, and I was present when he tested it at Friendship Airport in Baltimore. His system cost $2,000 and became the standard for civilian airports. He taught me there is usually a better, more economical, way to solve a problem.

He conceived of an entire air traffic control system. He drew boxes with lists of components, sent them to engineers to design, and make sure each interacted as a system. Since making crystal radio sets as a 10-year-old, he had followed all fields of electronics from vacuum tubes to transistors. He knew the cutting edges of navigation and communication systems and put them all together. I learned from him to put different components into a coherent whole.

Like my father, I am a conceptual thinker. I can just picture the whole system. Often in a proposal, I write the concept, the methodology and then the details, all linked to the basic idea. Once at a Land O'Lakes workshop, I asked the country managers to describe their projects conceptually. Almost no one could do it. I would try to coach them, and just say this is how to think about it in a few words. What I realized is that conceptual thinking is the way my brain works, and it comes to me easily.

Most of his colleagues thought my father was brilliant, and he probably was. But he would tell me that if you work 10% longer and harder than anyone else, you will succeed. He brought papers home every night to study after dinner. It was good advice.

Like me, he was not a good fit in large corporations. He spent most of his career as a private consultant, similar to how I have operated as head of the U.S. Overseas Cooperative Development Council (OCDC). While there was an organizational structure, I was basically on my own to develop relationships with the U.S. Agency for International Development (USAID), write legislation and design projects. Every day I came to work, I had the freedom to decide what I wanted to do to advance our common development agenda.

The values that I learned from my father include critical thinking, determination, focus and self-discipline. I learned a love of sailing, a willingness to take risks, and faithfulness and loyalty to my wife. These values helped me to become studious, and, like him, I learned to become an effective technical writer.

He was a founder and president of the Institute of Navigation – his first love. When we sailed together on the Chesapeake Bay, he preferred to plot the course on his charts while I skippered. On the other hand, my mother was lost as soon as we left the dock. Sailing is a good analogy for my father's influence on me. Sailboats go faster upwind and against the wind because of lift, not by going downwind. Going against the forces that drive most others takes boldness, originality and acting as a contrarian – an apt description of my personality.

My Mother, the humanitarian

I inherited a different set of traits and values from my mother, Elizabeth — Sissy to the family. While my father was a global leader in avionics, she was a local and statewide leader in Virginia. She told me the story of Ed Campbell taking on the case of four black children for the integration of the Arlington schools. Ed asked his wife, Elizabeth Campbell, founder of WETA Public TV, if he should take the case that was eventually combined with Brown v. Board of Education. "It might mean," he said, that "I will never be able to take another case in Virginia." She told him, "Do what is right." It taught me that some actions are worth losing your job or endangering your career over.

I was a high school student when my mother led the efforts for school integration statewide. Her efforts saved the public-school system after Governor Lindsey Almond pledged he would shut it down if one black child went to a white school, similar to the stand taken by George Wallace in Alabama.

My mother organized a statewide coalition of business, education and civic leaders called "Save Our Schools (SOS)." In racist Virginia, the best argument was preserving public education, not integration.

Always lady-like, she wore white gloves and a hat testifying before the legislature. Once she asked the wife of Governor Almond why he had backed down and allowed school integration to go forward. She responded, "He was a better lawyer than a politician."

She told me the story when four black teenagers entered Strafford Junior High in Arlington, Virginia, our home town. They had to walk through a gauntlet of Nazis who were waving their flags, and other angry white protesters. The mothers of the black kids gathered in the home of her friend, Theda Henle, whose upstairs bedroom window had a clear view of the school entrance. The black mothers took turns looking out to see if everything was peaceful. One of the women was uneasy, and mother asked her why? She said, "This is the first time that I have ever been in a white person's home."

I vividly remember those days when blacks could not sit at restaurants, had separate drinking fountains and were "fenced off" by a wooden wall built around Halls Hill, a former freeman's village. It taught me that while the worst ravages of racism may be over, it has a long path to real integration. Take a long view of societal changes, and value diversity.

I shared her passion for civic engagement. We were the only mother - son team although separated by 25 years that chaired and served on many Arlington boards - Planning Commission, Economic Development Commission, Committee of 100, and the Neighborhood Conservation Committee. She was the first woman chairman of the Planning Commission, and a pioneer for women leaders in Arlington.

Lady Bird Johnson came to Arlington often to see her daughter, Lynda Bird Robb. On one occasion, the First Lady sent a letter to the County Board suggesting that Arlington needed beautification.

The letter went to my mother on the Planning Commission, she attended the first White House conference on beautification, and led these efforts in Arlington for over 40 years. She brought roses to the county board meetings for each member when asking for her funds.

Honored with a plaque for Arlington beautification

I saw how small gestures could be so effective. When I led the fight against the proposed Portman high rise convention center in Rosslyn, we filled the back row of the courthouse, with each person holding a black balloon with only a simple sign that read: "265 feet."

In the early 1960s, she founded the innovative neighborhood conservation program which protects neighborhoods from encroaching commercial development. She sought an ideal test for this citizen-driven planning process. She said, "Arlington View was the perfect candidate, a black neighborhood in great risk, with many unpaved streets, no sidewalks, no curbs and gutters." Due to its location, many developers wanted to tear down their homes and build apartments. She said that the neighborhood had a "great nucleus of leaders" that opposed this development and wanted to prevent it. They were supported by neighborhood conservation funds and the community still thrives today.

It was a vivid demonstration of how my mother and I applied lessons from Margaret Mead, "Never doubt that a small group of thoughtful, committed people can change the world. Indeed, it is the only thing that ever has." All independent sector movements started with a few leaders and organizers.

Years later, I had lunch with Margaret Mead. I recall reading her book *Growing up in New Guinea* and studying her views on the importance of trial marriages. Many of my efforts are based on her principles, such as listening and open-mindedness, and the idea that a small nucleus of leaders can make dramatic changes.

I followed my mother's lead and chaired her long running Neighborhood Conservation program, I reorganized how projects were ranked instituting a point system, rather than log rolling between neighborhoods, and lobbied the county board to increase its funding from $1.7 to $10 million annually.

I acquired from my mother the ability to run a meeting *League-like*. I laughingly told friends that I was an orphan of the League, since my mother was gone so often running the Arlington League and its many committees. At dinner, we were given "talk tickets" to discuss what happened to us that day.

As a child, I remember the League meeting discussion in our living room on whether or not to recognize Red China. The League's organizational skills have worked well for me in creating and managing coalitions – whether local, national or international – and applying parliamentary procedures.

I have also inherited my mother's abundance of energy. Whether painting, varnishing our family sailboat, or putting up wallpaper, no one worked harder or longer than her. She gave me the values of altruism, cooperation, empathy, humanism and zeal. I was always her "blue-eyed baby boy." She died just a few weeks short of 100 in 2014. I hope to inherit her longevity.

University years

By high school, I knew that I was not going to be an engineer like my father, or a pilot like my older brother. My two passions were international affairs and politics. What better place to pursue these dreams than Washington, D.C.?

Unlike students today, I applied to only two universities: Georgetown and the University of Virginia (UVA). I was accepted at both, went to Georgetown's Foreign Service School, and later got a Masters in Planning on the G.I. bill from UVA.

Two professors influenced me the most. Dr. Carroll Quigley taught a required freshman class on the *Evolution of Civilizations*. I still have my class notes and both of his books, the second one entitled *Tragedy and Hope* on the history of Western civilization. He identified the seven stages of historical change in all civilizations: mixture, gestation, expansion, conflict, universal empire, decay and invasion. His breadth of thinking was overwhelming to me as a freshman.

He taught me how to read a book: study the index and go back to it regularly to see "how the author sliced up the subject" for flow and context. On exams, he would ask broad questions and say "spend one-third of your time thinking about the answer before writing down anything."

He said that there were only four types of questions:

Linear or straight line of events or eras: Paleozoic (plants), Mesozoic (reptiles), Tertiary (mammals) and Quaternary (man).

Waves or cycles: shifts between the preponderance of defenses like forts and WWI trenches, and offensive mastery such as skillful knights, Napoleon or Grant's flanking motions.

Hierarchies: civilizations or activities broken down from top to bottom: intellectual, religious, social, political, economic and military components.

Concentric or overlapping circles: mankind in the bullseye surrounded first by culture, then the natural environment, or overlapping civilizations, i.e. Canaanite and Minoan.

I use his conceptual thinking in a lecture I give, *The History of the World in Ten Minutes*. But, I added a fifth element, complex systems: cyclical activities repeating themselves as a process from planning, program development, monitoring to evaluation and repeating the process, or a log frame where a stack of elements interact – context, input, process, output, impact.

If Quigley were alive today, he would be on talk shows answering questions about the Western conflict with Islam in mostly Arab countries. Samuel Huntington, the Harvard professor who wrote *The Clash of Civilizations and the Remaking of World Order,* credits Quigley for his inspiration in writing the book.

My love of history can be traced to Carroll Quigley. As I have traveled to many countries, I read about their history to orient myself before a visit. My favorite historical event is World War I which set the stage for the 20th century.

I embraced Quigley's worldview that Western civilization balances individual rights and responsibilities. He taught me that the future can be better than the past and each of us has a personal, moral responsibility to make it so.

In times of trouble, he said, "Western society has been repeatedly rescued by the emergence of a sense of reciprocal obligation – a practical and moral covenant between individuals, reaffirming that they have both individual rights and responsibilities to others." Quigley was a demanding professor, giving out few high marks to students in his classes.

The second professor who influenced my values was Walter "Jack" Giles who gave me an intellectual grounding in constitutional law, the most exacting course in my sophomore year. He did not coddle us but expected us to approach class like a law school seminar. You had better be ready when he asked you a question about the class assignment. If you did not want to be asked, you could approach him before class and say "nolo contendere."

Two events stand out with Professor Giles. He was a huge Redskins supporter and did not give any exams if the Redskins were winning. They won their first six straight games and made all of us Redskin fans.

We were all 19 or 20, and the legal drinking age for hard liquor was 21. Each spring, he gave his famous Madison Martini Lecture. He would stroll into the room with a portable bar – glasses, tumbler, jigger, ice, Seagram's gin, Cinzano vermouth and olives. He would launch into the day's lesson: President Madison's contribution to the Constitution and his system of checks and balances. As Dr. Giles prepared pitchers of martinis, he explained how the ingredients – the olive, the vermouth and the gin – represented the three branches of government and the delicate balance between them. If one part is too potent, the balance would be destroyed, and the concoction ruined.

"Each true believer of martinis, including even your garden variety lush, is convinced that he knows how to make the perfect martini," he would say. "When you move into the realm of the first amendment's freedom of expression and association, I am the authority, and my approach is an absolute one, not balancing interests. Here, I am, indeed your perfect master." At the end of the presentation, he would pass out 128 drinks to the students. Dr. Giles would invite us to join him in a toast, "Gentlemen to the Republic!"

I learned the fundamental relationships of the executive and legislative branches as interpreted by the courts. I also learned "to stir, not shake a martini."

It is rewarding to be complimented by your professor in building self-confidence. To me, he wrote, "Your efforts throughout the year reflected very high standards and achievements, and I want to let you know that I believe you should be proud of them."

At Georgetown, I got to know many foreign students from the diplomatic corps. I found these "internationalists" were not rooted in their own cultures. They preferred Francois Hardy to the Beatles, seeing themselves as internationalists. Spending part of two summers in Grenoble and Tours, France to learn French, I contrasted my values with Europeans: a practical and at the time naive idealism and unremitting optimism.

At the urging of my older brother who was in the Air Force, I joined the Reserve Officers Training Corps program at Georgetown. I had never felt part of a group and I wanted to experience the camaraderie of a group. I joined Doud Rifles, the marching team where I was the *guide-on* as I was tall and very thin.

I found it hard to subsume my personality within the group, and almost got kicked out of ROTC at summer camp when I refused to rate fellow cadets. In my senior year, they gave me a chance to remain in the officer training program. I took the challenge and got the Commander's award for "Exceptional Leadership."

Commissioned as second lieutenant

Chapter 2: Life in the Air Force

I joined the Air Force in September 1965. I was an inept bachelor officer. I did not own a hot car, I did not drink beer, I did not like hanging out at bars, and was terrible at flirting especially with the country girls of Knob Noster, Missouri.

I felt totally out of my element. I was from the East and thought of myself as an intellectual. I was aghast at my first assignments when I arrived at Whiteman AFB when I asked to put up a bulletin board. Another duty was to collate manuals by walking around a table full of papers and stacking them up – this was prior to IBM sorters. I stayed by myself, read books and waited before going to missile training at Chanute and Vandenberg Air Force Bases. Maybe the authors and war novels I read fit my mood: *The Heart of Darkness, The Sound and the Fury* and *For Whom the Bell Tolls.*

I was a lost soul, bored, lonely and depressed, with only sailing on Lake Jacomo near Kansas City as an outlet. For a bachelor, you would think living in officer nurses' quarters would be great. But, men arrived at all hours, filled the TV room and disappeared into the nurses' rooms.

The World War II barracks was old, dirty and combined two adjoining small rooms with a bathroom in the middle. To brighten it up, I painted my walls purple and orange – only to learn later that the only approved official colors were drab green and pink.

I was not happy about living in Missouri or being an Air Force officer. I had a hard time socializing with fellow officers. Added to that, I constantly struggled with the very nature of my job, the daily practice with the missile launch sequences, and the possibility that one day I might have to actually launch a missile that would kill millions of people. The only thing I could think about was how to avoid doing it.

My non-conformity came out one day in an incident involving my tie tack. The clasp had a peace symbol on it and was normally hidden by my jacket, but when the air-conditioning broke down in the monthly Emergency War's Orders meeting, we were ordered to remove our jackets, and my tie clasp was exposed. I was immediately called out of the meeting asked to explain it to the base commander. I replied that the SAC motto was "Peace is our profession" and the symbol had been used to symbolize peace for thousands of years.

My superiors asked me if I was aware that it was also used by various "subversive groups" and I was asked if I was a member of any of them. I said "no" but admitted that I had worked for the McCarthy campaign. That did not go over well. Needless to say, I took the tie clasp off and did not wear it again. Of course, I knew the peace symbol was not ancient. In the 1950s, it was the logo for the British Campaign for Nuclear Disarmament and adopted by anti-war activists in the U. S. protesting the Vietnam War. The next month, the Air Force issued an official regulation on tie tacks.

I had not only supported Senator Eugene McCarthy on the Whiteman Air Force Base, I put posters inside my VW and parked it conspicuously at the Officers Club; organized a 14-car caravan from Whiteman to his rally in Kansas City, and I dared the Air Force to discipline me since I was fully familiar with the Hatch Act prohibitions on government employees and Air Force policies from engaging in political activities.

At Georgetown, I opposed the Vietnam War where Father Sebes was enlisted by President Johnson to give student lectures in its support. Father Sebes was a very popular professor. He was a favorite of Bill Clinton's, a classmate two year behind me. I remember asking Sebes, "What is the strategic value of Vietnam? The Germans had already invented synthetic rubber – about their only product."

If I had been assigned to Vietnam, I wondered if I would have defected to Canada. After the Air Force, I joined John Kerry's Vietnam Veterans Against the War, went to anti-war marches in D.C. and New York, and grew the longest sideburns possible as a late hippie. Vietnam and missiles were both depressing, and my mood reflected it.

Top secret mission

My personal *Catch-22* was an Air Force assignment that I could not opt out of, nor resolve its insanity.

The defense contractor for the Minuteman Intercontinental Ballistic Missiles (ICBMs) is Boeing Corporation. They were constantly modifying the equipment in the Launch Control Centers where we lived "in the hole" an underground command center with control over 10 ICBMs scattered around us in barbwire-fenced launch pads. The outlying missiles changed targets often, most frequently when our nuclear subs went off station under the arctic ice cap.

Each Minuteman missile has a device on the end of the first stage motor known as the "Command Signals Decoder "(CSD). This classified device decoded the enable and launch commands sent by the missile crew to launch the missile. It is essential to a successful launch.

In June 1968, the CSD on one of our missiles at Whiteman failed, or was thought to have failed – the targeting team was not sure.

41

Since it was not sure that this missile could receive and properly decode the launch commands, the entire missile was pulled from its silo by a large lifting device attached to a truck, lowered on a flatbed rail car, strapped down and then shipped 1,136 miles to the Boeing facility located at Hill Air Force Base, outside Salt Lake City, Utah.

ICBM on train flatbed

This was a big deal. According to regulations, the entire missile must be guarded at all times with two armed officers and one enlisted person. The Wing Commander at Whiteman AFB at that time was Colonel James Bryant, the brother of Alabama football coach Paul "Bear" Bryant. Col. Bryant was an alcoholic who ran the 510 Wing as his brother did his football program, with fear and intimidation.

Bryant selected Second Lieutenant Lew Brewer, a sergeant and myself for the assignment. On a hot Wednesday morning in mid-July 1968, we reported to the Air Police Office to be issued our weapons to guard this missile. We were handed standard snub-nosed .38 Smith & Wesson revolvers which were well worn and carried by missile crews. One could throw this handgun at an intruder with better accuracy than shooting it. The Air Police sergeant calmly said that these were the weapons requisitioned for your mission. We each took a handgun, six bullets, a holster and a belt.

We were driven to the rail spur that connected Whiteman to the main railroad line running across to Kansas City. We were told we would be met in the railyard at Kansas City and then hooked to our main train and be off to Utah.

We found the 56-foot-long Minuteman secured to a flatbed railcar with a second empty flatbed car just behind it. An engine was hooked to these two cars. We looked at each other and climbed up onto the empty flatbed. We secured our paper sacks of food and personal gear as best we could and waited. The engine tooted its horn and we started to move.

Our train conductor

It took about an hour and a half to reach the railroad yard at Kansas City. KC is a major rail hub for the entire United States, and the railyard is massive. Our engine was directed to a side track and we were uncoupled and watched as the Air Force engine headed back

43

to Whiteman. There we sat. It was around 10:00 AM and it was very hot.

I had no idea a railyard could be so hot. With no cover, the sun just burned down on us. The steel rails, the crushed gravel of the rail beds and the steel and wood of the flat car made it feel like we were in an oven. We sat there waiting and waiting. No one ever came near our two railcars and we had no way to contact anyone even if we had known whom to call.

At around 4:30 PM, a long line of cars began slowly backing down the main track toward our siding. We watched as it snaked around and headed toward our two open flatcars. Railroad men jumped off the train and coupled the flatbed carrying our missile to the long line of railcars. Our flatbed car was now at the rear of the train.

My crewmates in caboose behind missile

We could not see the engine from where we were. We were pulled along up to the main track and then backed into an old-fashioned red caboose. We were the last three cars on the train. We jumped into the caboose only to find it empty. Inside were wooden benches along two walls, a small toilet and a radio on the wall. No one was there but us. Then without any warning, the cars jerked and groaned and we began moving slowly down the rails.

Once we cleared the massive railyard, we began to pick up speed. As the train went around a big bend we were able to look up the track and see how long our train was. We were amazed: it had to be over a mile long as we could not see the engine at any time.

Missile in its container on flatbed

At first the breeze felt good after sitting in the hot sun for so long. But it did not take us long to find out that being the last car meant lots of black-grey dust and fine particulates. My nose quickly clogged up and I was gasping for air by hanging my head way out. The constant rocking and rolling of the cars was like being on a ship, and I wondered if any of us would get seasick.

The first night was not too bad. It cooled off when it got dark and we spent the time talking and getting to know each other. The next day dawned clear and hot. We were getting really dirty by this time, as all of the dust and dirt kicked up by the hundreds of cars ahead of us blew directly on us.

During the trip, I read *Spain, A Modern History by Salvador de Madariaga* which is still soot covered in my library – an apt book about what the author called the "follies" of the Spanish Civil War

Our route took us up into Nebraska, over to southern Wyoming and down into Salt Lake City. We rode on and played cards a lot; mostly hearts and rummy. The time dragged by and Nebraska provided nothing special in the way of scenery. I recall a young girl riding a horse next to the train at Lincoln, Nebraska. She was the only human along the railway that we saw the entire trip.

I was dirty, hot, tired and sleepy as we pulled into Cheyenne, Wyoming after dark and slowed down and finally stopped. We had no way of knowing how long we would be stopping. It was well after dark and we debated if one of us should get off to see if we could find someone to help us get some food. Ours had spoiled in the heat.

We were sitting on the flatcar next to the one holding the missile debating this issue when we saw movement. Someone jumped up on the missile's flatcar and ran toward the rear of the missile itself. The figure appeared at the rear of the missile dressed in dirty and ragged clothes and wearing a baseball cap. It was then we noticed he was also wearing a gun in a shoulder holster.

He came over and showed us his credentials. He was a cop assigned to the railyards to prevent hobos from stowing away on freight cars. He was dressed as a bum on purpose. "You scared the hell out of us," we told him. "You almost got yourself shot."

He smiled at us and said, "*No, you almost got yourself shot,*" and pulled out the biggest revolver I had ever seen. He laughed and said, "You should be ashamed of yourselves running around with toy guns."

We pulled into Laramie just before midnight and there was a store and a small diner across the street from the tracks. We were able to get some food before we chugged on up the tracks toward Rawlins, Wyoming.

We passed through Green River, Wyoming on Friday morning and almost froze to death. The temperature was 35 degrees and this was the middle of July. We rode across the edge of the Rocky Mountains and finally descended into the Salt Lake City railyard.

Once in the railyard, our three cars were uncoupled from the main train and hooked up to a separate engine, which pulled us into Hill Air Force Base. The engine backed us onto a rail siding and left us sitting there.

We looked at our watches and it was about 4:00 PM and it was again very hot. So, we sat and waited and waited. We noticed no activity in the railyard at all. We knew that if we were not picked up soon, we would be there for the weekend since the base is really a civilian facility.

About an hour later, an engine backed up and hooked up our three cars and we began moving. We were pulled into a huge hangar, the engine uncoupled and left.

Soon two men in Air Force uniforms walked up along with another guy in civilian dress. Introductions were made all around and our orders were checked. The Air Force guys left.

The civilian turned out to be an engineer working for Boeing. He took a small tool pouch and climbed up on the flatcar holding the missile. We watched as he took out his screwdriver and undid about eight bolts and then removed a cover from a panel on the side of the missile. Next, he took wire cutters, reached in and made several cuts. He pulled out a metal box, about the size of a loaf of bread. He handed it to us with a cheery, "Here you go, Lieutenants."

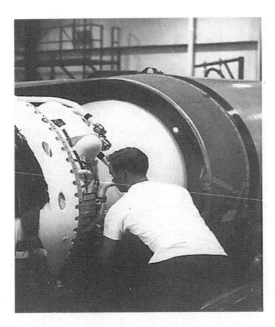

Removing the CSD

I looked at him and asked, what are you talking about? He replied, "I have removed the Command Signals Decoder from the missile and now you are to take it back to Whiteman and turn it in to your Codes Vault where it will be locked up for safekeeping since it can't be fixed. The missile will be shipped back to Whiteman and a new CSD installed there by your maintenance crews." The three of us just stared at him with our mouths open.

I blurted out, "Do you mean to tell us we just rode three days through the Great Plains on an open flatcar with little food or sleep for you to unscrew eight bolts and clip two wires? Why couldn't this have been done at Whiteman by our maintenance personnel?" His answer stunned me: "It could have been done at Whiteman, but Boeing has a contract with the U.S. Air Force that requires such work to be done only by a Boeing engineer here at Hill Air Force Base."

He looked at us and added, "Lieutenants, you do realize that you and your team cannot fly on just any military flight due to the classified nature of your 'package' and the requirement that you must be armed at all times." We had nothing but a paper sack to carry it in.

As a launch officer, I learned how to quickly sign dozens of *top-secret* documents every time we replaced a missile crew in the capsule. But, it was a little word "*crypto*" that made the "package" super classified since it contains launch codes. As such, it requires two-armed U.S. Air Force guards at all times when being transported.

We learned that Hill AFB had no aircraft assigned to it. There was only an Air Force Reserve Unit stationed here. Our best bet was to hitch a ride on any flight outbound. None were going anywhere near Whiteman but there was a flight to Nellis AFB in Las Vegas, Nevada.

The ops officer said, "There will be plenty of planes in Vegas over the weekend and you could easily catch one out Sunday or Monday for sure." We went back to our quarters and slept in a bed for the first time in what seemed like a week. As I lay there, I could feel the swaying and rolling of the train.

The next morning, we left Hill AFB on a C-97 for Nellis AFB in Nevada that afternoon. Upon arrival, we went immediately to the flight operations office to see about a ride home. We were not happy to learn that almost all of the planes that come to Nellis are fighters with only one or two crew.

There were no large planes scheduled to leave Nellis anytime soon. We were told that it was highly possible some transports would come in during the weekend and that we could probably get a "ride" out either late Sunday or Monday. We put our names on a "stand-by" list for any flight available. We were driven to the base headquarters office.

We explained our mission to the Captain on duty and asked that he provide us quarters and transportation until we could get a flight out. The Captain did not feel like it was his job to take care of us so we pulled out our mission orders from the SAC commander and handed them to him. After reading them, he was more cooperative.

He explained that he could put us up in the Visiting Officers Quarters and the sergeant would have to stay in the NCO quarters. I said, "That is not acceptable as we all three had to stay together due to our orders."

He left and came back and told us he had discussed it with his boss and that they would arrange rooms for us downtown in Las Vegas at the Sahara Hotel. We only had to charge the rooms to Nellis AFB. That sounded good to us so we accepted. He arranged for a vehicle from the motor pool to be brought around for our use.

We checked into the Sahara Hotel and were given well-appointed rooms. I could not believe our luck. Since our team was composed of two commissioned officers and one enlisted man, we could not stay in the same building on base. But the Air Force had no problem footing the bill for rooms in a luxury hotel. I did not mind at all.

The next morning, we drove back to the base flight line to check on flights. Nothing but fighters were parked on site. The operations officer told us there was a transport coming in Sunday and leaving late that same day heading for Kelly Field in Texas. He suggested we go down to Kelly as it was a training base and we would have a much better chance of finding a ride to Whiteman from there.

We decided to give it a try and put our names on the manifest to leave around 5:00 PM the next day. We went back to Vegas and enjoyed being tourists.

The next day, we checked out of the Sahara and headed to Nellis again. We did indeed have a ride down to Kelly Field near San Antonio.

We arrived at Kelly AFB to find everything pretty much closed down as it was Sunday night. The flight ops officer did not have any flights scheduled out on Monday heading east. We explained our situation and the need to get the CSD back to Whiteman ASAP.

After the three of us were put up at the Officers' Quarters for the night, the next day I called flight ops. He informed us that he could get us *back* to Nellis AFB. There was an Air National Guard C-119 leaving late Monday taking an Air Force ROTC group from Nellis to March AFB in California. He said our best bet would be to try to get on an Air National Guard flight going east out of March AFB. We agreed to give it a shot, so back to Nellis.

At Nellis, we were told the AFROTC group was our only choice out for days. We got set up on that flight and sat in the ops center waiting. We felt self-conscious sitting with a paper sack with "Top Secret" written on it. We got plenty of strange looks but no one said a word.

Our AFROTC group arrived and the pilot came out to get us aboard. We explained to the pilot about our team and the fact we were armed. We showed him our orders and he was most accommodating. We headed out to board the C-119 known as the "Flying Boxcar."

The C-119 was used in WWII to carry paratroopers into combat. It looks like it could not possibly fly with its high twin tails and the body of the plane seemingly suspended beneath them. It was a propeller-driven twin engine plane, and I thought it would be cool to fly on it. Not so.

The inside was mostly empty cargo space. We sat in the uncomfortable web seats that basically hung from the walls, common on almost all military cargo planes. The twin engines were so noisy you had to put your mouth next to someone's ear to be heard. The plane shook and vibrated. I was not sure it would hold together.

We sat on one side of the cargo bay and the AFROTC cadets sat across from us. They kept looking at the paper bag and the silly "Top Secret" written on it. Finally, one of the college students asked, "What's in the bag?" When I told him, we could not discuss it as it was highly classified, I think he thought we were messing with him. True.

We landed at March AFB near Riverside, California after dark. We asked at the flight ops center about flights going anywhere near Whiteman. There were none. We were told to check back in the morning. The next day we could not find a ride heading toward Missouri but we got another ride *again back* to Nellis in Las Vegas. Back and forth we went on our surreal odyssey.

From Nellis, we went to Brooks Field in California and then to Kelly Field in Texas. So far, these flights transpired over five days. I began to think we would never get home flying on military planes. We were stuck. One step forward and two steps back. Every time I thought we made progress getting back to Whiteman, we took two steps backward and further away.

Return home

It was now Thursday or six days since we had delivered the missile to Hill AFB. We were at Kelly Field in Texas a second time. Hurricane

Celia was bearing down on Texas, and all military aircraft at the base were relocating to other bases.

The base was home to the Air Force's top medical facilities. The flight ops officer told us, "I have some good news for you. There is an air evac flight scheduled to leave tomorrow for Scott Air Force Base in East St. Louis. They have room for the three of you. We could not believe our ears. Scott Air Force Base is located literally just across the Mississippi river from St. Louis. We would be almost home.

We arrived at the flight line the next morning ready to go home. The flight was on a military C-9A Nightingale that transported soldiers who had been wounded in Vietnam to the military hospital at Scott AFB.

We met with the nurses who would be on the flight and they told us, "It will not be pleasant." We did not care. I watched spellbound as litter after litter of wounded men were carried up the steps and loaded into the plane. We were finally told to board.

Looking over the deserted tarmac, we saw that it was the last aircraft leaving the base before the expected hurricane. *What luck at last.*

As we approached the steps to the plane, the pilot, an Air Force Major, stopped us. "Lieutenants, you cannot carry those weapons on board this aircraft." We showed him our orders and explained what we had in our Top-Secret grocery bag. He told us, he understood but that we needed to understand that these men had all just arrived from Vietnam. He could not have armed men on board. He was afraid one of the wounded men might try to grab our weapons.

We understood but we wanted to go home. "I will make you a deal," I said. "We will give you our bullets and you let us keep our guns. No one but you and we will ever know." He smiled and agreed. The four of us walked around to the far side of the plane. We quietly handed him all eighteen of our bullets. We boarded and prepared to go home.

The flight was not pleasant, just as the nurses warned. The wounded soldiers were strapped to litters stacked three high along both walls of the plane. IV's ran to each soldier's arm from bottles hanging overhead. They were in constant pain. I felt so sorry for them. The nurses were great. They took a lot of time with each man and tried their best to make them comfortable and keep their spirits up.

It made me realize how lucky I was to be on SAC "combat duty" in the middle of Missouri. In fact, some officers assigned to Whiteman refused to wear the "Combat Crew" badge because they had experienced *real* combat in Vietnam.

We landed at Scott AFB around noon. Just across the river was the new St. Louis Arch, the "Gateway to the West." We were only about 300 miles from home. We retrieved our bullets from the pilot and thanked him profusely.

We walked into the flight operations center and hurriedly called the base. I expected them to send a vehicle to pick us up or to authorize us to rent a car to drive to the base.

Instead, the base commander arranged for an Air Force U3-A to pick us up. We walked out to the plane and met the two officers inside. The pilot was a Captain who was being evaluated by a Major. The Captain was being discharged from the Air Force effective the next day. I wondered why the Air Force would go through the time and expense to do this unnecessary check. "How absurd!"

We carried the paper bag on board. The pilot asked us, "What it is that?" We told both officers the short version of our trip. They just howled. The pilot said, "That is why I am getting out tomorrow." He cranked up each engine and taxied out to the runway. We were almost home.

The runway at Scott AFB points directly toward the Gateway Arch and downtown St. Louis. We roared down the runway and lifted off heading straight toward the big arch. For a minute, I thought the pilot was going to fly underneath it. The arch had only been erected a few years earlier and was still quite a wonder. As we headed straight toward it, the evaluator asked the pilot, "What are you doing?" He replied he was going to fly under it. The Major went ballistic.

"What are you going to do, kick me out of the Air Force!" the soon-to-be-discharged pilot said as we flew straight toward the arch. The next thing I knew, we were looking face-to-face with people high up in the arch as we shot by and banked away. The pilot laughed and the evaluator shook his head.

We touched down around 4:00 PM and were never so glad to be anywhere. I thanked the pilot for the *"interesting ride"* and left him and his evaluator arguing over what he had done on the check ride.

We got a lift to the Code Vault and happily turned over the CSD to the officer in charge. He asked how our trip had gone. I was too tired to say anything more than, "It was interesting." We had been gone ten days. It took three days to get to Hill AFB by train and seven days to get home by military aircraft. The news of our trip was soon all over the missile crew force at Whiteman.

Filing our report

The more I thought about the whole episode, the madder I got. I could not believe the Air Force would go to the expense of shipping a missile over a thousand miles to have someone remove eight bolts and clip two wires. How could the Air Force justify taking three trained personnel off missile duty for ten days for such a mission?

I wrote up a full report questioning the need and expense for such a trip. I included a breakdown of costs: the train trip, air flights, lodging and salaries for ten days. There was a suggestion box on ways to save the Air Force money. Satisfied with our report, I slipped it into the box.

It was not long before we were summoned to Colonel Bryant's office. The Colonel held up my report and in his gravelly voice said, "Lieutenants, what is the meaning of this report?" We began to explain our reasoning, at which point Bryant stopped us by holding up his hand. He ripped up our report and threw the pieces into his trash can.

The Colonel said, "Lieutenants, let me make one thing clear to you. You launch the fucking missiles and I will run the fucking Air Force. Do you understand me?"

I already knew that the Air Force was not for me. I was there as a citizen soldier to do my duty, following the paths of my father and brother. This experience confirmed my dislike for large hierarchies and top-down authority. I was not good at submerging my personality within such organizations.

But, I value the military virtues that I learned during my Air Force tour: loyalty and the importance of good leadership; maintaining trust with your colleagues through integrity, respect and honor; and serving my country. It was really not until after 9/11 that I felt proud of my service. Unlike those Vietnam years, I am always amazed when I mention that I served when talking on the phone or at checkout counters, and just about everyone responds "Thank you for your service."

A COMMUNITY SALUTE TO
WHITEMAN AIR FORCE BASE

1968 UNOFFICIAL DIRECTORY & GUIDE
PUBLISHED BY BOONE PUBLICATIONS, INC.

Whiteman Directory Cover
Minuteman Test Launch at Vandenberg AFB

Chapter 3: Moral Dilemma of a Missileer

Same boredom, same Emergency War Order tests, same cheating, same low morale and same moral dilemmas not much has changed in the Minuteman missileers life since I pulled alerts 50 years ago.

In 2015, the headlines read: "Nuclear Corps, Sidelined in Terror Fight, Produces a Culture of Cheating" and "92 Air Force Officers Suspended for Cheating on their Missile Exam." It brought back a rush of memories.

The first report of cheating on a proficiency test this time was in January 2014, when 34 officers in charge of launching nuclear missiles at Minot AFB were caught and a major-general sacked for drinking too much and meeting "suspect" foreign women in Russia. On tests, they were cheating to get 90% correct; in my day, we had to score 100% and a single missed question resulted in a letter of reprimand and 15 hours of tedious retraining.

This time the Secretary of the Air Force told Congress that it was important for commanders to "ride herd" over junior officers. A colonel in charge said, "Get back to the basics and crush any rule violators." *Same old, same old*, I thought.

Nobody can monitor what is going on in a launch capsule, buried 60 feet below the surface. As one officer said, "Everyone is pretty friendly with each other. We talk about anything and everything. You're spending twenty-four hours with this person, after all."

At the forefront of gender integration in 1988, the Air Force began assigning women to serve with men on missile crews. The Air Force says there are *no reports* of sexual misconduct among the mixed crews. I emphasize "no reports," because I was acutely aware before this gender integration of missile officers and their wives being unfaithful to one another and exchanging partners. I am no prude but somethings do cross the line for me.

When I was on duty in the missile capsule, the space included a cot around which we hang wool blankets to create a space for "shut eye" breaks, since sleeping was not permitted on duty.

With the mixed crews, the cot was replaced with a real enclosed bed in 1991. "Babysitting" missiles took on new meaning — making babies. I know, since I lived in the first unisex bachelor quarters, we averaged one marriage a month, and sexual encounters were only slightly more discreet than that Best Little Whorehouse in Texas.

When I left the Air Force in the winter of 1969, I was an emotional wreck. I spend a month taking it out skiing on Ajax Mountain in Aspen while staying at the Snow Flake Lodge, a ramshackle boardinghouse.

Returning to Arlington, VA, I began putting into words my missile experience and how I felt. Writing was a great relief. No publications were interested in my story until I was contacted by Jack Limpert who for 43 years edited the *Washingtonian Magazine*. He forced me to do many rewrites and to tone down my anger.

In a note with one of these drafts, he wrote, "The important thing is to be as informative as possible to create a picture for the reader of what it's like to be a missile officer with as much detail as possible."

Once it was written, I feared the Air Force would retaliate with good reason, I later learned from former colleagues. So, I went to see Katherine Nelson in Senator Stewart Symington's office, the Democratic Senator from Missouri who was also the first Secretary of the Air Force.

The Senator met with me briefly, and I discussed the demoralization of the missile corps. Technically, I was still in the Reserves, subject to recall, and had signed a nondisclosure form promising not to reveal any secrets after I left the military.

At the Senate hearing before a Senate Committee on Armed Services in April 1971, Senator Symington surprised General Holloway, commander of the Strategic Air Command (SAC), with galleys of my article, which he handed to him.

Symington said, "This is an article written by a retired Air Force captain stationed in my home state, at Whiteman, about the morale of men who live in the Minuteman holes. Have you seen that article? His father is a scientist, and he is a graduate of Georgetown University. He seems to be one of those typically intense but sincere young men of the day."

"I do not believe so. I have seen others. I heard about it," General Holloway responded. Symington said, "If I send it to you, will you comment on it?"

Asked about *human reliability* in the missile corps – an issue that I raised in the article, General Holloway said there is "tight screening and keeping these people informed of the fact they are special." Symington said, "I am glad. I myself went down in some of these holes and looked around and felt it would be quite..." The General finished his sentence, "it would be a challenge."

Continuing, Symington said, "It would be difficult for me to handle that as a permanent job. The man who wrote this article – I had never heard of him before. He lives around here, so I asked him to come in. He did, and he backed up the article with more details."

The full article was placed in the Congressional Record and excerpts are below. The article cover for the *Washingtonian,* May 1971, depicts the entrance to a Minuteman launch capsule.

The message to go to war starts "Purple Dot... Purple Dot... Purple Dot... Bravo ...Zulu... Mike... Romeo ...Delta... Juliet..." The commander and his deputy go to a small red safe for the go code and launch keys. They insert their keys and the commander says:

Launch on the Count of Three.

One... Two... Three

The launch officer waits for the message. What kind of man is he? What does he think about? If the message ever comes, will he turn his key? On his own, could he start World War III? A Minuteman launch officer tells what he has seen and what he thinks.

Turning past the sign PEACE IS OUR PROFESSION, a visitor entering Whiteman Air Force Base is struck by the empty spaces and lack of activity. A 12,000-foot runway stretches to the horizon. Three obsolete aircraft sit lost in acres of concrete near the terminal. Old hangars by the ramp area are reminders of Whiteman's busy glider-training days of World War II. A checkerboard of treeless lots divided by potted service roads show where hastily constructed quarters once stood. A new elementary school, modern chapel, and bowling alley stand out as evidence that the base has been resurrected for a new role.

Whiteman is part of the other Air Force. It houses the 351st Strategic Missile Wing and supports the wing's 150 Minuteman missiles scattered in silos across the central Missouri farmland.

There are fifteen underground control centers, some of them 100 miles from the base. Each is linked by a network of cables to ten missiles. Above ground, security guards patrol for intruders. Signs on a barbed wire fence surrounding the buildings caution strangers in bold red letters: WARNING: RESTRICTED AREA. At night, floodlights cast intricately lined shadows from wires and antennae. Mushroom-topped ducts pump air filtered for radioactive and biochemical agents into a subterranean capsule.

Descending slowly into a sixty-foot shaft, two officers in dark blue uniforms with.38 caliber revolvers on their hips ride a freight elevator to the tomb-like enclosure below. They could be police officers except for a patch over the left pocket that reads "Missile Combat Crew." The launch capsule is entered by crouching through a five-foot-high tunnel. A tired, anxious-to-leave crew emerges to ride the elevator back to the surface. The deputy of the new crew, using all his strength, closes a massive blast door. Locked in, the new crew is isolated as if camped in a bank vault. Alone now, they take their guns off and switch into dungarees and casual clothes to wait out their twelve-hour shift.

A whirring deedle-deedle-deedle from a loudspeaker above the command console warns the crew that an important message is being sent. They scramble for red copy books and turn to the tabbed format - LAUNCH. After the message is validated, the crew opens a small red safe where two launch keys and the go code are stored. They compare the message with the go code and they match. Next, they are supposed to insert their keys and check with the other crews for launch timing. If two crews decide to launch and turn their keys, the missiles launch.

Under almost maddening conditions of isolation and boredom, a launch officer repeatedly mulls over his reactions to an actual launch message. Daily he practices the launch sequence from receipt of the message to the twist of his wrist above the launch key slot. Each time a part of his mind dwells on his role at unleashing the destruction at his command. He tries to cope with the moral implications of turning the key on millions of people.

Over a three-year hitch as a missile launch officer, I lived with the responsibility for carrying out the launch order. I didn't choose the duty. A computer at Maxwell Air Force Base singled me out "in the needs of the service." Before assignment at Whiteman, I graduated from Georgetown University as a commissioned ROTC second lieutenant. My selection for missiles must have been completely random, for I never took a college course in mathematics or science, and I showed a near total lack of technical or mechanical skills on an Air Force aptitude test...

Capsule life is Spartan. Once we are locked in and are in comfortable clothes, we sit. No entertainment is available to pass the endless hours. There is infrequent maintenance activity to relieve the monotony. There is constant equipment noise. The many alarms are loud enough to alert a hangar instead of gaining our attention in a tiny enclosed capsule. Rube Goldberg contraptions are devised to silence them. A capsule tour is long hours of quiet boredom.

To pass time crew members place endless phone calls to family and friends. Occasionally an officer takes a game or model airplane into the capsule. Certain crews are noted for the hobby shop atmosphere of their capsule. The only way to hear an important event, like the World Series, is to ask your security guard topside to leave an open intercom mike next to a portable radio. In the capsule there are high-frequency, ultra-high frequency, and low frequency radios, but none with an AM or FM band for missile music lovers.

Some crews sleep. It is forbidden, but the capsule is conveniently equipped with a GI bed. In order to isolate the bed from the lighted portion of the capsule, a tent of blankets hung by paper clips surrounds the bed. One crew member maintains the alert; the other sleeps. While this practice clearly violates the "Two Man Policy," which says crew members must at all times monitor each other's actions, sleeping is condoned by everyone. The term "eye-rest" is used to mollify those who are uneasy about breaking the regulation. Some officers have been known to "eye-rest" for twelve hours, not infrequently shaking off a hangover...

There also are continuous tests at the base, and since no mistakes are allowed, officers learn that playing square can be dangerous. A friend, Captain Mike Berk ... "missed" one of ten questions on a code-handling test. Actually, he knew the answer, but marked the wrong IBM card slot. His squadron commander gave him a letter of reprimand and fifteen hours punitive training. The general rule on missile tests is to compare answers so that nobody makes a mistake...

Checklists are designed to handle the normal and the emergency. They are tabbed and updated with any misplaced pages worthy of a letter of reprimand. Launch procedures are found under the category "Normal Operations."

In a crisis, the checklists get in the way. I was once checking blast valves which isolate the capsule during an attack. I pushed a button which should have had no actual effect. But the valves closed and fumes from a diesel engine, undergoing a periodic operational check, almost overpowered me. No time for a checklist, just reflex actions. After the emergency, an inspection showed the valves closed because a solenoid had been put in backwards...

Missile crew members have a different perspective from those higher up. We spend hour after hour sitting in front of the panel of ten missile ready lights. Our daily job does not involve inspection trips to the field or the hypothetical world of nuclear strategy. We live intimately with the ICBMs. We feel the presence of the missiles like a hen delicately tending her eggs...

We are not supposed to have consciences. Our job is to turn the keys, the mythical buttons of nuclear destruction. Our training consists of writing down the launch message and practicing the launch sequences over and over, Pavlovian conditioning. We've been told that the President and others with greater knowledge and wisdom will take care of making the decisions. All we do is pull the trigger.

The moral consequences of the job gradually seep into the conscience. The training period is hectic. During the first six months of pulling alerts, the Orwellian environment holds the new missileman's fascination. We tell ourselves that war is hell, so don't clutter the mind with personal feelings. With time that attitude changes, not because of what others say, but because we have so much time to contemplate our role in a nuclear war.

Some missile officers finally decide they want out. If a man goes to the chaplain and tells him he refuses to turn the key, his missile days are instantly over. There's a catch, however. Missile officers who claim a conscientious objection to participating in World War III might as well forget about a career. They'll get the worst imaginable duty, for the command does not want others to catch the disease...

No dialogue exists between launch officers and those who write and enforce the rules which govern capsule activity. Most contact is at briefings where crew members find it safer not to ask questions. The commanders talk and act behind closed doors. The standardization and training sections maintain blacklists of weak crew members. Missile officers treat them collectively as enemies. The idea is to remain anonymous to those in command. If someone gets a bad reputation, there is extra training and more standardization checks. More opportunities are offered for a mistake. The margin between passing and failing is narrow...

The only consideration I remember from a commander was a telephone call at Christmas to say, "Because of you, others are safe this day."

We know that if told to launch, the whole system of deterrence has failed. Our launching would be a postscript to a monstrous miscalculation or madness. With this in mind, we believe the launch message will never come. If the message ever does come, we will first assume it is a mistake...

Because crew members are not treated as human beings with failings and consciences, the missileman's life is one of playing the game. If a launch message interrupts the game, no one can predict the crew's response. I think many Minuteman officers will freeze. Some will query higher command for verification of the message. The rest will look into their souls.

After a decision to launch, how many missiles will leave the silos is another unknown. Reaction time to an enemy's attack ever shortens, but safeguards entailing additional procedures grow and grow. For example, earlier Minuteman systems armed the warheads by simply lifting a toggle switch; now a detailed separate procedure sends a coded message to arm the missiles.

Launch procedures change so often that an old one is no sooner learned than a new one arrives. An instructor told us that the constant changes were a device to keep Russian spies off balance. After all, if we who live with the system can barely keep up, consider the spy's difficulty.

The complicated launch procedures also presumably prevent a Dr. Strangelovian plot among missile launch officers. But four officers in a Minuteman squadron of fifty missiles could, without any authorization, start World War III. If four officers in two capsules decide to turn their keys and launch, no one could stop the launch. Even two officers in separate capsules with a mechanical device to turn the needed cooperating keys could launch the squadron's missiles...

America's missile officer corps is demoralized. Submerged in an organization devoted to the "glory days" of long-range bombers, SAC has forgotten about the special concerns of the missile people.

Reactions

For the record, General Bruce K. Holloway, commander of the Strategic Air Command, and the person who signed the orders for my top-secret missile trip, responded at length to Senator Stuart Symington:

"The principal premise of Mr. Weihe's paper, and the one from which most of his criticism stems, is that the life of a missileer is intrinsically monotonous and boring. I agree fully with this premise, but with little of the criticism...

As mentioned last week in my response for the record, SAC has recognized from the start the morale problems concerned with standing alerts in missile control facilities under necessarily rigid conditions of duty attention and job knowledge. The rules are very exacting, and there are many checks and inspections: operational readiness; maintenance standardization and compliance; and personal performance against comprehensive procedural checklists. There have been many things done to make life under these duty conditions more attractive, and to ameliorate the boredom which is so obviously, a problem....

We are continuing to work the problem, and there just isn't any substance to the allegations that 'America's missile officer corps is demoralized,' that it is 'submerged in an organization devoted to the glory days of long range bombers,' and that 'SAC has forgotten about the special concerns of the missile people."

My response

The great advantage of being an author is that you get to respond to comments on your article so I wrote: "The overall high morale of the Air Force tends to obscure the particularly low morale of the missile corps Having been an Air Force Captain with over three years' experience pulling alert tours in two Minuteman systems, I believe my opinions represent a consensus of those held by "launch officers at the operational level"...

I shared my article with Senator Jack Miller, a conservative Republican from Iowa and Reserve General in the Air Force who asked Holloway to respond as well. Holloway wrote, "As you can sense just from the tenor of this author's style and language, he is harboring some resentment and frustration. The maintenance of good morale and discipline in the very exacting circumstances of keeping missiles on alert year to year has been long recognized in SAC."

He added "It is, however, a continuing worry of mine – particularly against the alarming trends and behavior on the part of youth in general." I thought this is exactly the attitude of senior military that are unable to adjust to a new, more skeptical generation towards authority.

Air Force Times

The publishers of the *Air Force Times* read the *Washingtonian Magazine* article and contacted me to write a longer one from a military perspective. I was surprised that a military publication that is delivered daily to all branches of the armed services would want me to write an anti-military piece. The staff was trying to open up their publication to more provocative issues – and that certainly occurred.

My revised article appeared in the *Family Magazine* as an insert on November 17, 1971 under the title: "When Armageddon Comes

Will They Fire in the Hole?" The lead was printed over a cover of a nuclear mushroom explosion.

On the newspaper's front page, the USAF Chief of Staff, General John Ryan, attacked the *Air Force Times* for publishing my article. He characterized it as "inaccurate and misleading," and "an affront to the many dedicated men now assigned to SAC missileer duty."

He wrote, "If I understand your paper's function correctly, it is to pass accurate information to the Air Force people about things of interest that are happening in and around the Air Force. In light of this, our men and their families have come to regard the *Air Force Times* as an authoritative source of information. The Minuteman piece which you are now publishing seriously detracts from that reputation."

Of course, this headline meant that every missile launch officer immediately turned to the *Family* insert and read the article. Over 50 responses came pouring in, half in agreement; half opposed, and a dozen subscription cancellations. Here are samples:

Your description of the atmosphere of fear and paranoia was quite lucid and exact, Captain Alan Schlukbier at Malmstrom missile wing.

I wish to congratulate you for having the initiative and guts to print an article that tells the real truth about the Minuteman system...As the article points out, the morale is extremely low, job satisfaction non-existent and the amount of harassment very high. Again, thanks for the truth, Captain George Hardy.

I have rarely encountered such a hopeless mishmash of truth, half-truth and outright absurdity, Major James Hastings.

Unfortunately, many of Weihe's observations about crew duty are valid. I can verify several of the incidents he related and recall others. Paragraphs about test rules in the force, Standardization Board harassment of certain crew members, and a lack of experience or understanding by senior wing officers are painfully accurate to Minuteman crew members, Field grade officer.

Launch Control Center, requirements to follow Tech Order checklist to the point of absurdity, a managerial system based on fear of punishment as the prime motivation, missile launch officer.

I am appalled by your gross display of irresponsibility...That you would print such an article over the very strong objection voiced by General Ryan is incomprehensible, Major Lee Stanley.

You have performed a real public service. As a Missile Combat Crew Commander, I can personally verify the accuracy of the information, Midwest Captain.

Printing the article was an irresponsible act, Maj. Donald McCort.

Yes, the capsules are austere, the job is lousy one and the career visibility for a young officer extremely limited, Line crew member.

I believe one should set aside criticism of the article as to its factual inaccuracies and hence to dismiss the entire piece as uninformed muckraking. The crux of the matter is what he believes to be true...If it is found that these feelings, however, mistaken are widespread in the missile force, then correction of such a morale problem should become a matter of special interest to commanders at all levels, Captain John Trever.

71

I would say that 90 percent of the article is true. Having spent six years in the missile field, I speak with a little experience, Captain.

We were dismayed to read the Ted Weihe article. As former combat crew members, all previously stationed at Whiteman and personally knowing Ted, we were not surprised at the half-truths, inaccuracies, unsupported opinions, Major Lloyd Rowe and 21 other officers. (This letter came from Offutt headquarters, not Whiteman and clearly was designed to please the higher-ups. I recognized none of the names on it.)

The article presents it like it actually is, allowing for minor differences found within various wings, Officer.

The article smacks of sensationalism from front to back...I do not intend to make missiles a career, but you can be sure there is at least one missile crew member who intends to turn his key when properly ordered, Capt. Richard Homberg.

It is worth a thousand SAC staff studies, Former Crew Commander.

In fact, because of my articles and the inquiry from Senator Symington, SAC commissioned 19 former ICBM launch officers to review life and regulations in the capsule. It did change some policies such as allowing TVs and radios for launch crews.

When a *New York Times* reporter went to Warren AFB in Cheyenne, Wyoming, where he was given a carefully scripted tour and officially-approved interviews, someone slip my article under his door.

In "H-Bomb Duty: Alert for Armageddon" on April 4, 1972, Anthony Ribley wrote: "Into this orderly, programmed remote world last

November came an article that sent shock waves through Air Force circles in Washington. Written by a former launch control officer, it was printed in the twice-monthly supplement to the Air Force, Army and Navy Times, which is called 'Family.'

"The launch-control officers have been relegated to a bureaucratic dehumanizing way of life which leads to demoralization and unreliability in our deterrent force,' wrote Ted Weihe, a former officer. Such a comment struck at the heart, for the launch-control officers man a central battle station in the nation's nuclear shield. The officers at Warren AFB, "for the most part say that the article was too dark, too depressing," he concluded.

I was asked by the National Committee for a SANE Nuclear Policy to write a book against ICBMs. I rejected the offer and felt that I had done my duty in exposing the hypocrisies in my Air Force service. More curiously, I was contacted by an alternative New England newspaper several years later. They wanted me to write what if Nixon decided to launch the missiles; I turned them down as well. I wanted to get on with my life and career and put this past experience into the past.

The *Bulletin of the Atomic Scientists* (November 1980) quoted my thesis on the moral dilemmas of launching Minuteman missiles. It said, "Moving from the carefully controlled milieu of the laboratory into the reality of operating nuclear strategic forces, some insight into these problems can be gained from the 1971 report of a former Air Force deputy missile crew commander, Ted Weihe, on life in the hardened silos of the U.S. based missile force. *Even healthy humans who are not subjected to extraordinary stress or grinding boredom may contribute to the human reliability problem in the military because of control difficulties inherent in all bureaucracies of size.*"

A 2014 Rand study commissioned by the Air Force concluded that the typical launch officer was "exhausted, cynical, and distracted on the job." ICBM airmen had high rates of sexual assault, suicide, and spousal and child abuse, more than double the rates of court-martial than Air Force personnel as a whole. In 2014, a former Minuteman launch officer told a reporter from *Mother Earth* that having a bunch of disillusioned guys babysitting such terrible weapons has "been talked and bitched about for a *long* time.

Bob Peurifoy, director of weapon development at Sandia National Laboratories who introduced build-in missile safeguards, said," The risk of accidental launch is small. But, if you want it to be zero, just take them off alert." He added that "an accident is waiting to happen."

In December 1997 under the SALT nuclear arms agreement, the last Minuteman II silo at Whiteman AFB was destroyed. Prior to the arrival of the first B-2 Stealth bombers, the Air Force removed the warheads and begun to demolish the 150 launch sites. In many ways, the SALT agreements promised an end of the Cold War standoff. But, additional ICBM reductions have not occurred.

While walking on the third floor of the Senate Hart building in 1990, I came across a four-star Air Force General. I asked him, "How many generals had four stars." I was surprised when he answered, "39 and 11 in the Air Force." Then, I noticed that he wore a missile badge and told him that I had served at Whiteman AFB. He said that he was assigned with his equivalent in the Soviet Air Force to dismantle the missiles and that they blew up one of the silos at Whiteman.

I read later that the Air Force just removed essential and useable equipment from the launch facilities and left the rest and just filled the elevator shaft with concrete. They became big party scenes with empty beer and liquor bottles scattered around. It was hard to believe that the Air Force just abandoned it "as is" and left it open to the public.

Views widely shared

I am no longer alone in my views; many retired senior military generals have spoken out, saying that Minuteman ICBMs are an obsolete deterrent. In the *Washington Post Magazine* (December 7, 1997) entitled, "The General's Conscience," by three-star General George Butler who rose to be chief commander of America's nuclear forces said he dutifully planned and rehearsed for atomic war. And somewhere along the way, he began to question the moral meanings of his work.

While in the Air Force, Butler did not question the value of nuclear weapons as deterrence. But, after leaving, he wrote, "Nuclear weapons should be abolished. They do not provide security to Americans or anyone else. The theory of nuclear deterrence, the bedrock principle of U.S. national security during the Cold War, is costly, wrongheaded and dangerous." Sixty retired American, Russian and other generals and admirals supported his call for the elimination of nuclear arms.

Former Secretary of Defense (1994-1997), William Perry in his memoir, said, "The United States can safely phase out its land-based intercontinental ballistic missile (ICBM) force, a key facet of Cold War nuclear policy...These missiles are some of the most dangerous weapons in the world. They could even trigger an accidental nuclear war." He described the incident 40 years ago when a malfunctioning computer indicated 200 ICBMs on their way from the Soviet Union in which the president had less than 30 minutes to make that "terrible decision."

ICBMs are still trigger-ready to launch. Installed in 1996, nuclear arming has changed with more potential targets that can be added in seconds through REACT, Rapid Execution and Combat Targeting.

During his presidential campaign, Barack Obama said, "Keeping nuclear weapons ready to launch on a moment's notice is a dangerous relic of the Cold War. Such policies increase the risk of catastrophic accidents or miscalculation." He said that because the United States is the only nation that has used these weapons, we have a "moral responsibility to see a world without them."

Early in his presidency, he called for taking Minuteman missiles off hair-trigger alert, but deferred to Cold War holdouts in the Pentagon. Obama won the Nobel Peace Prize partly due to his landmark 2009 speech in Prague. He said he would take concrete steps to "reduce the role of nuclear weapons in our national security strategy." Yet, the Pentagon is committed to the modernization of nuclear weapons over the next three decades at an estimated cost of $1 trillion.

By taking my case to Congress, the Air Force and public, my choices validated life-affirming values in dealing with a crisis of conscience. As I left the Air Force, I was sure that there would be an accidental launch. To this day, I know about incidents of Minuteman unreliability that have not been declassified. Those of us who were part of the Strategic Air Command are amazed that nuclear weapons have not been used and major cities not destroyed.

The issue of control of our nuclear arsenal returned with the election of Donald Trump as President and his loose cannon temperament. I contacted Bruce Blair who organized a list of over 30 former missileers who were concerned about Trump with his finger on the proverbial "Red Button."

The joint statement read: "We are former nuclear launch control officers, or 'missileers.' We sat nuclear alerts in underground missile launch centers. It was our job to turn keys to fire nuclear-armed missiles if the president so ordered us. Once we began alert duty, we took orders from the president and no one else.

Only the president can order a nuclear launch. That order cannot be vetoed and once the missiles have been launched, they cannot be called back. The consequences of miscalculation, impulsive decision-making or poor judgment on the part of the president could be catastrophic.

The pressures the system places on that one person are staggering and require enormous composure, judgment, restraint and diplomatic skill. Donald Trump does not have these leadership qualities. On the contrary, he has shown himself time and again to be easily baited and quick to lash out, dismissive of expert consultation and ill-informed of even basic military and international affairs—including, most especially, nuclear weapons."

On the Brink

On February 11, 2018, I made a presentation to the forum at my Unitarian Universalist Church of Sarasota. I said,

"For nearly 50 years as a former Minuteman ICBM launch officer, I have lived with the fear of nuclear war. On duty for three and a half years, our war plan was to hit every city in the Soviet Union and many in China. At Whiteman Air Force base, we had "special packages" to destroy Moscow and Beijing. It was called MAD – Mutual Assured Destruction. The US was prepared to annihilate 600 million people or 100 Holocausts. We would not only kill Russians, but friendly states like Norway and Austria through fall out.

The war plan – called Single Integrated Operational Plan or SIOP – was to carry out a pre-emptive strike against the Soviet Union based on warnings. As a launch officer, I practiced pre-emptive war

against the Soviet missile bases often. Hit them before they hit us. While in the alternative command center. I looked at how many nukes were targeted on various cities: 1/3 had a single nuke, 1/3 two nukes and the rest, more than 2 including one target with 17 nukes. Launch officers asked not to know which cities that they would strike – but basically all of them.

I knew that I would never launch the missiles. I decided to keep this decision totally within me, not telling anyone. So, as a release, I questioned everything about the job that seemed ridiculous – and there was plenty of it…

There have been 32 US confirmed accidents involving 1,200 nukes. Some noteworthy ones are:

- The accidental dropping of three nuclear bombs in North Carolina,
- A near launch of Soviet nuclear torpedo during Cuban missile crisis,
- The Jet-fueled fire of a nuclear-armed attack plane,
- The crash of a nuclear armed B-52,
- The silo explosion of a Titan II which launched its nuclear warhead several miles, and
- A flock of birds mistaken for 250 incoming Russian missiles.

These accidents or miscalculations due to them could result in retaliatory nuclear war. The president, senior military officials in Russian or the US have less than 30 minutes to react to an incoming missile attack. President Trump is accompanied by the so-called nuclear football which is supposed to show civilian control. But, the reality is that his authority is delegated to senior military leaders in a highly classified directive.

What can be done to lower these risks? We could move our nuclear posture from assured destruction to minimal nuclear arsenal –

probably less than 50 nuclear bombs though former nuclear planners have suggested 450 warheads.

The ultimate goal should be zero nuclear arsenals worldwide. A UN resolution to eliminate nuclear arms has 120 country signatories. The first steps are to reduce the numbers of nukes and protect them better from terrorists – especially tactical nukes which are smaller and easier to steal.

Yet, the US and Russia are rushing to "modernize" their arsenals at the cost just for us of $1 trillion over the next decade.

For 70 years, modernization has meant the ability to carry out first use or a preemptive attack. Trump's new National Posture Review (2018) said that officials perceive US nuclear capabilities as inadequate. They want to create low-yield nuclear weapons (less than 20 kilotons) – the same as Hiroshima - as a deterrent as well as new nuclear-armed cruise missiles and a replacement for B-52s as a long-range bomber. Trump wants to opt out of the START treaty when it expires in three years that mandates reductions of the nuclear stockpiles. Modernization also raises the likelihood of renouncing nuclear testing ban.

We are on the brink. In 2018, the Hawaii incoming missile warning and the similar one in Japan could have resulted in retaliatory nuclear strikes. Trumps taunting of Kim Jogn Un with "My button is bigger than yours" or his misguided thought that we could win a nuclear war is scary.

Congress could put restraints onto Donald Trump and future presidents. They have the Constitutional war-making powers. Yet, Congressional hearings on the subject by only the military witnesses confirmed the total delegation of nuclear war to the president.

To move away from the brink– that Obama said he would do but did not – is to take ICBM missiles off trigger alerts. There is no rational need for Minuteman ICBMs, except as a hollow threat of first use.

There only purpose is for a pre-emptive strike. The next step is to renounce the first use of nuclear arms.

Other initiates could include:

The Senate should approve the Comprehensive Test Ban Treaty. We should begin new START talks to further reduce US and Russian nuclear arsenals. We should not deploy ballistic defense systems in Europe and Asia since these systems encourage more offensive missiles and probably are not effective. Anti-ballistic systems in Europe are a major reason for Russia to rearm.

We need to reactivate programs to get rid of loose nukes, especially tactical nukes or stored missiles – such as the successful Nunn-Lugar program in the former Soviet Union.

But, all of that is not enough – and we are entering a new spiral of nuclear arming.

Some of the steps to reduce risks are advocated by Global Zero. Global Zero is an international movement with 300 national leaders and 450,000 citizens worldwide.

I have participated in two publicly release letters by former missile launch officers by Global Zero – warning about the instability of candidate Trump and urging Congress to limit his authorities such as prohibiting first launch.

The question that has not been addressed by any president or senior military official is: "Does any government have the moral right to bring its people or the possibility of all humanity under the shadow of nuclear destruction?"

Russia and the US possess doomsday weapons, 'Is there any justification to have them, to threaten their use or to maintain them?'

This is a moral issue of our times that has not, nor it appears will not be addressed."

For 50 years, I have been dogged with worries about a nuclear strike or nuclear accident, and my fears have not gone away.

Chapter 4: An International Career

When I returned from the Air Force, I felt that classmates who had avoided the draft such as by joining the Peace Corps had a major head start over me. It took me a year to find a job, but first I needed political experience and proof of my writing abilities.

I wanted to work on the Hill, and I knew Jack Lewis, a staffer for Senator Bill Spong (D-VA), so I decided to ask Jack for leads. He asked me, "Have you ever written a speech, or a press release?" I said, "No, but at Georgetown, all exams had to be written; there were no multiple-choice questions."

He suggested that I contact the manager of Bill Battle's campaign for governor. I did, and I volunteered to write speeches and press releases. My most noteworthy subject concerned the under-utilization of Dulles International Airport. The speech I wrote started with "In the lush green fields of Chantilly." I was told never use the word "lush" in a political speech.

After the primary, I was offered a job at $100 a week writing press releases and managing the Battle campaign in Northern Virginia. He lost. Later, I participated in Dorothy McDiarmid's campaign for Congress. She lost. I then helped manage Ed Holland's race for state senator. He won.

INGAA

With this meager experience on my resume, I applied for a writing position at the Interstate Natural Gas Association of America (INGAA) through the Georgetown placement office. Former Congressman Walter E. Rogers (D-TX) interviewed me and hired me as a Capitol Hill reporter. He and his sons had all gone to Georgetown.

My boss was Bud Thorp, who said, "My recommended candidate was a drunk, but a good writer." He basically tried to get me to quit by making me rewrite and rewrite again every paragraph that I sent him. It was wonderful on-the-job training.

I wanted to learn to write quickly and dictate stories over the phone like reporters, so I took a part-time job at the *Global Newspapers* as a political writer, which meant that I would be attending night city council meetings. In hiring me, the editor said, "Ted marches to his own drummer."

"No Growth"

A group of Arlington activists – Bradley Byers, Gerald Barney and Tom Floyd -- began to question unrestrained growth in the metropolitan region. They testified before the David Rockefeller-led Commission on Population Growth and the American Future in April 1971. Rockefeller was so impressed when the three testified that he wrote out a personal check of $3,000 to Arlington Co-Opt.

The D.C. metropolitan area was expected to grow by six million over the next two decades. The Arlington Co-Opt group wanted to form a regional citizen's organization to address land use planning to better accommodate this population growth. Generally, growth was controlled by developers with little say by citizens.

Initially, I volunteered to organize candidates meetings about growth in Arlington. I wrote my first proposal to the Agnes and Eugene Myers Foundation to form a regional Co-Opt. Founded in 1944 by these former owners of the *Washington Post*, it funds non-profits in the D.C. area. After receiving the grant, I hired myself to run the Coalition on Optimum Growth (Co-Opt), which advocated citizen engagement on development issues.

In this role, I organized citizens to speak out on zoning ordinances, participate in master planning, and held demonstrations against excessive high-rise development. I sent out press releases and a monthly newsletter that linked civic organizations into a coalition to share information and successful strategies. Developers called us "No growth."

Co-Opt views on development

I wrote the Co-Opt philosophy in a pamphlet entitled, "What Happens When Developers Plan a City," which challenged the notion that development always expands the tax base without considering its public costs in infrastructure such as sewers, water, fire protection, and other services. It was illustrated by Rudy Wendelin, creator of Smokey Bear.

These efforts united fiscal conservatives concerned about rising tax rates and environmentalists who opposed construction of sewer systems that are essential for urban sprawl in rural areas. As an example of these efforts, Julie Mangis and I prepared an alternative citizen's plan for the development corridor in Arlington with much lower densities than proposed by the official planning staff.

I was successful in getting the Arlington County Board to engage Robert Muller at the Urban Institute to study of the costs and benefits of Rosslyn, across from D.C. It concluded that it would take more than 20 years for the county to absorb the costs of development and result in higher revenues.

I tried to stop the construction of an extra Metro stop in Arlington because it would generate too much density. I got support from the transportation committee, but only one vote on the five-member County Board.

I had a Nader law student intern research the interstate compact for the construction of the Metro system which required jurisdictions to fund additions, but did not allow them to recover any funds for deletions — in this case, saving Arlington $20 million. The student lawyer showed me that this hard-to-achieve compromise formula could be challenged since it was adopted without public hearings. I learned that sometimes, inaction is the best course of action.

This experience taught me how to mobilize citizens and build coalitions that, in turn, can successfully impact political decisions. We were able to defeat plans for a new downtown on Wisconsin Avenue in D.C. We also analyzed and challenged a regional computer program that inevitably indicated the need for more highways and defeated a proposed bridge across the Potomac.

On the downside, I saw how money and developers can intimidate local elected officials, including the chairman of the County Board. When I tried to change the zoning ordinances to restrict "McMansions" in Arlington, the developers fought hard to prevent the changes. It took 11 years of organizing and an enlightened chairman, Chris Zimmerman, to adopt the revised ordinances.

League of Women Voters

From the Co-Opt job I learned to be a self-starter. My next position was as a lobbyist and writer for the national League of Women Voters. Here my editor and executive director was Peggy Lampe. If she didn't like one of my Hill articles, she stamped it "bullshit" without any explanation. That certainly made me write more clearly.

Another lesson I learned – You can never be certain what Congress will do. Several Leaguers kept encouraging me to oppose the inclusion of tobacco in Food for Peace programs. I told them that it was impossible; the tobacco lobby was too strong. On the House floor, an unexpected amendment passed that removed tobacco from the program. I had to write them apologetically that I had been wrong.

My most noteworthy effort was to co-chair the National Clean Air Coalition and lobby for the enactment of the far-reaching 1970

Clean Air Act that put in place new technologies like the catalytic converter and smokestack scrubbers as well as the monitoring of air quality to protect the health of the most vulnerable: asthmatics and young children.

As the international affairs lobbyist for the League, I formed "The Floating Crap Game," a coalition of religious organizations, non-profits and labor unions, who met periodically in the Methodist building across from the Supreme Court. At the time, the major issue was how much US aid goes for security and military programs compared to humanitarian ones. We felt there was an imbalance as a result of the Cold War that favored "security" funding to anti-communist but often corrupt regimes.

USAID

As leader of this non-government coalition, I went to all of the key markups of the legislation. Jean Lewis who was the deputy in USAID's Legislative office and I collaborated on upcoming foreign aid floor amendments. She invited me to sit in the Diplomatic Gallery during House and Senate floor action prior to televised CSPAN.

With the election of Jimmy Carter, Jean Lewis, who had been a secretary to Congressman John F. Kennedy (D-MA), became the Assistant Administrator for Legislative Affairs at USAID. She asked me to join her as one of her Legislative Assistants. I got letters of support from Congressmen Dante Fascell (D-FL) and Joe Fisher (D-VA) who helped clear my name by the Carter White House. At the League, I had worked with Fascell on reforming Revenue Sharing, and helped get Fisher elected. I was Jean's only pick; the rest were campaign workers referred from the White House.

Jack Sullivan, who headed the transition team, set my salary based on my previous salary at the League of Women Voters as a GS 13.

The liaison positions had grades of 14, 15 and 16, so I was the lowest in pay.

A staffer to former Senator Yarborugh (D-TX), Alex Dickie had a grade 16 level of pay. His biggest responsibility was to stay in touch with Speaker Jim Wright, a fellow Texan, on scheduling of the foreign aid bill. Henry Poole, a grade 15, came from the staff of Senator Morgan (D-NC), and John Waggle, also a 15, came from a prominent Georgetown family, who raised funds for Democratic candidates.

I felt I had to work harder than the others to prove myself. Unlike my colleagues who saw their roles as going to USAID meetings and offering "political advice," I worked the Hill and established rapport with key staffers.

At the League of Women Voters, one of my mentors was Judy Norrell, whose father and mother were members of Congress representing Arkansas. She told me to find an office that you can work out of. She spent her Hill time at the office of Wilber Mills (D-AR), who was chairman of the Ways and Means Committee. He became famous for jumping into the Tidal basin with stripper Fannie Fox, a caper which did not prevent his re-election in 1974.

I was lobbying for the grain reserve to offset the losses of markets because of the boycott of the Soviet Union due its invasion of Afghanistan. I worked closely with Secretary of Agriculture Bob Bergland, whom I got to know well over the years.

A key supporter of the reserve was Matt McHugh (D-NY) on the Agriculture Committee. Matt came from a mostly urban upstate New York district and strongly advocated for school and infant feeding programs. McHugh wanted to move to the more powerful Appropriations Subcommittee on Foreign Operations.

Totally out-of-line for an official liaison officer of USAID in basically lobbying on behalf of a Congressman, an internal matter of the legislative branch, I discreetly helped him get the appointment. After that, I became an ex officio member of his staff. His staffer, Garry Bombardier, was my inside source of the subcommittee's inner workings, critical to funding USAID and its program budgets.

In 1978, I was told that I would not be promoted because there were only a few slots open, and they did not want to reward political appointees. This infuriated me and I appealed the rating with a USAID attorney, Mike Hager, who took my case and represented me at the Promotion Appeals Review Board.

To the board, Hager wrote, "The Executive's stunning victory on the House Appropriations bill Monday owes a great deal to your imagination and vigorous efforts. Your active contacts from the outset with Congressman McHugh and his staff did much, I am sure, to promote and sustain his leadership. Your regular involvement with the religious and other non-government organizations contributed to their constant state of mobilization. Finally, your fresh ideas for specialized 'talking points' papers provided ammunition for all of our friends."

Hager praised me for my efforts to improve the USAID Congressional Presentation (CP) and said that "many of the innovations in this year's CP are partly or wholly Ted's. One vital contribution stands out as Ted's idea and as a design element he executed himself. He edited 23 office inputs for consistency and clarity. But, the lacking element was the Agency's essential humanitarian mission, 'the narrative was devoid of people.'

Each section needed the human factor to balance the straightforward discussion of dollars, programs and projects. "Ted then hit on a solution: simple vignettes to precede each major account summary. In the weeks, which followed Ted not only undertook primary editing of budget sections reducing the text by more than half its original length – but he drafted the vignettes – carefully selecting them from a variety of sources and double checking their accuracy with appropriate agency offices. "

Hager concluded, "Ted worked quietly behind the scenes to help Matt McHugh, a liberal Congressman from Ithaca, gain the vacant seat" as a member of the Foreign Operations Subcommittee. McHugh's role on the subcommittee was critical to USAID. He has developed into our most supportive member of the subcommittee. After he got on the subcommittee, Ted suggested that McHugh meet all of USAID's assistant administrators, an innovation no other member of Congress has ever been enticed to do."

Hager detailed my efforts in developing close working relationships with Representatives Paul Simon, Don Pease, Dante Fascell and Senator Chuck Percy, our strongest supporters of USAID. I worked with the "good guys" on the subcommittee – McHugh, Lehman, Wilson, Conte, Burke, Stokes – for a common markup strategy rather than relying exclusively on Obey to cut a deal with Chairman Long.

He noted that I enlisted McHugh to educate relatively new members of Congress about the foreign aid legislation and originated the idea of hosting a series of members' breakfasts with Governor Gilligan, the USAID administrator.

During floor consideration, Hager pointed out that I suggested and then undertook the preparation of a floor action book – "never before attempted by the administration on a foreign aid appropriation." These became handouts and were used by supporters during the eight days the bill was on the House floor. He also drafted "Dear Colleague" letters for members in which they answered charges by opponents, not leaving any unanswered.

After House action, he turned to the Senate, and worked closely with Senator Hatfield (R-OR) to increase USAID's agricultural account by $5 million. "In summary, Ted's work was not only outstanding, but exemplary. Much of last year's legislative success for USAID and foreign aid is the result of Ted's efforts." I got the salary performance increase, but not a full step up from 13 to 14, but that was to come.

Jean Lewis, the head of the Legislative Office who hired me, left to take over the legislative office of the Government Services Administration in which there was a funding scandal. It left me as the only active and Hill focused legislative aide.

Doug Bennet moved over from State and became USAID Administrator. He brought with him Genta Hawkins, a career foreign service officer, who had interned with Congressman Dave Obey – a powerful member of the foreign operations appropriations subcommittee. Genta did not know the Hill like I did and relied on me. She said, "I always gave Ted a long leash."

She and Doug depended on me for Hill intelligence, and I had lots of inside information from Congressman Matt McHugh's office, such as getting markup drafts prior to official committee markup sessions – a leak and a coup.

Genta Hawkins recommended me for a full grade increase from 13 to 14 in December 1979. She wrote, "Throughout the FY 1979 legislative cycle, Mr. Weihe has made a number of noteworthy contributions helping to get the Agency's legislation through Congress. As an experienced legislative strategist, Mr. Weihe understands the necessity for immersing himself in the substance of issues involved and has consistently done so.

Weihe possesses a high degree of initiative, intelligence and sincere dedication to the Agency's programs and objectives. He is also imaginative and provides much of the spark in our office. He has consistently performed above his grade level. I believe that his enthusiasm and outstanding work performance should be rewarded with a full grade promotion."

The next legislative cycle in 1980 would test Genta Hawkin's reliance on my "initiative" and "imagination" when I accompanied Congressman Bill Lehman (D-FL) to Haiti and later engineered the Food for Furniture Amendment. I needed that long leash.

Self-confidence, independence, creativity, leadership, originality and boldness are some of the values that enabled me to launch a successful international career.

Chapter 5: Undercover Trip to Haiti

During the Easter Congressional break in 1979, I accompanied Congressman Bill Lehman (D-FL), along with Lucy Hand, chief of staff from his Congressional office and Sergio Bendixen, the director of his Miami office to visit USAID projects in Haiti. The trip was a cover for the Congressman and his staff to see what would happen if Judge James Lawrence King deported 5,000 illegal Haitians from his Miami district. The court case was pending at the time. They feared deportees would be jailed in inhuman conditions when they returned to Haiti.

**U.S. Ambassador William B. Jones,
Bill Lehman and Sergio Bendixen (left to right)**

We were accompanied by a Miami TV crew ostensibly there to document the Congressional trip, but who got up early one morning to photograph Baby Doc's notorious prisons and who were reporting live about the Tonton Macoute and military repression. Sergio Bendixen made clandestine phone calls to local relatives of the U.S. detainees and met secretly with them to find out what would happen if their relatives were deported back to Haiti.

We stayed at El Rancho, a luxury hotel in elegant Petionville, a suburb of the capital surrounded by mountains with swimming pools fed from filtered, fresh-water springs. As I was walking to my room the first evening, the electricity failed and I had to count the doors to reach my room. After that, I carried a small flashlight with me on overseas trips.

To keep up the fiction of our trip, we visited several USAID projects including an open-air, under-the-tree school, doctors' clinic in "Brooklyn," one of the poorest shantytowns along the Port–au-Prince Harbor, and an Israeli project that attempted to swap small plots divided up among brothers to consolidate them into more workable farms. We visited a Catholic charity that, to my surprise, provided contraceptives. I have never seen such poor people – with a possible exception of a later trip to South Sudan.

We met with Al Furman, the USAID mission director, and Ambassador William B. Jones, who was soon to retire. The ambassador held a formal dinner for us including business leaders that ran local shops for making baseballs and Gucci belts (later these companies left due to corruption and violence).

The ambassador invited me to help "tune" his sailboat, which he planned to sail to New England. We took a brief sail in the harbor, but the sails were so sun struck that they split as I tightened the boom vang. I thought how unsafe the ambassador's voyage might be since he appeared to know little about sailing or sailboats.

Bendixen found out about a Haitian USAID worker who had been deported and was located outside of Port-au-Paix. The Congressman insisted that the Embassy hire a plane to fly us there, much to their consternation. As he was a member of the Foreign Operations Appropriations Subcommittee, they could hardly refuse.

We went out to a small six passengers, banana-shaped airplane, whose pilot had to put a stick under its tail so that the plane did not fall backward when we boarded. We flew across Haiti where I took pictures of the barren hills and brown runoff since top soils were washing away. When we came to the dirt runway, the pilot buzzed the field to get the cows to move off.

Runoff and top soil losses due to removal of forests

As we touched down, a car pulled up and the Congressman and his two staff members got in and drove off to find the Haitian USAID worker to interview him. I was standing there alone when four appointed mayors arrived for the official visit which the Embassy had arranged. I was dumbfounded but recovered as best I could. I told them that the Congressman had gone to another location, that he wanted to see, and that I would be their official guest until he returned.

We met briefly in their tiny offices, and then I got a tour of the small town, its markets and docks, especially appreciating the wooden gaff-rigged boats that took passengers over to the island of Ile de la Tortue. As I was walking down the main dock, I asked in a loud voice, "When is the next boat to Miami?" A stranger in perfect English pointed to an anchored powerboat with gasoline Gerry cans along its deck and said, "It leaves in a couple of hours." Port-au-Paix was the major jumping-off place to go to Florida. There were no police or coast guard in sight to discourage such illegal trips.

To my great relief, the Congressman and staff returned and we visited the United Fruit cannery ruins and the harbor. They apologized to the mayors and we returned to the airplane. The pilot again put the stick in the back of the plane as we boarded. I was the co-pilot as he revved the engines, and we began bumping down the dirt runway.

All of a sudden, the pilot put on the brakes and reversed propellers for a sudden stop. He taxied back and got out of the plane. He took a wad of paper out of the speed indicator which tells when the plane has sufficient speed to take off. As we again took off, he said, "I wanted to make sure no dust clogged the air speed indicator."

I asked the Congressman why he and his staff had disappeared earlier. They had driven to a road construction project and tracked down a recent returnee who worked at USAID, and they interviewed him. He had told them, "My biggest problem was that I had taken out loans from friends for the trip to Miami and they wanted to be repaid. They beat me up." He told them as soon as he saved enough money by working for USAID, he planned to take another illegal boat to Miami. He said, "I have debts to pay." During our visit, we found no official repression of Haitians deported from the U.S.

Haiti is the poorest country in the Americas. We saw poor people in the street collecting and eating rotten food. Haiti is nearly a hopeless country for development projects which fail due to low levels of education, poor agricultural land, few jobs, bad governance and corruption.

What I learned is that what you see is not necessarily what reality is. Many underground secret Voodoo societies are more powerful than the officials. I witnessed a Voodoo ceremony where the high priest ate the head of a chicken. Drunken revelers clogged one of the streets we were on; we were told to be patient since they can turn on foreigners.

In the evening, mission director Al Furman asked, "Do you want to see the local sights?" I didn't know that meant visiting a whorehouse and being asked to dance awkwardly with a muscular prostitute – I could not wait to leave.

As we were about to leave, we went to the Haitian White House which resembled a Woody Allan set with machine guns behind some bushes out front. It was later destroyed in the 2010 earthquake. We met with Baby Doc, dressed in a plain khaki uniform without medals, who seemed intelligent. He feared the socialist revolution taking place in Grenada, which the Reagan Administration later invaded and removed from power.

In a class action suit on behalf of Haitians without visas, District Judge James Lawrence King condemned the Carter Administration policies that "were offensive to the very notion of constitutional due process and equal protection."

With the change in administration to Reagan, mass deportations against newly arrived Haitians began in 1981, with 35 cases per day being processed in locked courtrooms without lawyers. Its goal was to expel 6,000 Haitians by October 1981.

The U.S. helped Baby Doc flee to France with a hopeful but ultimately failed effort to establish democracy. My view is that Haiti is nearly hopeless and needs financial support and humanitarian assistance indefinitely. It is a graveyard for effective development assistance projects with few true successes and little prospects for broad economic prosperity.

As a result of the trip, I got a close look at Senator Ted Kennedy's primary challenge to Jimmy Carter. Several senior USAID officials resigned to join his campaign, showing disloyalty in my opinion. Bendixen, a native of Peru, chaired Senator Kennedy's 1980 Democratic primary race in Florida. Since my current political position depended on a Carter win, I was not pleased when he left Lehman's staff to run the campaign. He formed the foremost polling firm about Hispanics in the United States and Latin America.

Bill Lehman retired in 1993. His seat is now held by Debbie Wasserman Schultz, former chair of the Democratic Party. He was known as "Alabama Bill" due to his frequent TV ads for his auto dealership that he had relocated from Tuscaloosa, Alabama. Congressmen and staff consulted with him regularly when they were thinking about buying a car. He died in March 2005.

I recall a conversation about Haiti at one of my first days as a political appointee at USAID. A career staffer said, "We should continue to support Baby Doc since he is anti-communist." I responded, "only with humanitarian aid. Didn't you hear that President Carter ran on human rights and cutting off aid to repressive dictators?" It is one of his lasting legacies that I helped implement by supporting the people, not governments of dictators and tyrants.

Sergio Bendixen, Bill Lehman, Lucy Hand, reporters, myself Weihe, Al Furman (left to right)

Chapter 6: Saving a Million Lives

It is hard to imagine saving a million lives. But I can start by telling how I saved one.

At Georgetown University, I often took friends out on my Shearwater catamaran.   Mike Fagan, who grew up in Hibbing Minnesota and played in Bob Dylan's high school band, was my crew and his roommate Joe Flude joined us. In April 1963, when it was rather balmy, we decided to take a six pack of beer and Mike brought along his guitar for an evening sail down the Potomac.

We got becalmed south of the Wilson Bridge, but were in no hurry and could wait for some wind. As we sat there, we saw a speed boat in the channel going fast, about a half mile away. We heard what appeared to be an explosion and screams. I asked Mike to paddle while I steered toward the sound and we saw a man in the water.

"On the way", I yelled to him to get our bearings. I said, "How many are there?" and he responded "two." He said, "I can hang on a few minutes longer. Go right." He meant upstream. He was hanging on to a buoy and I did not know how much longer he could hold on. We got him into the boat and started up stream but we didn't see anything but debris. He said, "She's gone. She's gone."

He seemed very anxious to get to shore. He was very cold and his face was bloody. As we paddled, he changed his story, "I was alone," he said, but we remembered hearing a female voice and his words. He told us, "I hit the windshield of the boat." We flagged down a tugboat and they put him ashore at the Old Town Yacht Basin.

We wanted to believe him, but the more we discussed it, we knew he lied. It took a while to paddle to Alexandria where we found a late-night boat owner and called the Coast Guard on his radio. The police arrived and we each gave separate depositions.

The police found the tug boat and crew. They said the man sought medical help when he got ashore, and promptly got off their boat. The next day, the Coast Guard found the bow of the speedboat im-- bedded in the buoy. The harbor policeman said, "The buoy is eight feet out of the water. It's heavy and it's made to stay there." After dragging a net around the buoy, they found the women's body, Mary Dole.

The man we saved disappeared. In the next day's, *Washington Post*, it said that the "Maryland State police today were investigating a mysterious Potomac River boat crash that killed a woman and injured a man who was rescued but later disappeared."

Several days later, he turned himself into the police and said that he had taken a lot of pain pills and passed out for two days. He told them, "Mary was driving and that I went to the stern to check the stern light." We knew he was lying since his bloody face went through the windshield, and we had noticed that the stern light was working before the crash. He was not charged with manslaughter. In hindsight, I wish we had tried to save Mary first.

Saving lives with food aid

My trip to Haiti helped me appreciate how desperate people can be for food when I saw them scrambling to pick up rotten fruit that merchants threw out on the street. There is nothing more important than adequate water and food to save the lives of refugees and starving people.

In the winter of 1980, there were huge refugee crises in Pakistan with the Soviet war in Afghanistan, in Kenya with the Somalia attack on Ethiopia, and Thailand in which refugees fled conflicts in Cambodia and Vietnam. They desperately needed food aid.

In December 1979, Kathleen Bitterman at the U.S. Department of Agriculture (USDA) managed food programs. She sent an internal memo to various offices including mine that Congress has appropriated all she expects and a push for the extra funds would be "supererogatory."

She reflected Chairman Jamie Whitten's view that the Appropriations Committee had done enough. Whitten (D-KY) was known as the "Permanent Secretary of Agriculture," who dictated agricultural policies in detail and was feared throughout USDA.

With the refugee crises worsening, the President submitted a request for a supplemental of $122,600,000 on February 12, 1980. It was based on a memorandum by Tom Ehrlich, the overall foreign aid coordinator, that said, "We have just completed a careful review of the most urgent food needs around the globe. The results are alarming. Substantial amounts of food must be shipped soon to prevent widespread death and suffering. Unfortunately, our ability to meet these urgent food needs is extremely limited and will remain so until Congress passes the $122.6 million PL 480 Title II supplemental you requested in February."

His attachment indicated there were 1,950,000 refugees and drought victims in need of emergency food. These emergencies prompted Jimmy Carter to personally call Jamie Whitten twice to urge action on the supplemental. But, Congress acts slowly since all of the appropriations subcommittees must hear and consider a host of additional supplements for various government programs, most significantly the military.

By June 1980, the food situation continued to worsen. Without consulting the White House or senior administration officials, I explored some options for getting the full Title II humanitarian supplemental.

When the Agricultural Appropriations Subcommittee marked up the bill in early June, I asked Congressman Matt McHugh (D-NY) to increase the humanitarian food aid account. He got an agreement to shift $15 million from non-emergency (Title 1) to emergency food aid (Title II), but I told him that was not enough.

I took him to lunch at the Democratic Club and said, "Isn't there a way to move some money from another appropriations account to fully fund the emergency food aid." We discussed cutting a gasification plant project, but he said, "You can't do that. It is located in the subcommittee chairman's district."

Food for Furniture Amendment

As I explored options, I discovered that Congressman Andy Maguire (D-NJ) had a bill to cut $229 million in the GSA furniture account because of a scandal that agencies went there at the end of the fiscal year and got furniture whether they needed it or not.

Congressman Andy Maguire

104

Senators Jim Sasser (D-TN) and Tom Eagleton (D-MO) had a similar cutting amendment in the Senate. I thought why not cut the furniture account by $100 million and increase Title II by $42 million and save $58 million for taxpayers

As the legislative strategy was moving forward, USDA's Deputy Food Aid Coordinator, Mary Chambliss said, "It was too late to ship the food aid by the end of the fiscal year, September 30th."

I asked Bob Chase who handled food aid for USAID, "If I can get the money, can you deliver it?" He said, "Yes, just do it." Since I was not coordinating my actions with the White House or others, I kept Genta Hawkins, head of legislative affairs, and USAID Administrator Doug Bennet informed. I knew that an internal fight within the administration would doom the effort.

At my urging in late June, we formed a "PL 480 Working Group" that was led by David Dreyer of Andy Maguire's staff. He drafted the initial amendment and "Dear Colleague" letter. His list of proposed co-sponsors did not include Floyd Fithian (D-IN) who at my suggestion became the key sponsor, lead spokesman and face of the amendment.

Congressman Floyd Fithian

Andy Maguire was from an urban district. Floyd Fithian represented an agricultural district in Indiana, was on the agricultural committee and had just returned with Rosalynn Carter from visiting refugee camps in Thailand. Maguire recruited Fithian. We wanted to make it bipartisan, so they recruited Congressmen Ed Derwinsky (R-IL) and Silvio Conte (R-MA), both of them were on the Appropriations Committee.

We came up with the title -- "Food for Furniture Amendment" since it had a whimsical twist. Without a doubt, Andy Maguire did the most cajoling and recruited co-sponsors such as Bill Gray (D-PA) and Howard Wolpe (D-MI) who were also concerned about the food crisis in Africa. Maguire and Fithian were close and worked well together since they were members of the "1974 Watergate Class."

The problem was there being no precedent to shift funds from one account to another in a supplemental appropriations bill. Maguire and Fithian went to the Rules Committee to ask them to allow the floor amendment.

As they were speaking at the hearing, there was a roll call vote on the floor. They both walked to the chamber with Rules Chairman, Eddie Boland (D-MA) – famous for the Boland amendment that cut off money to the Contras and resulted in the Iran Contra scandal. When they returned to the committee room, Boland moved to allow the amendment – a new Congressional precedent to the Jeffersonian Rules of Order!

It is hard to beat the Appropriations Committee on the floor since members go to them and ask for money for their districts. The subcommittee chairmen are called "Cardinals." They control the purse strings for these projects so we knew we had an uphill battle. Each section of the supplemental appropriations bill is handled by different subcommittee chairmen who work together to try to head off any floor amendments.

Fithian issued several "Dear Colleague" letters which pointed out the food crisis, the savings by cutting the GSA furniture account, and helping struggling American farmers by shipping surplus food overseas. The letter said, "Without the full amount of the Title II supplemental, it will be nearly impossible to address in an adequate and timely fashion the pressing needs of millions of hungry and displaced persons."

Another Fithian letter with 21 co-signers said: "We intend to offer an amendment that will reduce overall expenditures while replenishing critically needed PL 480 food aid to Africa, Southeast Asia and the Near East. The amendment will also provide a boost to farm incomes that have been depressed by excess supply, caused in part by the Soviet grain embargo. We expect a net savings to be $58 million.

The Senate Subcommittee on Federal Spending Practices has uncovered mountains of used furniture piling up in 78 GSA warehouses. Yet there is still funding available for furniture procurement."

We were uncertain about the $100 million in the GSA account since it was not a line item. I asked Congressman Don Edwards (D-CA) to write to the GSA Administrator who wrote in response that there was a surplus of $103.4 million.

I contacted outside lobby groups to write to Congress -- Bread for the World, National Association of Universities and Land Grant Colleges, Farm Bureau, Interreligious Taskforce on U.S. Food Policy and others who were part of a foreign aid coalition that I had put together.

I contacted State Department officials: Victor Palmieri, assistant administrator of the Refugee Office, and Dick Moose, assistant administrator of the Africa Bureau, who sent letters of support to

Fithian on the importance of the additional $42 million in emergency food aid.

Palmieri pointed out the famine and refugee crisis in Kampuchea, Somalia and Ethiopia. Moose's letter said that $14 million was needed for five countries in Africa: Mauritania, Somalia, Uganda, Zimbabwe and Gambia.

Prior to the appropriations debate on the floor, I got the U.S. Ambassador to Somalia to sit in a meeting room off the House floor, and Andy Maguire would round up members to talk with him. I told the Ambassador, "Don't talk policy, just tell them how bad the refugee situation is."

Just before floor action, Fithian sent out another Dear Colleague letter for "MEMBER'S ATTENTION FLOOR ACTION TODAY" that said, "Our amendment will convert furniture to food while saving the federal government $58 million."

The Food for Furniture amendment came up for floor debate on June 17, 1980. Fithian and Maguire worked the Democratic door; and Conte and Derwinsky, the Republican door. Their handouts caused chuckles as members read them. It said, "Vote YES on Fithian, Maguire, Derwinsky, and Conte Amendment. Our amendment will rescind $100 million in GSA furniture purchasing authority for 1980. Our amendment will increase by $42 million U.S. Food for Peace commitments to nations with large refugee populations. Our amendment will increase government purchases of surplus grain from the American farmer to offset the surplus caused by the grain embargo.

OUR AMENDMENT WILL RETURN $58 MILLION TO THE U.S. TREASURY"

The Fithian amendment was the first order of business. On the floor, he said, "The amendment would eliminate the purchase of unnecessary furniture, convert the money to critically needed emergency food aid and repay or refund to taxpayers $58 million. "

As planned, Congressmen Gilman, Maguire, Derwinsky, Simon, McHugh, Courter, Solarz, Edgar and Conte spoke in favor of the amendment.

During the debate, Fithian said, "I have worked with the State Department, with USAID people and with the administration on this. They tell me that the Department of Agriculture is geared to make the purchases; that USAID is, indeed, geared to see that the money gets to the needed recipients and that the figure which I offer in this amendment, the $42 million, would be administratively within the realm and easily within their administrative capacity."

This was not totally true, the agriculture staff said it was too late. The dispute was over timing. Passage of the supplemental was critical before the July 4th recess in order to deliver the food aid.

Subcommittee chair, Tom Steed (D-OK) opposed the amendment. He said that, "There is no such thing as a free $100 million just lying around unused. It has a commitment, and if it is taken out, it will be taken out of the funds of agencies." He said, "The mess at GSA has been pretty much cleaned up. They did have some trouble and the new people in charge have frozen acquisitions and tried to resolve a lot of these contracts."

John Myers (R-IN) raised the issue that we would be taking furniture from the Veterans Administration, but Maguire was ready with his response that the VA buys its furniture directly and not through the GSA. Maguire responded, "We have an 18-agency study and the agencies themselves have looked at this matter and have determined that there is excess and that the furniture is not being dealt with in a budget conscious fashion...there are plenty of desks waiting in the warehouses now."

Matt McHugh (D-NY) made the point that it is not just emergency food aid, but its critical to maintaining stability in the countries where these refugees are growing in number in particular Pakistan where refugees are flowing in from the Russian invasion of Afghanistan.

Steve Solarz (D-NY) mentioned the dire situations in East Africa. Maguire said that he had just returned from there and "tens of thousands of people in Somalia refugee camps" are in desperate need for food.

Paul Simon (D-IL) said, "Twenty years from now when historians look back on this session of Congress my guess is that they are going to judge this as a Congress which had as its major thrust a concern about safety. I suggest that also, in seeing to it that people who are hungry get food in their stomachs, and they are not amenable to overtures" from the Soviet Union.

As chairman of the Appropriations Committee, Jaime Whitten had the privilege of the floor to speak last before the vote. He opposed the amendment since, he said, it will cost $33 million in net outlays. "We need to examine the situation at GSA to know the facts and there are serious questions about the viability of this amendment."

Then, he exposed the rift between USDA and USAID, referring to a letter he received in June. "A further complicating factor has been the operating lead times required for the effective operation of title II programs. Under usual procedures, commodities must be ordered a full six months before they will actually be distributed to recipients. Programming and time constraints preclude the larger request and we will not be able to use even these amounts if funding is not provided within the next few weeks. That was 16 weeks ago."

There was a group of conservatives, rebel Congressmen who sat at the Republican desk. They did not go to committee hearings but knew all of the parliamentary procedures and tied up the floor, especially liking to attack foreign aid.

Bob Bauman (R-MD) was a leader of this group. Bauman was recognized as an articulate and formidable opponent of the Democrats who controlled both Congress and the White House at the time. His status as a champion of conservative Republican causes fell when the FBI accused him of soliciting sex from a 16-year-old male prostitute after which he lost re-election by a wide margin.

He said, "Mr. Chairman, as I understand it, this amendment will save lives, help our farmers, and save the taxpayers $58 million. That sounds good to me." These comments brought conservative Republicans to support the amendment. He struck the words from the Record which members can do through "Correction of Remarks."

The amendment passed overwhelmingly, Ayes 346, Noes 47 and not voting 40. The Noes were mostly from the House Appropriations Committee that did not want to displease Chairman Whitten.

Albright's Disciplinary action

Prior to the vote, Fithian placed a call to Rosalynn Carter since they had traveled together to inspect refugee camps in Thailand. He wanted her to get her husband to support his amendment. Madelaine Albright returned his call and told him that the White House would not support the amendment. Albright worked under National Security Advisor Zbigniew Brzezinski, and later become the first woman Secretary of State during the Clinton Administration.

Fithian spoke to Mark Rohner of the *Gannet News* who published an article with the headline, "Fithian says Carter team all mixed up." He said, "When the administration asked Rep. Floyd Fithian, D-Ind, for help with the Food for Peace funding, he agreed to take up the fight. But while carrying off an unusual maneuver to get the money approved, he discovered some in the Administration were working against him."

The reporter said, Fithian had learned several days earlier that the administration wasn't entirely behind him. After the Rules Committee vote, Fithian said, "I thought we really had a chance to win this thing," so he persuaded White House lobbyist Frank Moore to enlist the help of Rosalynn Carter.

"However, Fithian said he later received a call from an aide to Zbigniew Brzezinski, White House national security adviser, Madelaine Albright telling him the Administration could not support my amendment.

"I told her I was totally flabbergasted at her comments and what she ought to know is that this (the amendment) was an administration request in the first place. I don't take on the chairman of the appropriations committee lightly."

At my urging, I had USAID Administrator Brian Atwood contact Fithian who said in the article, "He was with me but he couldn't go all out."

After the floor action, Fithian raised the issue with Agriculture Secretary Dale Hathaway. He said, "Hathaway, nonplussed by the news that other members of the administration were working against him, promised to look into the situation."

Later, Hathaway said, "OMB was apparently worried about whether it was a proper procedure to shift furniture money into Food for

Peace... I don't care about the technical niceties, I want to get the hungry people fed," Hathaway said, contradicting his own staff.

It did not take Madelaine Albright long to find out who was behind the amendment. She called Brian Atwood and told him to "fire Ted Weihe." Brian responded that she would have to fire him first. She ordered him to write letters of discipline to Palmieri and Moose.

On June 19, 1980, two days after the amendment was approved on the House floor, Brian Atwood wrote the Acting Secretary of State on "Departmental Discipline on Congressional Matters." He justified Administration opposition to the PL 480 money. "The embarrassment was created when Dick Moose and Victor Palmieri wrote independently to Congressman Fithian strongly endorsing his effort." But he said the letters were not appropriately cleared.

"This kind of activity when it is juxtaposed against the Administration's official position on the Hill simply makes us look terribly disorganized. When the White House called Fithian to discourage him, they were confronted with the news that the State Department strongly endorsed his amendment. He remains convinced that the Administration will sabotage his efforts on the Senate side (we will of course do nothing to undercut Fithian's amendment in the Senate)."

This letter was Madelaine's price since Brian Atwood knew of my efforts to enlist both Moose and Palmieri in the legislative effort. I got a call from Brian Atwood that the White House prohibited me from doing anything in the Senate and to stay away. When Maguire called to ask for the strategy in the Senate, I had to tell them that "The White House ordered me not to step inside the Senate."

We knew that the Senate would knock out the Food for Furniture Amendment" since Senator Tom Eagleton's (D-MO) planned to cut the entire amount of $220 million in the GSA furniture account. So, the funding would be decided in the conference between House and Senate.

After the Senate passed its version of the supplemental bill without the Food for Furniture amendment, Fithian wrote the House-Senate conferees to support his amendment: In passing the P.L. 480 provision in H.R. 7542 by the overwhelming vote of 346 to 47, the House recognized that the need for food assistance has become desperate.

Last Friday an agriculture department official reported that the conditions in East Africa have gone from bad to worse. *Somalia now harbors over 1.5 million refugees, about 40% of the original 3.7 million population. In the Karamoja region of northeast Uganda, 100 people a day die of starvation. The critical rains in Kenya started late and continue to be poor and widely scattered. And there is little prospect for early improvement. During the next year, East Africa will need at least 1 million tons of food over and above normal aid and trade levels.*

As you also know, the massive incursion by Vietnam into Thailand to attack refugee camps has again thrown that area into turmoil. Of about a million-people receiving food aid prior to the invasion, 400,000 were in camps that have not been destroyed.

In Pakistan, the Afghani refugee population has reached 1 million and is expected to top 1.5 million within six months.

These statistics are difficult to grasp in human terms. The suffering is incalculable. But we must do what we can. I urge you to stand fast on the $142.9 million Food for Peace provision in the House Bill, H.R. 7542.

Food for Future Amendment approved

At the opening of the appropriations conference between House and Senate passed bills, Rules Committee Chairman Eddie Boland walked in and told the conferees that the House would not accept any changes in the House food aid provision "that was overwhelmingly approved by our membership." That was it!

On July 9, 1980, *The Christian Science Monitor* wrote: "In a display of clever maneuvering, Congress cut spending while boosting its package of emergency aid to the world's destitute. The decision casts a lifeline to hundreds of thousands of hungry, homeless refugees."

With enactment, Bob Chase went to work getting food aid to refugees and drought victims.

After President Carter's disastrous rescue mission to get American hostages out of Iran, Secretary of State Cyrus Vance resigned since he opposed the mission. Senator Edmund Muskie (D-ME) was appointed and confirmed as the next Secretary of State.

I saw the change at State as an opportunity to get back at the White House for opposing the Food for Furniture amendment. I kept tabs with Bob Chase and his ability to program all of the extra food aid. He provided me with a summary of where the $43 million in food aid was sent.

In a memorandum, I sent to Maguire, Fithian and other supporters, I said, *"All of the funds were expended without difficulty. The additional money resulted in a doubling of assistance (99%) in food delivered to three major refugee crisis areas: Kampuchea, Somalia and Pakistan. It also provided an increase of 63% in emergency food assistance to East African countries experiencing a severe drought. Five countries (Cape Verde, Kenya, Sudan, Zaire and Zimbabwe) which might not have received any assistance also benefited from the additional PL 480."*

I encouraged the White House to respond to a telegram by Art Simon, Executive Director of Bread for the World. Lynn Daft of the White House Policy staff wrote the letter and I assume Madelaine Albright did not know about it. In her September 23, 1980 letter, Daft wrote, "I very much regret that actions taken by Administration representatives left the impression that we opposed additional funding because we were concerned the assistance might have come too late.

As you know, Congress approved the $142.86 million before the July 4 recess. Furthermore, the entire amount of the supplemental fund has been obligated and the food purchased is being shipped to needy people in developing countries to meet urgent humanitarian needs."

Next, I engineered a letter from Secretary Ed Muskie to Maguire and Fithian since both were in tough House races where Reagan had the momentum in the presidential race. I drafted the letter and sent it confidentially to Dick Moose and Victor Palmieri who were still fuming about the disciplinary letters placed in their personal files.

In November 1980, Muskie wrote: *"Several months ago, you and several of your colleagues made a special effort to achieve passage of the full amount of emergency food assistance in a supplemental appropriations request by the Administration. This measure made major contributions to achieving our foreign policy and humanitarian objectives. It is now possible to write to you not only to express the Administration's appreciation, but also to let you know how precisely the supplemental funds were used. As a result of your action, more than 300,000 tons of American food has reached Africans and Asians who might otherwise have suffered crippling malnutrition or even starvation."*

Muskie listed the amounts of an additional 23,000 tons of food aid to Kampuchea, and 46,000 tons to Afghan refugees, 33,000 tons, that with the suffering both in Cambodia itself and in the refugee camps along the Thai border would have been much worse."

He said, "46,000 tons went to Afghan refugees, now numbering more than one million, in camps in Pakistan." For these victims of Soviet aggression, "it is safe to say that without our assistance their plight would be desperate. Half the additional funds went to emergency food supplies in Africa to Somalia, Uganda, Ethiopia and Tanzania.

Muskie closed the letter, "I deeply appreciate your support in this critical area and I very much hope that you will continue to support necessary food aid initiatives in the future."

When I met Andy Maguire after he left Congress and headed a USAID-funded NGO, I thanked him. He told me that the amendment was, "His crowning achievement as a Congressman." He framed the letter from Ed Muskie on his office wall.

I asked Bob Chase with the extra food aid, how many refugees and starving people do you think we saved? He said, "At least one million."

Some bold and unorthodox initiatives are worth the risk of getting fired. The loyalty of my bosses, Genta Hawkins and Doug Bennet attest to their willingness to stand up for me, and commitment to supporting this life saving effort.

To orchestrate this effort, there had to be inside information on the evolving food crisis, help from a group of staff who convinced their members of Congress of its merits and worked as a team, write and insert the amendment into the Congressional Record, gain bipartisan sponsors, enlist outside advocates, prepare multiple dear colleague letters, understand the rules of the House, use whimsy to get other members attention as they came to the floor to vote, and find powerful allies like Eddie Boland who assured its approval in conference.

That is why I loved my job in USAID's Congressional Office where I built strong relationships with members and staff, and particularly was given the freedom and support to advance our humanitarian mission.

Chapter 7: Palestine: The Seeds of Violence

The late Senator Paul Simon (D-IL) and my friend said, "Members of Congress generally travel too little to broaden their understanding, considering the importance of the decisions they must make."

The Senate and House Appropriations Subcommittees on Foreign Operations make hundreds of decisions each year about US interests, activities and priorities that span the globe. They fund billions of dollars in overseas programs ranging from the operations of our embassies to famine relief. "There is no substitute for seeing some of this work in person and in context," says Senator Pat Leahy (D-VT), long-time chair of the Senate Foreign Operations Subcommittee.

Because of my close relationship with Congressman Matt McHugh and over the objections of Ed Powers, staff director of the House Appropriations Subcommittee on Foreign Operations, I hitched a ride on Air Force Two with "United States of America" emblazoned on its side for the 12-day tour of the Near East from April 3-15, 1980.

My role was to encourage the four members of congress to visit USAID projects, especially on the West Bank or Palestine. Words matter in terms of the region: West Bank and Gaza are the neutral terms used by USAID; Occupied Territories is more accurate by international law, and Judea and Samaria by Israeli settlement groups.

Prior to our trip, we were briefed by Assistant Secretary of State Harold Saunders who had drafted the Camp David Accords and Jimmy Carter's Middle East envoy Sol Linowitz. They asked us to be "frank" about illegal settlements on the West Bank as impediments to peace.

119

Congressional delegation in front of Air Force Two

The Palestinian issue was a grand reason for the grand tour. The Camp David Accords had been signed by Egyptian President Anwar El Sadat and Israeli Prime Minister Menachem Begin on September 17, 1978, following twelve days of secret negotiations at Camp David which led to the Egypt-Israel Peace Treaty. But, the Palestinians were not present and now the hope was to bring them into the peace deal.

A congressional trip, known as a CODEL, gives lawmakers first-hand knowledge of matters relevant to their legislation. I can attest to why past U.S. presidents miss this cherished perk to fly on Air Force One, more than anything else.

I had a first-class trip in the back of the presidential plane to Paris, Cairo, Jerusalem, Tunis and Madrid and had more fun than upfront with the Congressmen, wives and staff. I sat with the regular folks, mostly Army escorts.

For a stopover, I got to spend a weekend in Paris to deal with jet lag and visit Notre Dame on Good Friday with Congressman Matt McHugh and his wife when the "thorns of Christ" are exhibited only on that day. I hit the bars on the Left Bank and took a boat tour of the Seine in the Bateaux-Mouches.

I rested up in our first-class accommodations at the beaux arts Hotel Inter-Continental on the Tuileries, Heliopolis Sheraton Hotel on the Nile, and the King David Hotel overlooking Jerusalem. I never touched my passport at airports, my clothes were hung up before I arrived at hotels and there was an all-night hospitality suite with booze and snacks manned by military escorts. Just in case of an emergency, we were accompanied by our own Marine Corps doctor.

We were given guided tours by the most noted archeologists at the Pyramids of Giza and an archeological tour of Luxor in the upper Nile at the ancient city of Thebes with the tomb of Tutankhamen in the Valley of the Kings and the majestic temples of Karnak.

We got private tours of Jerusalem and Bethlehem led by its mayors, and a briefing on the Holocaust at Vad Vashem for martyrs and heroes by its senior archivist. I was most impressed that they were trying to identify every victim of the Holocaust, especially difficult for young children in Eastern bloc countries with poor record-keeping.

I walked through the souk where I bought a bowl for my wife and toured the Punic ruins in Tunis. I was at a restaurant where a West River sailing friend, Alan Getson, hunted me down to say "hello." He sent me an official newspaper clipping that said, "The American Congressmen have a deep respect for Bourguiba," the aging long-time Tunisian dictator.

At the time, I thought that this might be my only trip to the Near East so I slept little, going out after the formal receptions or dinners at the Ambassadors residences to see Jerusalem and Paris.

Being in the back of the Air Force Two had a huge advantage. I got to know William Gemma, Associate Administrator for Health Affairs at the National Institute of Science who had established the Emergency Medical Services in Cairo with Dodge EMS trucks. Before his program, if you were hit by a car in Cairo, it was "*inshallah*," translated as God willing or tough luck.

Now there is a "128 call number" and standby EMS emergency vehicles for first aid to take you to the hospital. At the Cairo airport, we were met by Dr. Sad Fouad, Undersecretary for the Ministry of Health who wanted to give us a personal tour.

On the way to Cairo, we passed an EMS station, and I said "Let's do an inspection." We met two young men, talked with them about their first aid courses and checked the EMS truck to see if they had the required supplies. Both of us were impressed as was the minister. As we were about to leave, he got on the radio, broadcast to other EMS crews about our official visit, and gave the two men we met an instant salary increase.

After a tour of the old town, dinner and choking on a tobacco smoking hookah, the minister said, "Would you like to go to Giza?" I knew that it was already on our tour so I said, "No, I would rather sail a dhow." Wooden dhows are common along the Nile carrying heavy supplies up and down the length of Egypt. They have one or two masts with lateen sails. I wanted to sail one.

It was after midnight when we got to the Nile. The minister tapped hard on the bow to wake up the crew. Then, I said, "You must tell them that I want to skipper the dhow, not be a passenger." William Gemma had never been on a sailboat before, and we sailed an hour tacking back and forth in a gentle breeze. I landed the dhow perfectly to the applause of the crew. The minister's driver waited and took us to the hotel about 2 AM.

We met with world leaders in each country, which was the major purpose of the trip: U.S. Ambassadors, Prime Ministers, Ministers of Defense, senior USAID officials, heads of NGOs, and the entire Tunisian cabinet. The delegation met with Israeli and Egyptian Prime Minister Menachem Begin and President Anwar Sadat, Israeli Defense Minister Ezer Weisman and Foreign Affairs Minister Yitzhak Shamir, Labor leader Shimon Peres, Egyptian Prime Minister Mustafa Khalik, and Defense Minister and chief negotiator, Hassan Alie.

Our return flight was from Madrid and for some strange reason the presidential plane could not take off because of the wet runway. So, on the final night of this "potentate" tour, the back of the plane guys took the four Congressional wives to dinner and dancing at the Casa Funada. Their Congressional husbands were too exhausted at that point.

On arrival back at Andrews Air Force Base, there were government cars waiting with a name sign for each of us, a driver, and an open trunk for our baggage ready to take us home. Joan Lehman, wife of Congress Bill Lehman (D-FL), had a gift shop in Miami. As we waited for our bags, box after box of merchandise came down the conveyer belt; all tax and duty free to sell in her shop.

Palestinian Question

In 1978, Begin, Foreign Minister Moshe Dayan and Defense Minister Ezer Weizman, came to Washington and Camp David to negotiate the Camp David Accords, leading to the 1979 Egypt–Israel Peace Treaty with Egyptian President, Anwar Sadat. Under the terms of the treaty, brokered by Jimmy Carter, Israel handed over the Sinai Peninsula in its entirety back to Egypt.

The peace treaty with Egypt was a watershed moment as it was the first time an Arab state recognized Israel's legitimacy and Israel effectively accepted the land for peace principle as a blueprint for resolving the occupation of the West Bank conquered in the 1967 war.

Prime Minister Menachem Begin and Congressman Matt McHugh

This initial peace treaty in the Middle East did not address the occupied territories and was without participation of the Palestinians. The critical issue at the time was, how does the U.S. deal with the Palestinians but not Yasser Arafat, head of the PLO? Years later, he would be engaged under the Oslo Accords.

Our CODEL included two key appropriators (McHugh and Lehman) with leverage on foreign aid and the chairman of the powerful Rules Committee (Butler Derrick D-SC). It was thought that the Congressmen would be listened to since they funded the accords at $2.5 billion annually. We were to urge Israeli officials to suspend the "illegal" settlements on the West Bank prior to the upcoming summit with President Carter on Palestinian autonomy. President Carter was scheduled to meet May 26, 1980 with leaders of Israel and Egypt to discuss how to resolve the "Palestinian Question."

Matt McHugh who lead the delegation said the May deadline for autonomy talks makes "the timing of the trip especially relevant. The success or failure of the autonomy talks will have an enormous impact on the stability of the region, which in turn will have important consequences for our country. Although Israel and Egypt have already resolved a number of difficult issues, formidable obstacles to a negotiated settlement remain."

And, so it remains today. With the coming to power of the Likud Party and Menachem Begin in 1977, the number of Israeli settlers in the occupied territories reached 20,600 by 1982; and over 600,000 in 2017. In our meetings, we could see the "changing facts on the ground" as Begin once said. He was the founder of Likud, the rightwing party that includes religious and occupier parties in its ruling coalitions. They continue to expand despite the pleas of our delegation and subsequent administrations.

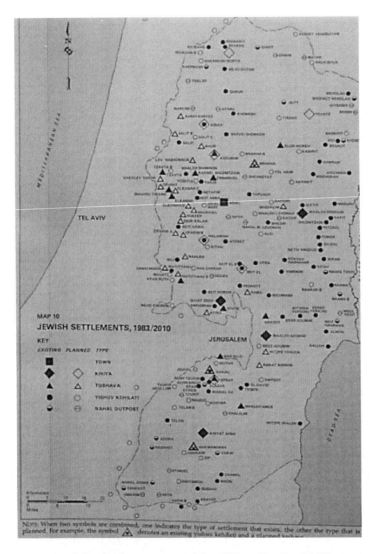

Jewish settlements on the West Bank, 1980

In my trip report, I wrote: "In Israel, the CODEL concentrated on the settlements question in occupied territories and came back with a balanced, if more complex perception of the importance of the issue. Israeli officials stressed that the settlements related to their security. The argument that Jews should be able to settle anywhere or that they have a historical right to settle these areas was less convincing.

The visit to see West Bank projects, the reception at the Consulate at which West Bank mayors talked with the CODEL, and the meeting with opposition leader Perez were invaluable in broadening the array of viewpoints on this issue. While individual members of the CODEL came to the issue differently, the CODEL tended to conclude that Israel's security argument has some validity particularly in the short term in resisting terrorism. However, the settlement policies are hurting the prospects for peace and are a deterrent to Israel's security over time."

It was clear from our meetings in Egypt, as the U.S. Embassy political officer said, "The glow was off the treaty and it would be hard for Egypt to welcome normalization with Israel if there is no progress for Palestinian autonomy."

Most Israeli elected officials told us that the government supports settlements for historic and security reasons. They said we are "doing it now" since time is short for settlements. They totally opposed a Palestinian homeland which "would become a PLO state and lead to the destruction of Israel."

Prime Minister Begin said that he was opposed to a separate state and that "we have a perfect right to live there and that Jewish people must live in groups to protect themselves." He gave me a copy of his book, *The Revolt: The Story of the Irgun*, about the Jewish underground in Poland. The book he told me would be "good night reading" to put me to sleep. Begin was responsible for blowing up a wing of the King David Hotel, where the CODEL was staying, in order to drive out the British with the goal of forming an Israeli homeland.

Foreign Minister Fonmin Shamir said that the "substance of life here is to create new cities and new settlements. And we continue to do it everywhere.'" Congressman Matt McHugh told him that the U.S. sees settlements as "an obstacle to peace," but they were intransient in their views.

Delegation meets with Shimon Peres

Labor leader Shimon Peres told us that autonomy should be tried first in Gaza. He was opposed to settlements in highly populated Arab areas so that Israel can remain a Jewish state. He told us Jerusalem would remain under Jewish control, united and it was "not negotiable."

In our meetings with Elias Freij, the mayor of Bethlehem, he said, "the settlements are a matter of life and death to us." He said that "only 10% of the West Bank was suitable for cultivation, yet the Israelis have taken 27% of it – besieging Bethlehem and Hebron." He said look at the population growth trends over the next 70 years, "Israel will become like Rhodesia."

On a tour around Jerusalem, the embassy political officer, Charles Hart, pointed out how the Israelis were redrawing the boundaries "like a star shape" to include Israeli settlements in unpopulated areas between major Palestinian villages.

The CODEL visited two West Bank USAID-funded projects in which Tom Neu of American Near East Refugee Assistance (ANERA) told us that, "there was a land rush by Israelis as more Jews are purchasing land." We visited the ANERA chicken feed cooperative and the AMIDEAST Arab College of Nursing. They said that approval of their projects was used to reward or punish villages if there were rock throwing or other disturbances against Israeli settlers.

ANERA staff and CODEL at chicken feed cooperative

It was clear that the settlement question was intransigent at this optimistic time just after the signing of the Camp David Accords. While I expected that the right wing and settlement movements were not interested in a separate Palestine, it was the left or labor movement that I found to be disappointing. Basically, they argued that we must have Israeli settlements or Kibbutzim in the Golan Heights and fertile Jordan valley to protect the borders.

Their optimism on the Gaza first option was appealing, but none of us foresaw the rise of Hamas after the Oslo Accords that recognized the PLO as the voice of the Palestinians. The Israeli settlements in Gaza were dismantled with many protests. This withdrawal demonstrated how politically difficult it would be to remove established settlements on the West Bank.

General Kahalani and me in front of a destroyed Syrian tank

The CODEL helicoptered to the Golan Heights and we met with the soon-to-be General Avigdor Kahalani, a hero of the Yom Kippur War on the Syrian front. He and seven of his remaining tanks of the 77th Brigade stopped the massive Syrian tank advance, destroying 1,000 Russian-made tanks. I am pictured next to him at the last Syrian tank that got half way up the hill they were protecting.

He told us that it took between 10 and 15 hours for back up Israeli reservists to arrive at the scene, largely held up because of the stream of Israeli settlers clogging the roads.

While the solutions to the Palestine Question are well defined in terms of land swaps and security arrangements such as in talks by President Clinton, there has never been the Israeli and Palestinian political will to accept them. With two Intifadas (both of which I witnessed), security walls, and rapidly expanding settlements, there may not be a viable two state solution anymore.

Palestinian cooperative project

At the time, I did not think that I would ever return to Palestine. At a CODEL reception for NGOs, however, I met ANERA President Peter Gubser, his local representative Henry Selz, and his director of cooperatives, Adnan Obeidat – all of whom I would work closely with in designing a cooperative project on the West Bank, four years later after leaving USAID.

When I was the head of cooperatives at USAID, I knew about ANERA's support for cooperatives on the West Bank and Gaza. My invitation to join the ANERA board came from Denis Neill after he stepped down as Assistant Administrator of USAID Legislative Bureau under the Ford administration just prior to my joining the office. He formed his own company and became a well-known lobbyist in the 1980s for Egypt, Jordan, and other recipients of U.S. foreign aid.

Denis tried to recruit me for his firm, Neill and Co., but I felt uneasy about working for him – with good reason since, I later learned, he operated an offshore account for an Egyptian arms dealer, former General Kamel Mohammed Abdel Fattah.

Denis Neill was indicted in December 1995 and convicted in March 1997 for $4 million in unreported profits and evading $1.4 million in taxes. At his trial, the jury heard what it was "like to rub elbows with foreign dignitaries at black-tie parties and be exposed to the life of a successful arms dealer." He served 18 months in a minimum-security prison.

I think that you can sense when to avoid job opportunities. Denis was willing to lobby in unscrupulous ways. I observed this when he bragged about wild parties he organized for Congressman Charlie Wilson (D-TX). Charlie, as nearly everyone called him, was a tall and handsome womanizer in Texas boots, a member of the appropriations committee, and later the subject of a book and a film, *Charlie's War*. He had a huge picture in his office in which he was riding a horse with Mujahedeen crossing from Pakistan into Afghanistan.

After my appointment to the ANERA board, I approached Peter Gubser and suggested U.S. cooperatives could help strengthen West Bank cooperatives and bring better understanding of Palestinians to Middle America where most U.S. cooperatives exist. He arranged for two small grants including one from Merle Thorpe's Foundation for Middle East Peace for an assessment tour.

I selected a team of cooperative leaders led by Gordon Lindquist, president of MSI insurance, Phil Hein, chairman of the Farm Credit Services of St Paul, and Sam Bunker, former Ford Foundation representative to the region and head of the rural electric coops international programs.

We began with visits to cooperatives in Jordan, arranged by the Jordan Cooperative Organization (JCO) which financially supported the West Bank cooperatives including its 39 employees. Jordan retained "formal" authority to administer the occupied territories until the Oslo Accords when it reverted to the Palestinian Authority. Israeli military authorities were really in charge of all activities including approving or disapproving cooperative projects.

We visited a machinery cooperative that shared agricultural equipment with farming groups, a cooperative bank where nearly every farmer was in default, and the most unusual cooperative was an extended Christian family cooperative with 1,000 members. This cooperative provided college loans to family members, arranged for funerals and financial support for family widows.

ANERA's Adnan Obeidat arranged our visits in the West Bank and Gaza where we went to nursery, poultry feed, housing, fishing and electric coops. Our conclusions were that the cooperatives were functioning relatively well given difficulties by the Israeli military occupation authorities.

On the trip, I drove through Israel with Adnan Obeidat. We stopped at his family's village that was destroyed in the 1948 war. We walked up the hill and he noted that the nearby Kibbutz was named for his ruined village with only stone blocks and wild bushes remaining.

Gordon Lindquist, Adnan Obeidat, his assistant and Phil Hein

Later, Adnan arranged for a meeting with elder Arab leaders in the Pasha's room at the American Colony Hotel, founded by a Chicago-based Christian utopian society in 1881. Its communal residence was converted into the hotel. At this and other meetings, if Adnan did not think that those we interviewed spoke strongly enough against the occupation, he would pull this information from them.

After the meeting, we went to the bar in the American Colony catacombs, a favorite place for foreign journalists. Everyone easily identified the Shin Bet secret agent at the bar. In 1992, the PLO and Israeli representatives met at the hotel where they began talks that led to the historic 1993 Oslo Peace Accord.

Our U.S. cooperative delegations learned U.S. NGOs were providing the cooperatives with valuable services, but the recently elected Likud government was applying more restrictions as land was being confiscated by the Israel settlers.

U.S. cooperative delegation at ANERA vegetable market project

The cooperatives were operating under complicated administrative laws from Jordan and Israel, the latter unwilling to register new cooperatives. We noted that the overriding concern expressed by Palestinians was the Israelis seizing land with government incentives and financing.

We tried to make our observations and conclusions as mild as possible. I recorded our discussions with Palestinian cooperative leaders which universally criticized occupation military authorities. They would not register new coops, harassed trucks that transport their products to Jordan with intrusive inspections, arbitrarily closed bridges and roads, did not issue building permits and delayed approvals of NGO projects--and those only to favored villages.

I wrote the report which was edited by Carol James and asked the publication staff at the National Rural Electric Cooperative Association to print it. A Jewish staff member refused, so I turned to Carol's friend, Michael Moss, who produced the document.

We shared our report with USAID officials who liked our efforts to support Palestinian coops. They forwarded the report to the US Embassy which, in turn, presented it to Israel authorities. Based on our conclusions, I wrote a proposal for $1.4 million on financial management of cooperatives. Our embassy said that they would prefer not to use any "political chits" to get the occupation authorities to approve it.

We had met with the Histadrut officials during our assessment. Since the 1930s, this powerful labor union supported Israeli cooperatives. I asked Wally Campbell, president of CARE, to call the Secretary General of the Histadrut. On the trip, Daniel Rabinvich told us that his family survived on CARE packages after the 1948 war for independence. He contacted the Israeli military authorities on the West Bank and urged their support.

To get final approval, there was one condition: we would have to return to the West Bank and Gaza to get "the official Israeli perspective." For this delegation, I selected Bart Harvey and Bob Fischer, both with Agricultural Cooperative Development International (ACDI). USAID funded the second trip. It was strange going to the same cooperatives, with an armed Israeli official with us, conversations were stilted.

My guide to Israeli cooperatives and the kibbutzim movement was Yehuda Paz who emigrated from Brooklyn as a young man and changed his name to reflect his life's work trying to bring peace to Israelis and Palestinians. On each of my trips, I visited many kibbutzim including Yehuda's that was on the border of Gaza. He took me to an Arab cut flower cooperative in Israel.

Later, we exchanged speaking engagements at an International Cooperative Alliance (ICA) conference that I hosted in D.C., and he invited me to an Israeli cooperative conference where I spoke about US cooperatives.

One of the project goals was to try to bring Israeli and Palestinian cooperative leaders together since they had similar people-centered perspectives and democratic governance. While there were informal exchanges of technology such as drip irrigation and some limited trade, my efforts failed because of the deteriorating political situation that drove the two groups apart.

Yehuda and I shared a similar career in promoting cooperative development around the world. We believed that cooperative can play a role in enhancing peace. And, we agreed it is hard to bridge deep political, ethnic, and social divides.

Project underway

In June 1985, the Palestinian cooperative proposal was approved. It focused on financial and management training as well as agricultural credit.

Since most cooperatives were created and linked to Jordan, there had not been any training of cooperative officials since the 1967 war. There were 280 active Palestinian cooperatives, and the goal was to create more disciplined management and to change the way they dealt with donor grants, for example, to charge commercial rates for donated bulldozers to clear land. Otherwise, it would be impossible to replace them when they wore out. Clearing land was critical since the Israeli authorities could confiscate land that was not tilled.

I visited Gaza to see strawberry, vegetable and fishing cooperatives. It resembled a "war zone" with Israeli soldiers at key intersections and huge towers protecting Israeli settlements. I witnessed a riot where tires were burning at the university.

Later, it became a real combat war zone with Israeli military incursions and Hamas rockets. I observed that most women were conservative with full veils and gloves, unlike more Westernized, educated and secular women on the West Bank. Because of the tight border security, the project limited its support to five Gazan coops.

With Adnan Obeidat, I visited an olive press cooperative where an old man carried his basket of olives and dumped them in the hopper. His son was at the other end with large flasks to collect the oil. I told Adnan, "That seems very inefficient." He said "Ask him" which I did, "Why do you put your olives in the press and have your son collect your oil?" He responded, "Because I know the taste of my olive oil." "Do you mean you can tell your oil from that of your neighbor's field?", I asked. He responded, "Yes."

I thought about it. Connoisseurs can taste the differences between wines in various fields in Burgundy, why not olive oil in the West Bank?

We selected a recently retired Nebraska farm credit president, Don Hovendick, as project manager. He had no international experience and, despite our briefing, allowed the Israeli customs officials to stamp his passport. This meant he had to wait six months to get a new one in order to travel to Jordan to coordinate the project with the Jordan Cooperative Organization (JCO).

He hired a financial staff person who directed bids to family members for what were supposed to be competitive bids for official equipment, vehicles, etc. I learned that in the Arab world, if you were in a position to help your family or friends, it was expected, not seen as nepotism.

What I did not know initially was that Don Thomas, president of ACDI, had made a deal with Hovendick that he would be there for the first year, and Don Thomas would replace him. Hovendick left for what he said were "personal reasons," but by then I knew the arrangement. I was flabbergasted.

I had tried hard to keep Thomas away from the project since he was very pro-Israel. He was being pushed out of his job at ACDI, looking for a soft landing and wanted to go to Jerusalem because his wife was a Pentecostal Christian, a sect whose members are often possessed by the Holy Spirit with clapping, dancing and speaking in foreign tongues.

He was not really engaged in the project, leaving it to staff. He spent most of his time driving his wife around since she could not drive and playing tennis with the Israeli registrar of cooperatives – not endearing to our Palestinian clients.

In 1985, I wrote a monograph on the project. It noted that the cooperatives, established in the 1920s, had reached 34,000 members. Most are agriculture (129) and fewer are housing (92) and village electric (14). At the time, there were 50 employees of the Jordan Cooperative Organization, many of whom I later found out were "ghost" employees since JCO had no official presence on the West Bank.

Each year, I asked Matt McHugh to include supportive language in the foreign aid appropriations report, always careful to first run it by AIPAC, the pro-Israel lobby. In 1988, I arranged to travel to the West Bank when Matt McHugh was on a tour sponsored by Jewish organizations in his district. I caught up with him on Saturday, the Jewish Sabbath, since he had a free day. We visited several project sites including a children's nursery in the Kalandia Refugee Camp. I vividly remember an 8-year-old girl going into hysterics assuming we were Israelis. Many families had experienced military repression and home searches.

I asked Matt not to say he was a congressman, but he proudly wrote his name in the guest books. Instead of asking about the projects, he took the opportunity to ask "political questions" and gauge the viewpoints of these Palestinian community leaders. I made a small loan to Matt so he could buy some handicrafts at the Refugee Camp where Palestinians girls are taught needle work to maintain their traditional culture. He reimbursed me in a letter that said, "The work of the coops is very important especially when instability is on the rise."

We wanted to create financial discipline and profit-centered management. These efforts were undercut by donors mostly from Europe who wanted to show solidarity with Palestinians, but did not understand that cooperatives were group businesses, not charities.

After the initial three years and numerous visits to the project which I coordinated on behalf of different cooperative organizations, I wrote a major extension for $9 million. The project continued for ten years.

While I think that the project had positive impacts, the project managers were ineffective, mostly they were staff-driven and inexperienced in this difficult environment. I learned how important it is to select the right Chiefs of Party.

With the Intifada (uprising in Arabic), it was hard to hold joint training sessions because of road closings that prevented travel by both staff and participants. Dave Davies, the project trainer with excellent "Saudi" Arabic, shifted courses to go to the participants where they lived. He produced training manuals and pamphlets.

The most effective training took place in Cyprus on agricultural marketing, export controls, and standards, including new opportunities to export to European countries which were pressing Israel for better market access for Palestinians.

A project evaluation found that the Intifada and withdrawal of Jordan from the West Bank in July 1988 adversely impacted the ability to train and strengthen the cooperative management and accounting systems.

The evaluators noted that the rapid turnover of chiefs of party in the projects initial years resulted in differing development objectives. However, they were impressed by the local staff who had developed solid training curricula and courses. They found that 28 managers, 81 directors, and 451 members had received training among the 192 active cooperatives in the West Bank and five in Gaza.

Palestinian dairy project

My next two trips to the West Bank were on behalf of Land O'Lakes. From 1997 to 2000, the company managed a $1.7 million project to help sheep and goat producers in Ramallah, Jericho, and Jerusalem areas. Its focus was extension and training for small dairies and producers including a ram breeding revolving program to upgrade sheep genetics.

Like the first project, it was adversely impacted by the second Intifada when roads closed and cities and villages were cordoned off. I went to Hebron where Jewish settlers had occupied the bus station and later built a settlement in the middle of this Palestinian city of 200,000. I watched as an Israeli soldier grabbed a Palestinian youth and put him up against a wall to frisk him.

In Nablus, what I found amazing is that within this white stone city without a tree, there were sheep and goats in small shelters, totally out of sight. I visited the soon-to-be developed dairy in the city that was run by a devout Muslim with a crease on the bridge of his noise that demonstrated faithfulness in repeatedly bowing to Mecca. It was known as the "Hamas dairy," signifying its source of Saudi funding.

Violence was on display or just below the surface. Our car was stoned by youth as we left Nablus since it had Israeli tags. Despite a PLO scarf displayed on the dash, they assumed we were settlers. I asked the driver to back out, rather than go up and talk to the 10-year-old stone throwers.

Village meeting on breeding sheep

At a project village, the women staff trained Palestinian women in their homes since they tended and milked the animals. The men received training in breeding by the project manager, Wahib Tarazi, a veterinarian. His staff called him "Doctor Wahib."

This was one of the few projects that reached out to Bedouin women. Much of Arab culture is based on the "desert" Bedouins where women are isolated, even now as they live in villages, not as nomads under animal-hide tents. Two Bedouin brothers that I met would either be goat or sheep herders, but never both.

Bedouin customs are pervasive in the Arab world. When offered Turkish coffee, shaking the cup indicates you were finished otherwise they kept filling your cup. Pouring precious water over your hands before eating with only your right hand was Bedouin. If they did not think you were eating enough, they would reach over and place more meat on your plate.

I asked Adnan Obeidat to take me to meet a Bedouin in his tent. We were greeted with trepidations since he assumed that we were Israeli officials. As we sat on fancy rugs, he proudly showed off one son after another. We could see his two daughters and wife peeking around a corner in the tent.

It was hard to meet a Bedouin woman. I got to know one who was helping her Bedouin community form a women's coop. She was well-educated because her father thought it important. She was fascinated with lions and other mammals that she had never seen and wanted to visit a zoo. On my second trip to the project, I bought an illustrated book on large mammals to give her. She had a hard time accepting a "gift" from a Western man. We arranged for an exchange in which she gave me some of her Bedouin needlework.

Land O'Lakes project staff

Palestinians are a welcoming culture and among the best educated in the Arab world. In the West, some think of them too often as terrorists and do not appreciate their culture, struggle, and hardships as a result of occupation and ever growing Israeli settlements which dot the hill tops while they prefer living in the traditional valleys.

Any optimism that I had was dashed with the violence of two Intifadas, the assassination of Yitzhak Rabin, and the collapse of the Clinton-led peace talks between Ehud Barak and Yasser Arafat for a two-state solution in July 2000.

The seeds of violence were evidenced every time I visited Palestine. It only gets worse. I asked the local Palestinian staff why land was so critical to their future, instead of education and work. They simply said, "It is the heart of our struggle."

The "two state solution" is nearing a point when it is not feasible with the increases in Israeli settlements. Are not values of peace more sacred than land? Are not peace and co-existence, the essence of true democracy?

My experiences in Palestine challenged my optimism that most human problems can be solved. It is hard to overcome the power of extremism, terror, lack of political will, and sectarian and religious differences. Achieving peace and reconciliation is difficult and, in some cases, may be impossible.

Chapter 8: Mr. Cooperative

With Reagan's election, I expected to be fired in February 1981 since I was a Carter political appointee.

To my surprise, the new USAID administrator was Peter McPherson whom I knew well from working together on Title XII BIFAD land grant university legislation. I stood up at an NGO meeting and said, "we need to tap the expertise of universities in the fight against hunger." Several NGO leaders saw such projects as funding professors' travel and studies rather than frontline assistance.

After passage of BIFAD, Peter and I divided up the members on the House appropriations subcommittee– he approached conservatives like Jack Kemp, and I approached liberals like Matt McHugh for university research funding on hunger issues.

Peter McPherson at Capitol Hill Food Day

McPherson wanted me to remain in Legislative Affairs until his new team arrived: Jack Murphy from Senator Goldwater's staff and Michelle Laxalt, the daughter of Senator Laxalt (R-NV), as his deputy in her first real job.

Michelle could not understand "why a liberal Democrat should be in her office." Once she arrived at work with a formal dress over her arm and tell us that she would see "Uncle Ronnie" at a White House event that evening.

Michelle Laxalt so exasperated David Obey, chairman of the House appropriations subcommittee that controlled USAID funding, she was prohibited from entering his office. In 2013, former New Mexico Senator Pete Domenici admitted he had an affair with the then 24-year-old Michelle and was the father of her son. She had been an intern in his office.

I knew McPherson's Deputy Jay Morris from Prince George's politics. He was Peter's "hatchet man" to ferret out political appointees who had burrowed into the civil service. Newly arrived Republican appointees were aghast when Morris sat next to me at USAID parties.

Jack Murphy was a political disaster and did not know the difference between an authorization and appropriations bill. Prior to administrator's senior staff weekly meetings, I wrote out his remarks so he seemed knowledgeable. Jack Murphy was sent off to the legislative office at NASA which seemed like a safe post until the Challenger disaster. He fought for me when he was asked to leave USAID's legislative office and said "Ted cannot survive with Michele Laxalt being there."

A few months later, McPherson called me up and said he could not keep me in legislative affairs any longer but had a position as his special assistant for cooperative development. After he hung up, he called a few minutes later to tell me it would be temporary until a friend of his, Herb Wegner, former head of the World Council of Credit Unions, was available for the post. Tragically, Wegner died of AIDS after serving two years in USAID. I attended his funeral.

McPherson's invitation launched my cooperative career. I got to know the cooperative development organizations and immediately carried out evaluations of their programs. It was a perfect fit for me especially because there were so many different types of cooperatives that gave me a challenge to comprehend and understand.

Cooperatives fill in holes that private companies believe are not profitable, like rural electric cooperatives with fewer customers and are costlier in the delivery of electricity, or credit unions that serve lower income groups that are not "bankable." Cooperatives fit my values of service, organized not-for-profit but for the benefit of members.

I remained as the Coordinator for Cooperative Development until May 1982 when I did the "Washington revolving door act" and became the first executive director of the U.S. Overseas Cooperative Development Council (OCDC) and led it for the next 23 years. When I was approached for the job, I cleared it with a USAID's ethics officer who said that it was not a conflict of interest since I had not officially sign the cooperative grants.

Oversea Cooperative Development Council

Since 1963, this group was the official USAID Advisory Committee on Overseas Cooperative Development or ACOCD. In 1968, with declining USAID support, ACOCD severed its ties with USAID so that they could advocate on the Hill and lobby senior USAID officials. I renamed it OCDC to simplify the acronym.

Congress controls USAID funding, and as a lobbyist, I was able to dramatically increase cooperative development funding from $25 million in 1980 to $400 million by 2010, mostly through legislative actions and positioning OCDC members for grants to Eastern Europe and the former Soviet Union.

As Paul Hazen one of my OCDC successors noted, Ted "triggered a 12-fold increase in cooperative development funding." He said, "The world is a better place today because of Ted's hard work and perseverance."

In addition to legislation, I advanced cooperative development as an appointee to the USAID Advisory Committee on Voluntary Foreign Aid (ACFVA). I served on this committee through four administrations – two Republican and two Democratic over 17 years. It was created by Harry Truman after World War II for coordinating voluntary relief to Europe. It was a great platform for advancing people-to-people assistance. I got to know all of the USAID Administrators and senior USAID officials, and opened their doors to US cooperative delegations to make our case.

The USAID administrators appreciated my service on ACFVA where I led many task forces, arranged for speakers and suggested meeting topics. When I retired I was honored to have so many appreciative comments about my contributions.

USAID Administrator Brian Atwood said, "Your personal leadership of ACFVA has been instrumental in creating a collegial and effective working relationship" between non-profit organizations and USAID.

Administrator Henrietta Fore said, "The time, energy and expertise you have given underscore the American people's desire to provide economic and humanitarian assistance and a better future for men, women, and children around the world."

Andrew Natsios wrote, "As chair of ACFVA's Strategic Plan Subcommittee and as a member of the Global Development Alliance, Constituency Building, Gender, Millennium Challenge Account, USAID Organization and Procurement, Humanitarian Assistance, Higher Education Partnership, Civil Society, Results, Non-presence, and Future of Foreign Assistance Subcommittees, you have been instrumental in moving the Agency's and ACFVA's agenda forward. I appreciate the many hours you devoted to this work."

Andrew Natsios and ACVFA members

Administrator Rajiv Shah wrote, "Your expertise and perspective played an important part in the Committee's deliberations and achievements."

As an ACFVA member and at other USAID meetings, I made a point of asking questions to senior officials or outside speakers about cooperatives. This strategy as an advocate is how I got the title, "Mr. Cooperative." They knew that if there was any issue or question about coops, just call Ted Weihe. And, they did.

I testified before Congress on the importance of cooperatives overseas since they shared the same values as US coops, such as the Wright Patman Congressional Credit Union in the House or a local agricultural coop in their districts. I reassured them that a "little bit of money goes a long way" for these self-help, democratically-run businesses.

I served on congressional fundraising committees and held low-key fundraising events with cooperative PACs, more to thank members like Matt McHugh, Doug Bereuter and Ben Gilman for their support and international leadership than raising significant campaign funds.

**A Tribute to Matt McHugh
for his Work on Behalf
of the World's Needy**

Invitation for McHugh Fundraiser

I served and chaired various cooperative organizations: United Cooperative Appeal for fundraising, the Hall of Fame to select and honor coop leaders, Cooperative PAC and the Cooperative Month Committee to celebrate coops in October. I had a strong relationship with Judy Ziewacz who headed the Cooperative Foundation, and from 2017 to 2018 was president of the National Cooperative Business Association. Whenever she called, I volunteered to help her promote cooperatives domestically and internationally. We focused on cooperative basics – whether in the US or abroad. Her husband, Rick Merril, was especially important to me since he cleared my name at the White House as a political appointee at USAID.

As executive of a diverse set of cooperatives, I became familiar with agriculture, consumer, housing, electric, telecommunications and credit unions. I read many historical books about cooperatives in the U.S., Europe and elsewhere: The Farm Credit System, Rural Electrification, Land O'Lakes, Ocean Spray, Tri-Valley Growers, Tree Top, Sunkist, etc. Armed with mini-facts and anecdotes, they prepared me for a cooperative point of view or story.

When my wife and I went to the grocery store, I pointed out cooperative products and looked through the displays particularly at the fruit and vegetable tables for imported cooperative products. At artists' coops, I asked how the board functions? In the chocolate aisle, I asked customers why they picked out their bars and did they know they were produced by small farmer coops? At REI or Ace Hardware, I asked the checkout cashiers if they knew they worked for a coop? It made my wife crazy.

I visited many cooperatives throughout the U.S. Most were effective local or regional cooperatives though there have been many consolidations, conversions to stock companies and bankruptcies. I learned from their successes and failures and applied these lessons in helping cooperatives abroad. I attended and spoke at U.S. cooperative conferences on the importance of foreign aid and how U.S. cooperatives were helping the poor overseas.

Monbazilla Cooperative Winery

On vacation in France, I stopped by small wine cooperatives along the Midi-Canal and visited the Monbazillac cooperative winery, formed in 1940 and located in a chateau. I would ask our local guide if that was the first Raiffeisen cooperative bank in town on the corner. Raiffeisen are the oldest and original banking coops in Europe. I cheered the round-the-world sailboat race sponsored by Crédit Agricole, a large French banking coop.

I visited multi-purpose rice cooperatives in Japan, electric coops in the Philippines and Bangladesh, coffee coops in Costa Rica and Ecuador, farm supply coops in Colombia, medical doctors' cooperatives in Brazil, kibbutzim in Israel and credit unions in Central America, Chile, Malawi and Kenya.

I am not naïve about cooperatives. They have a mixed record in developing countries with major exceptions such as credit unions, electric coops in the Philippines and Bangladesh, dairy coops in India and Fair-Trade coffee coops in several countries.

The reasons for failures are paternalistic laws, legacies of colonialism, Marxist models, easy credit, poor management, corruption and over reliance on donors.

Outside of a few countries in the developing world, there were few that were truly member-owned and member-financed – two key concepts for success. For coops to grow, members must contribute financially through delivery of their products – a small percentage is monetized as member equity in long term revolving funds. The lack of member equity, in my opinion, is the most significant stumbling block to prosperous cooperative formation and development, a subject that I have written about extensively.

I used to think that there were two models of cooperatives – those with roots in socialism or capitalism. OCDC sponsored a 1984 conference by the world's leading cooperative practitioners to answer that question. In *Why Cooperative Development*, we concluded that there is only one model which includes: focus on members, private group business, needed services, open to all, fulfilling unmet gaps, and sound management. The major obstacles remain interference by governments, subsidies or donations, and few development experts who understand them.

Using the report as a basis, OCDC organized an international conference in the same year at a forum by the International Cooperative Alliance (ICA) in D.C. There were 85 participants from 25 countries in which various papers were presented by leading experts.

In the conference report, *Why Do Cooperatives Succeed...and Fail*, we wrote about the factors that lead to success or failure. A major finding was the lack of trust by members for a group-led enterprise. The conference was the first interactive and open discussion by the ICA attendees who at other meetings made only formal presentations. A delegation from Bulgaria, still under Communist rule, did not participate in the discussions because they were authorized to only present "official views."

This experience gave me a skeptical opinion of the ICA, formed in 1895. It is one of the oldest international organizations. The worldwide organization propounds universal principles, holds conferences and advises governments on cooperative legislation. It is heavy on ideology and accepted so-called cooperatives from the Soviet Union and Eastern Europe as members. These cooperatives were not coops in any meaningful sense, but government entities. Delegations were full of spies.

At an ICA conference in Berlin, I presented a paper on how US cooperatives support Fair Trade coops. I wanted to visit this historical capital. Most European cooperative leaders did not know that US agricultural cooperatives had assisted many of the cooperatives in developing counties that were able to participate in Fair Trade programs. USAID remains the largest funding source for cooperative development overseas.

OCDC was unsuccessful in opening up new sources of development funds for U.S. cooperatives at the World Bank, Multilateral Investment Fund, and U.N. development agencies. But, I did enjoy trying to access funding from the International Fund for Agricultural Development with visits to Rome.

Towards the end of my formal cooperative career in 2006, I drafted, *Cooperatives: Pathways to Economic, Democratic and Social Development in the Global Economy* as an accumulation of my experience, thoughts, successful models and observations.

Over the years, I had gathered key cooperative documents so I knew where to go to find a quotation and make cogent arguments for cooperative development. I wrote it in a few weeks. Another year passed before its publication as OCDC members and outside experts reviewed conclusions and added their own perspectives. Susan Schram, who led the OCDC drafting effort, wrote of the draft, "Your vision and insights were invaluable."

I learned a lot in visiting cooperatives. I recall a conversation with Gordon Lindquist, a cooperative leader from Minnesota who said, "When you see them, you know them." That became my mantra.

It is easy to see if the coop is manager-controlled. Are members of the board invited to meet with you? Only a few questions are needed – how many members attend the annual meetings, do they financially contribute, what value does the coop bring to its members? Are operations transparent? Are your books audited and can I see your balance sheet?

In a similar vein, I learned how to assess development projects. How do staff interact, are schedules posted on the wall, are activities focused or haphazard? Are managers committed to the project or more interested in an overseas life style? Is the project conceptually sound and organized for success?

Poorly designed projects are easy to spot. For example, in 2005, I did an assessment of a cooperative in Arusha, Tanzania that was run by women, had an expensive donated large milk cooling tank, and just enough processed cheese to fill a small refrigerator. The project manager did not understand that a cooperative must be economically viable, not a charity. While the women in the village deserved assistance, the scale was too small, milk production too low, and the market too limited.

At a cooperative in Uganda, the project manager dominated the discussions, did the financial accounting instead of coop staff, and the five-person board discussed what the image of a cow should look like on a proposed yogurt cup. They came for the meal and hoped the French Embassy would donate the yogurt machine.

155

I am tough and honest in evaluations which in some cases meant that the cooperative organization did not want me to do more evaluations. At village internet centers in Ethiopia, they were using old computers and equipment and did not charge enough to maintain staff and upgrade equipment. It was a matter of time before they failed.

On the other hand, I visited a women's savings group in rural Ethiopia where they were proud to save a few cents a week and record it in their passbooks so their children would have uniforms to go to school. At a credit union in Malawi, the entire village turned out with men, women and children lined up in different sections to watch a proud board of directors dedicate the new building that they built.

A women's savings group in southern Ethiopia

I visited ten successful rural electric cooperatives in Chile where the boards were politically mixed with a strong business focus. Members were willing to increase their rates so the electric coops could finance line extensions to their neighbors.

In Costa Rica, I went from one coffee coop to another, each formed through the Alliance for Progress in the 1960s; the coffee plantations were operated collectively, well run, and successfully exporting specialty coffees in a jointly held company.

At an Israeli kibbutz, I was escorted by the founder of drip irrigation who advised me, "Photos are forbidden." Many of these coops were shifting to manufacturing such as eye glasses or Dr. Scholl's inserts which were more financially attractive than reliance on agriculture.

These positive experiences are etched in my memory. It makes me proud to have raised significant resources, written about, represented, designed and managed cooperative projects in over 35 developing or transition countries. They fit nicely with my values: cooperation, care for others, democracy and self-reliance through group action.

OCDC board meeting in New York, 2000

A Look at the Overseas Cooperative Development Council

The mission of the Overseas Cooperative Development Council (OCDC) is to strengthen the ability of member organizations to promote cooperative development in developing countries and emerging democracies.

OCDC represents eight cooperative development organizations, including CHF International.

Members currently have multi-year projects in 67 countries from Albania to Zambia. Programs of member organizations include technical assistance and training in agriculture and natural resources, business, community development, civil society, disaster and reconstruction, energy and rural electrification, finance, public policy and advocacy, and telecommunications.

A recent initiative of the OCDC was to bring together international officials and experts in rural development from the International Fund for Agricultural Development (IFAD), headquartered in Rome, and cooperative development organizations for a two-day workshop called "Working Through Cooperatives and Credit Unions to Reduce Rural Poverty" this September.

A reception on Capitol Hill was sponsored by Doug Bereuter, Chairman of the International Monetary Policy and Trade subcommittee and by CHF International. IFAD President Lennart Bage affirmed the important role that cooperative organizations and credit unions can play in rural poverty reduction.

Ted Weihe has been Director of OCDC since the council's founding in 1982, and was recently commended for his longstanding service to the council. (See photo.)

COOP
U.S. Overseas Cooperative
Development Council (OCDC)

At a recent workshop, Ted Weihe was recognized for two decades of service as Director of the Overseas Cooperative Development Council. Judith Hermanson, 2002 Chairperson and Vice President of CHF International, presented a commemorative plaque.

Honored in 2002 for two decades of service

Chapter 9: Advocate for Cooperatives

On her first day, Beth Sheehy, my new assistant, came into my office. I asked her, "What do you want to accomplish while working for me?" She said, "I want to pass legislation."

That conversation started a process that resulted in the Support for Overseas Cooperative Development Act, the first major rewrite of the USAID mandate in 39 years.

Cooperatives were enshrined in the original and still current Foreign Assistance Act of 1961 by Senator Hubert Humphry (D-MN) who wanted to share the successful US cooperative experience with developing countries. Section 601 recognizes the role of cooperatives as free enterprises along with labor unions, credit unions and savings and loans societies.

Sheehy had just returned as a Peace Corps volunteer in Kazakhstan. Her father worked for the House Intelligence Committee. A red head, beautiful and very independent, I only needed to write the legislation and provide some guidance to get the bill rolling. Very determined in her ways, she had turned down the offer of a new car if she would not go into the Peace Corps.

Advancing cooperatives was a job I had achieved with amendments and report language in every major piece of foreign assistance legislation over 20 years, but I had never attempted to write a freestanding bill. Usually, I found supporters on the committees to add an amendment here and there, but to pass independent legislation is tough.

Usually, the bill would have to be written in a House Foreign Affairs Subcommittee, reported out of the full committee, gotten approved for floor action by the Rules Committee, and gone through a similar process in the Senate, reconciled in a conference committee and signed by the president. I knew the process well - but it was uphill. But there are short-cuts.

It was made tougher as no major rewrite of the original foreign assistance bill had passed since 1961 despite many attempts, all of which I had been engaged in. At each rewrite effort, I retained the current cooperative mandates. So, there was no major foreign aid legislation in motion that I could attach the provision to.

The only way to succeed was to present a bill that was non-controversial, placed or attached to another bill on the House consent calendar which for passage took a two-thirds positive vote, or unanimous consent. The bill could not be opposed by the administration though its support was unnecessary. The bill had to be non-threatening, have broad political support, expand USAID's mandate and require a comprehensive implementing study.

The sponsor, in this case, Doug Bereuter (R-NB) was a moderate Republican whom the administration needed on other major issues such as rapprochement with China and support for multilateral development banks– two subcommittees that he chaired.

Why would Doug Bereuter sponsor such a bill? Earlier, he authored a provision that "Cooperatives provide an opportunity for people to participate directly in democratic decision-making." Bereuter wanted to become chairman of the House Foreign Affairs Committee, and as a moderate would be up against Henry Hyde (R-Il), who under House rules could move from chairman of Judiciary to Foreign Affairs Committee. Hyde was famous for the Hyde amendment to prohibit government funding of abortions. He led the impeachment against President Clinton.

Another candidate was Chris Smith (R-NJ), who like Bereuter, was seen as moderate in an increasingly right shift of the Republican Party. To prove his effectiveness, Doug Bereuter was looking for opportunities to take legislation to the floor since the Republican leadership would choose between him, Hyde, and Smith.

The House International Relations Committee (it changed its name several times) had become increasingly irrelevant as most legislation passed through the Appropriations Committee. Moving legislation to the floor would add prestige to the committee. It was important that the provision be freestanding so I decided to revise an outmoded Section 111, enacted in 1978, calling for USAID to support cooperatives "to strengthen participation of rural and urban poor in their country's development."

Over the years, cooperative development programs had expanded from agriculture to include electric, telecommunications, housing, health, community and insurance cooperatives, yet they were not mentioned in the USAID mandate. Since 1963, USAID had not carried out a major study of cooperatives. The legislation would be an opportunity to educate USAID staff about the important role of cooperatives in development.

I needed a Democratic co-sponsor and approached Earl Pomeroy (D-ND) who was a strong cooperative supporter. The next step was for Bereuter and Pomeroy to send a Dear Colleague letter to gain additional co-sponsors. We were able to get six – Congressmen Gejdenson, Lantos, English, Hall, Gillmor, and Gilman. The sponsors straddled the political spectrum from liberal Democrats to moderates to very conservative Republicans. Bipartisan support is an advantage with coops since they are not seen as ideological – left or right, Republican or Democrat. The bill, H.R. 4673, was placed in the Congressional Record on April 13, 1999.

Ben Gilman and me at World Food Day

The outgoing Foreign Affairs Chairman Ben Gilman (R-NY) had a passion for micro-enterprises in which small loans are provided mostly to women to operate family enterprises. His bill, H.R. 1143, was approved in committee and reported out for floor action on April 12, 1999. Nothing happened for the remainder of 1999. It was not until September 2000 when the committee was able to place the micro-enterprise bill on the House consent calendar.

Our strategy was to attach H.R. 4673 on the House floor to this popular micro-enterprise legislation – avoiding the requirement to report it out of committee separately.

On September 19, 2000, Doug Bereuter took the floor and introduced the bill as an amendment. He said, "This measure is a bipartisan effort. Specifically, this bill will give priority to funding overseas cooperatives in the following areas: agriculture, financial systems, rural electrification and telecommunications infrastructure, housing and health."

He said, "Cooperatives are voluntary organizations formed to share mutual economic and self-help interests of their members. The common thread among all cooperatives is that they allow their members who, for a variety of reasons, might not be served by traditional institutions to mobilize resources available to them, and to reap the benefits of association."

He cited successful cooperative projects to sell fruits and vegetables in war-ravaged El Salvador, credit and savings groups in Macedonia, and rural electric cooperative networks in Bangladesh.

Consistent with his earlier legislation on the role of cooperatives in promoting democracy, he said "they create an opportunity to routinely vote for leadership, to set goals, to write policies and to implement these policies. Cooperative members learn to expect results from their decisions and that their decisions can and do, in fact, have an impact on their lives."

At the conclusion of his remarks, he thanked "the Overseas Cooperative Development Council (OCDC) for its contributions to this measure."

Congressman Earl Hilliard (D-AL) said, "Credit unions and cooperatives give people more opportunity to help themselves. By promoting business enterprises and financial institutions which operate through the democratic decision-making process, the Congress can play a critical role in encouraging broad-based economic and social development, both at home and abroad."

Chairman Ben Gilman (R-NY) said, "The bill's purpose is multi-faceted. It encourages the creation of agricultural and urban cooperatives in electrical, telecommunications, and housing fields as well as the establishment of base-level credit unions. It will foster the key values of self-reliance, community participation, and democratic decision-making in programs that directly affect member lives."

The bill was approved in the House by unanimous consent.

I don't think Beth Sheehy and I ever expected to get the bill this far. Now, the rush was on to see if we could get it passed in the Senate. The clock was quickly running towards Congressional adjournment.

On the same day that the cooperative legislation was on the House floor, a delegation of Minnesota credit unions, led by its lobbyist John McKechnie, met with Senator Rod Grams (R-MN), the most conservative Republican ever elected from Minnesota. He agreed to sponsor the bill and placed it into the Congressional Record as S. 3072 on September 19, 2000.

The last scheduled markup of the Senate Foreign Relations Committee, chaired by Jesse Helms (R-NC) was October 5th. Beth and I rushed around Senate offices and got Senators Chuck Hagel R-NB), Russell Feingold (D-WI), and Richard Durbin (D-IL) as co-sponsors.

I was standing in line for the mark up in the small committee room in the Senate section of the Capitol. Chuck Hagel walked by, and I thanked him for his sponsorship. He said, "It's about time we passed this cooperative legislation." In his press release, he said, "Cooperatives can help bring stability, economic development and democracy to the post-Sept 11 world. USAID can tap cooperative methodologies to bridge ethnic and sectarian differences to build communities in areas that are rife with conflict."

There was a final hiccup, the administration wanted to change a single word by omitting "universal" access for rural electric and telecommunications cooperatives. U.S. utility cooperatives are based on the principle of universal coverage in the service area, not isolated systems. The change in wording meant that the bill had to go back to the House for this slightly different version. This action proved to be routine, and the bill became law on October 17, 2000 when signed by President George W. Bush.

USAID Cooperative Report

The Support for Overseas Cooperative Development Act required a comprehensive report for its implementation. But, as the legislation was moving ahead, there was no USAID coordinator for cooperative development. The vacant position would not be filled by a career officer, but by a RSSA, meaning using another agency's excess positions to fill the slot.

I was asked to suggest candidates, and two were selected. A recently retired USAID employee who had supervised some cooperative work in Uganda was the initial candidate, but he asked for so many conditions that he was rejected.

The second choice was Tom Carter who had spent nearly 20 years working with India dairy cooperatives through the NCBA international foundation and later as a Food and Agriculture Organization (FAO) consultant.

Tom Carter

With Carter in place, the drafting of the report began with three joint USAID-cooperative taskforces on agriculture and financial services, infrastructure, and housing and community services. I served on each of them. A survey was taken of cooperative projects in each USAID region and a survey of country and international organizations that support coops – the U.S. provided the most support and Canada, second.

Between 1971 and 2001, USAID funded eight U.S. cooperative organizations for $1.12 billion in projects with central grants of $105 million in over 60 countries. By 2016, the total for cooperative central grants ballooned to over $220 million.

The report laid out these lessons: importance of forming coops based on universal principles, autonomy from government, good laws, transparency and honest management, member loyalty, commercial viability and sufficient time to allow sustainability.

The most important aspect of the report was to set the future of the centrally-funded cooperative development grants, soon to be imbedded in Requests for Assistance (RFA) in a five-year funding cycle, but often extended another three or four years.

The new focus of central cooperative grants would be:

(1)   Innovative approaches to key coop issues,

(2)   Applying lessons learned from successful coop development,

(3)   Stages of development towards commercial financing and joint ventures with US coops,

(4)   Support for each of the sectors in the legislation, and

(5)   Better evaluations and impact assessments.

The Support for Overseas Cooperative Development Act is the culmination of our legislative efforts.   It represents my belief that sharing the successful experience of US cooperatives overseas should be at the heart of our foreign aid programs.

Cooperative earmarks

USAID is organized by regional bureaus and country missions, the centers of bureaucratic power. Regional bureaus want the most resources compared to central bureaus. The mission directors want to cut central programs and distribute the money to specific country programs they control. That approach makes it difficult for NGOs and cooperatives to develop their own initiatives, otherwise, they would have to shop around missions for funding.

When missions or regional bureaus did not want to fund cooperatives, I wrote or promoted cooperative earmarks: $10 million for low cost housing in Central America, $20 million for electric utilities in the Caribbean basin, $2 million for volunteer programs in Poland, $10 million for worldwide dairy development, $2 million for rural electric utility training in the Caribbean, $1 million for development education, and others. I particularly recall these examples:

I worked with Jerry Connally of the Senate Foreign Relations Committee (now a Congressman from Virginia) who staffed the President Carter-appointed World Hunger Commission from 1978-1980. The Commission was supposed to spend a year publicizing its report to the general public. Senator Bob Dole (R-KS) held up the study on various points. Jerry had been a Jesuit missionary and chaired the NGO working group for the Rome Food Summit, and I knew him well from local politics.

In 1981, I suggested to Jerry, now with Senator Joe Biden's staff, that he insert a provision in the foreign assistance act to create a USAID program on Development Education, which would not violate a prohibition on USAID propagandizing. Initially, USAID refused to fund the program, so we earmarked $1 million to launch it. OCDC, National Rural Electric Cooperative Association (NRECA), National Cooperative Business Association(NCBA) and the World Council of Credit Unions (WOCCU) all tapped this program, which grew to about $2 million annually, to education their membership on the importance of foreign aid and ways to end world hunger. Many U.S. NGOs tapped this popular USAID program over a dozen years to educate their constituencies.

A veterinarian, Senator John Melcher (D-MN), a great friend of cooperatives, sponsored rural electric cooperative and the national consumer cooperative bank legislation. He authored the Agriculture Aid and Trade Act that linked food aid and long-term U.S. agricultural markets; many agricultural cooperative leaders participated in these trade missions. The number of this bill

(Senators can reserve bill numbers) was the same as his tank division in Patton's army. When I thanked him, mentioning the bill number, S. 659, he handed me his tie tack with a Dragon armored vehicle on it, saying "anyone who mentions my old unit, I give them my tie tack." I still have it. I remember when visiting his office, you got to pet his two-friendly golden-hair, short tailed Minxes (Abigail and Eddie) that had the run of the office and hallways.

At our urging in 1987, Melcher inserted a provision in the foreign assistance bill that earmarked and tapped locally generated food assistance currencies to create a cooperative bank in the Philippines. Sam Bunker of NRECA led an OCDC team to study its creation with an emphasis on financing their hundreds of electric cooperatives. Although the World Council of Credit Unions was part of Sam's team, they submitted a separate proposal to finance credit unions which the USAID mission funded instead.

Sam Bunker was not pleased with this backhanded action. He was always a team player, previously worked at the Ford Foundation, and important to me since he was my contact when I was hired at OCDC and initially reported to him. He arranged for me to have the benefits of NRECA as a reimbursable employee, and for the housing of OCDC offices at NRECA without charging overhead from our members. Sam was the son of a famous diplomat, Ellsworth Bunker who was President Johnson's ambassador to the Dominican Republic after the U.S military intervention there and was Johnson's last ambassador to Vietnam.

As USAID moved away from funding infrastructure, a $35 million earmark ($5 million each from 1988 to 1993) required USAID to support rural electrification programs in Latin America. In 1987, the provision was sponsored by Senator Bob Kasten (R-WS), a member of the Senate Appropriations Committee, when he was up for re-election. He noted his support for rural electric cooperatives in his campaign that was acknowledged and praised by Bob Bergland, former Secretary of Agriculture, Democratic Congressman and General Manager of the National Rural Electric Cooperative Association. It may have helped Kasten in his very tight re-election.

Mike Findley, who specialized in Latin America, left Dante Fascell's (D-FL) staff, and represented Florida Power and Light (FPL). FPL provides power to electric cooperatives in Florida. In 1988, we earmarked $2 million for the regional training facility of electric utilities in English-speaking Caribbean countries. The British electric company left the region, and each country had to establish their own small utility. These utilities created a regional training center located in Barbados. With the earmark in hand, Sam Bunker negotiated with the center in which they were to use trainers from FPL and NRECA. The center just took the money eliminating any U.S. training, so I did not renew the earmark.

In 1974, I attended the first U.N. Habitat Conference in Vancouver, Canada on behalf of the League of Women Voters where I drafted language on civic participation in human settlement activities for the U.S. delegation, then headed by Carla Hills, Secretary of HUD. As a follow up action, a U.N. Agency for the Habitat was created in 1976, located in Nairobi, Kenya. The US had never given voluntary contributions to Habitat so I wrote a $2 million earmark with report language that the agency should work more closely with U.S. NGOs such as the Cooperative Housing Foundation (CHF). I got a call from their US legal representative complaining about the language. That was first and last U.S. contribution to Habitat since they refused to work with CHF.

For Land O'Lakes, I wrote a paper on the importance of milk and meat as high protein foods for victims of HIV/AIDs. Senator Paul Wellstone (D-MN) introduced an amendment to the Food for Peace program in June 2002 that earmarked 100,000 tons of non-fat, dry milk that went to mothers and children suffering from HIV/AIDs in the Caribbean.

Earmarks are the way to get cooperative programs launched, and if successful, they receive substantially more funding. A USAID evaluation concluded that dairy development and livestock projects in Africa were ineffective. In 1982 and 1987, I engineered two $5 million earmarks for dairy development that enabled Land O'Lakes to expand programs in Africa and later Eastern Europe.

In subsequent years, similar report language on the importance of dairy for small poor farmers strongly encouraged USAID to continue the programs at $5 million annually. Congressman Dave Obey (D-WI) and Senator Pat Leahy (D-VT) sponsored it since they had many dairy cooperatives in their districts and knew their value to family farmers. Missions now competed for the dairy program money as I found in Rwanda when I met with the mission director.

By the 1990s, there were fewer foreign aid authorization bills and more reliance on the appropriations committees for report language and earmarks. My core responsibility at OCDC was to assure central funding of cooperative programs. I quietly met with the head of the central bureau where coops were funded – often in an out-of-the-way restaurant over lunch. I would cut this deal: I will organize NGOs to push for report language to assure $50 million for your NGO office in exchange for assurances that cooperatives would get at least six million.

Over 20 years, these central grants funded people-to-people projects and initiated worldwide NGO child survival, micro-finance and strengthening of non-profit organizations to become more affective development organizations. I found many non-profit allies for these legislative efforts.

I preferred this approach because I understood how it worked. Foreign aid appropriations reports are full of directive report language, but the directives are not all equal. The chairmen and ranking members of the House and Senate subcommittees invite other members to send in report language to get their support for the overall bill. Timing is critical, the subcommittee does not begin its markup until it has the budget figures (302b allocations) at which time lobbying members becomes most important.

After the funding bill passes, USAID's legislative staff sits down with the four key staffers on the appropriations committees and they review which of the many directives to implement. The deal is that USAID will support directive language by the key members, and if USAID does not, the committee chairs will earmark them next year. If you have the support of Chairmen – at the time, Leahy in the Senate and Obey in the House for your language -- it is a done deal. This inside knowledge of how it works came from having worked in USAID's legislative office.

People-to-People Assistance

I advocated that U.S. bilateral assistance should come from the American people, especially well-known organizations, many of which began in the US to help the poor and expanded their international efforts, such as Heifer International, Winrock International and Save the Children, all of which began by providing assistance to poor families in the Appalachian region.

Save the Children was formed in 1932 to help children in the Appalachians during the Great Depression and was modeled on the Save the Children Fund which had been established in Britain in 1919. Other organizations were formed in America to help Europe recover from World War II such as CARE and Lutheran World Relief. They represent American values of compassion.

In contrast, multilateral funding from the U.N. Development Program or Development Banks such as the World Bank or Inter-American Development Bank do not promote U.S. values and mostly fund host government programs. The World Bank destroyed many cooperatives through providing them with subsidized credit through cooperative banks in which farmers most often did not repay them.

I knew many of these non-profit CEOs from my service on USAID's Advisory Committee on Voluntary Foreign Aid (ACFVA). Often, I would team up with my favorite NGOs in proposals.

I opposed increased funding to for-profit contractors that just did USAID work, but had no grassroots in America. In this regard, I wrote legislation that shifted resources from government-to-government to private non-profit organizations. At a USAID contract employees conference in Ocean City, I spoke against the overuse of contractors and some of their abuses such as hiring former USAID mission directors to manage projects somewhat like inside trading.

I was a strong supporter of Senators Claiborne Pell (D-RI), Joe Biden (D-DE) and Congressman Ben Gilman (R-NY) who set minimum funding levels for USAID for NGOs that increased over several years to 17%. As a young foreign service officer, Pell had seen what NGOs did to help Hungarian refugees after the Soviet invasion. The administration stymied this shift in resources by counting funds to local agencies of government ministries.

In reaction to the minimum funding requirement, USAID decided to require matching funds from U.S. NGOs (called private voluntary organizations, or PVOs in USAID parlance). This requirement became known as the "privateness test" in which PVOs would be required to match government funds with 20% of their own cash. As a member of the Advisory Committee on Voluntary Foreign Aid and leader of a PVO taskforce, I fought this requirement because PVOs raise public funds for disaster relief, child adoption and similar programs, very seldom for USAID projects.

When the House Appropriations Subcommittee on Foreign Operations prepared to require the 20% requirement, I approached Will Painter of David Obey's staff to exempt cooperative development organizations in the legislative provision since I argued they were mostly operated through trade associations with limited fundraising capacities.

PVOs continued their opposition to the 20% privateness test which USAID made a requirement in Requests for Proposals. Through persistence, we were able to create a loophole in which contributions from PVO local partners are counted as part of the cash as well as their in-kind contributions. Thus, it became relatively easy to achieve the matching requirements.

At a House Foreign Affairs markup, I was sitting next to Gilman's aide, and I gave him an amendment that required USAID to account for how much assistance went through government channels compared to NGOs in Latin America. The goal was to make USAID officials consider which assistance channel was most effective: directly to USand local NGOs as opposed through host government programs.

With Senator Mac Mathias (R-MD), I wrote legislation that earmarked $50 million in the Reagan Administration's Caribbean Basin Initiative for people-to-people assistance. The hard earmark was adjusted in conference to assure that at least $50 million in locally generated counterpart funds, passed through NGOs.

For Eastern and Central Europe programs under the Support for East European Democracy (SEED) Act of 1989, I wrote mandates to support credit union development, Farmer-to-Farmer volunteer programs, and the use of NGOs "to the maximum extent practical."

Similarly, I made sure the Freedom Support Act of 1992 for the former Soviet Union Republics supported "the creation and development of private enterprise and free market systems." Communist so-called cooperatives were not voluntary, nor owned by farmer members. They were agents of government for top-down five-year plans. US cooperatives were well poised to assist in their transition to free market-style coops.

The expertise of major U.S. cooperatives was appropriate for former Socialist countries because their citizens were well educated, they needed advanced Western technologies to catch up, and many were disillusioned with what might be called "mis-development" due to state communism. The emerging business leaders needed and wanted our expertise in market-oriented management.

Blowback from USAID administrators

My advocacy for people-to-people programs resulted in two key blowbacks from USAID. I took on two close colleagues: USAID Administrators Peter McPherson and Brian Atwood.

In 1988, Congress cut USAID funding by 5%. I wrote legislation that directed that the cuts must come from government-to-government programs. I led a coalition of 75 church, non-profit and cooperative organizations to require USAID to reverse funding priorities, shifting funds to people-to-people programs, and rolling back seven years of increasing government-based assistance. The 5% of USAID's $13.2 billion budget ($660 million) would be redirected to people-to-people programs.

I recruited Senator Claiborne Pell (D-RI), Congressmen Dave Obey (D-WI) and Ben Gilman (R-NY) as sponsors. While foreign aid is unpopular, I noted that people-to-people programs by non-profit organizations are strongly supported by Americans through their giving, service on voluntary boards, and broad appeals in disaster relief abroad. Many are rooted in American religious traditions.

My rationale was that private sector programs are more effective in reaching the poor; they create long-term bonds and friendships and reduce government programs that dampen private sector development. These basic values permeate all of my legislation actions over my career.

I wrote about these values in a publication, *Achieving the Cooperative Promise: How to Do More with Less Foreign Aid.* When USAID Administrator Peter McPherson read it, he called me hopping mad. He asked, "How could you undermine government programs which are critical to development?" I pointed out that "assistance for security and military USAID had doubled, but humanitarian programs had stagnated." These efforts in shifting resources from security to humanitarian programs were generally successful.

In the second incident, USAID's regional bureaus under the budget office of Larry Byrne decided to eliminate the $50 million in central funding to NGOs and cooperatives. Along with my NGO allies, I drafted a letter by the strongest Congressional supporters of USAID. In the letter, they opposed the cuts at the same time that Senator Helms was trying to dismantle USAID.

I told Kelly Kemmerer of USAID's legislative office that if the cuts stood, I would make sure that Administrator Brian Atwood had to address the issue at all of his upcoming Congressional hearings. As I was walking around the Hill, a black official Buick pulled up, the window came down and Brian Atwood leaned out and said, "I give up, you win."

Advocacy abroad

My advocacy for cooperative legislation extended to overseas efforts. I participated in but was not listened to in the initiation and development of CLARITY, an academic exercise in reforming cooperative laws. This was a case where OCDC did not follow my lead as a political professional. The OCDC taskforce preferred to rely on a law firm for its design.

Cooperative Law and Regulation Initiative — CLARITY — was supposed to help national cooperative movements create a more favorable legal and regulatory environment.

Created in 2005, CLARITY focused on developing a cooperative-led process for legal reform based on enacting key principles, assessing them and applying them. It was devoid of political perspectives and coalition building -- foundations of political advocacy.

CLARITY was better than formalistic model laws advocated by the International Cooperative Alliance (ICA) and the Cooperative College in England that over-emphasized the role and promotion by governments, rather than grassroots formation and member control.

These model laws were based on 1908 British law, part of its colonial history where the goals were to control the "natives." A recent example was when I visited and reviewed the new cooperative law in Tanzania. Government officials wrote the law as a way to deal with corruption in cooperative management and imposed onerous regulations that inhibited any ability of coops to become member-owned enterprises.

The core problem with CLARITY is than none of its authors had any political experience domestically or internationally. The exercise was interesting, and a retrospective ten years later in 2014 proved my point – it had little if any impact.

In contrast, I was successful in the Philippines with a proposal to the National Endowment for Democracy, which unlike USAID is geared to advocacy of democratic reforms. The triumph of the peaceful People Power Revolution and ascension of Corazon Aquino signaled an end to authoritarian rule in the Philippines. During her presidency, the country went through radical changes and sweeping democratic reforms. Aquino abolished the 1973 "Marcos Constitution" and dissolved the Marcos allies-dominated Congress. She created a Constitutional Commission to draft a new constitution.

Since cooperatives and NGOs were part of the Peoples' Movement, they successfully inserted a provision in the constitution for a unified agency for cooperatives. Under previous regimes, cooperative laws and registration were divided and controlled by various agencies: sugar coops under agriculture, electric coops under their rural electric authority, etc. The cooperatives wanted a single administrative and support agency. The challenge was how to implement this new constitutional mandate.

I travelled to the Philippines and selected two cooperative leaders, Luis Corral and Francis Nacianceno who I found to be politically savvy. They would lead the reform efforts. I walked them through observation of how lobbying worked on Capitol Hill, ways to design lobbying workshops in the Philippines, and sent them to Washington State and Wisconsin where they met up with two of the most effective state cooperative lobbyists. Unlike most countries, US cooperative laws are mostly state-based.

Cooperative lobbying workshop in Manila

Together, we organized Cooperative Government Affairs Conferences in the Philippines. With its transition to democracy, the banking system was still broken and corrupt. Marcos had taken billions of funds paying for U.S. base rights, transferred them into his personal accounts in New York, and issued the equivalent in local currencies. This fraud was uncovered by the USAID Inspector

General Jim Durnil whom I got to know well when he headed the rural electric international programs.

As a consequence, it was impossible to transfer US currency to Filipino banks. So, I carried $50,000 in cash through the airport in Manila to fund the workshops. I did not declare it, fearing a mugging as I left the airport.

In February 1988, I led cooperative political action workshops in Manila, Baguio, Cebu City and Quezon City. I taught local cooperative leaders lobbying techniques like coalition building, letter writing and advocacy. I was accompanied by Karl Kottman, Executive Director of the Washington State Cooperatives Association.

Our counterpart host was Aracio Lozada, president of the Cooperative Union and former retired commander of the national police. He had formed credit unions throughout the Philippines so that his policemen were less likely to take bribes between paychecks.

At the Cebu City workshop, I met with one of his police colleagues who asked me if I wanted to see the local sites. I said, "Sure." We were given a tour of strip joints by this police chief. There were three Jeeps with dozens of guards in front and more in back with M 16s. As we arrived at a strip joint, guards surrounded the entrance and rear doors. We were sandwiched in between and walked into the dimly lit cabaret with a dance stage up front. Filipino girls can wiggle, but it was painful to watch. Several did not abide by the three-point rule.

I thought this was nuts. Despite the armory of guards in three jeeps, I did not feel safe since policemen were targeted and killed by the Marxist insurgency. Interestingly, many of these rebel leaders later became cooperative leaders as part of the Aquino reforms.

Cooperative government affairs conference in Cebu

The outcome of the workshops was an agreed-to National Development Manifesto to enact the new legislative mandate. As a result, the central registry and cooperative support office was created, staffed and led a burst of cooperative formation focused mostly on agriculture and rural credit unions to help alleviate poverty.

The opportunity to change laws comes along seldom and generally with a change in government. Reforming laws takes political action in which few outside experts either have the experience or knowledge as political advocates. They may be supportive of local cooperative leaders *at most* but cannot create the conditions for change.

Outside events may be more critical. In Kenya, the International Monetary Fund (IMF) required the dismantling of marketing boards that controlled top-down cooperatives. Most coffee coops immediately went out of business when government support and subsidies were removed. Independent cooperatives survived on their ability to respond to member needs, not government officials or donors.

One size does not fit all. Credit unions want to be considered part of the financial sector, regulated (unlike micro-credit enterprises) and not part of the general cooperative law. Ministries of electricity and telecommunications seldom want or encourage cooperatives so there is an absence of cooperatives in these fields.

Cooperation with Japanese coops

My final project in the Philippines was to try to encourage Japanese agricultural cooperatives to initiate similar overseas programs as US cooperatives. I wrote the proposal funded by the Japan-U.S. Foundation. The idea was that, since Japanese cooperatives were part of the conservative government, they had the power to advance similar cooperative assistance programs, especially in Asia.

Delegates to Japanese workshop

A US cooperative delegation was selected to go Japan to discuss our development efforts and invite representatives from Japanese coops to come to Washington D.C. to meet USAID officials and cooperative development organizations. I recall a visit to a rice cooperative in which it provided many services; in fact, if you were a farmer, you had to be a member. It really was not a voluntary organization.

The Japanese prefer multipurpose cooperatives which were created by General MacArthur during the occupation as a way to dismantle former landed warlords. At one coop that I visited, they offered a marriage counseling service to encourage young urban women to move, marry, and live in rural areas.

Many educated Japanese women do not want to live on farms, preferring to stay at home with parents and live single lives. The lack of women was apparent in visiting the cooperative offices where junior male employees were expected to spend all hours honoring and serving their bosses – with long commutes home. More often than not, these professional men came home, collapsed on weekends, saw their kids on Sunday then returned to an office grind for the remainder of the week. After a workshop, I observed the junior staff member at a restaurant filling the glasses and catering to the senior cooperative officials.

The final event was a joint workshop in Manila where Filipino cooperatives made suggestions on how the Japanese coops could help, especially in the production and export of organic crops to Japan. Japanese are real foodies and love natural foods. Reflecting on these events, I think the Japanese agricultural leaders preferred to make their case for high tariffs on US rice imports, not helping overseas cooperatives. This advocacy failed.

Coalition Building

In legislative advocacy, coalitions are essential. While at the League of Women Voters, I co-chaired with Larry Minear of Lutheran World Relief what we called the "Floating Crap Game." It was a coalition of religious groups, labor unions, non-profit organizations and cooperatives including credit unions and rural electric coops. In a letter Cheryl Morden, North American Director of the International Fund for Agriculture Development, she recalled, "My first memories of you go back to the "floating crap game that used to meet periodically... I especially enjoyed the verbal jousting between you and other development cognoscenti and key congressional staff."

This coalition was my first contact with cooperative lobbyists with whom I would eventually work. The biggest issue at the time was the balance between military and security programs compared to humanitarian assistance. We wrote joint letters and walked the halls to shift aid resources to humanitarian programs.

In 1976, there was a well-funded effort to create a lobbying coalition called New Directions with Russell Peterson as president, and Margaret Mead as chair of the board. It failed quickly but not until I had the opportunity to have lunch with Margaret Mead.

With the election of Ronald Reagan, I co-founded Action for World Development with Frank Balance that organized international businesses and non-profit groups at the Chamber of Commerce. The focus was to support foreign assistance by telling members of Congress how much U.S. business is generated by these overseas programs such as purchases of Food for Peace (PL 480) for US commodities and providing humanitarian aid. We listed companies and amounts for each state.

Since World War II, the large relief organizations, called voluntary agencies or VOLAGS, were located in New York. They were a clubby group, but in the 1970's many new NGOs were forming such as Africare, Overseas Education Fund of the League of Women Voters, Winrock International and others. They were scrappy and headquartered mostly in Washington D.C.

They wanted to form their own coalition which was initially called PAID – an awful acronym for Private Agencies in Development. PAID and the VOLAGs group combined, and the offices were moved to DC. I helped found this coalition which became InterAction – a large successful coalition of over 140 non-profits. It effectively represents relief and development NGOs.

I wrote legislation and helped form the Debt for Development Coalition that allows countries to pay dollar-dominated debt in local currencies for NGOs to preserve nature parks and carry out development projects. The coalition ceased operations in 1996. Its efforts resulted in $200 million of external debt canceled and leveraged $27 million in local currencies for development. This provision remains imbedded in the annual appropriations act.

My usual role in all of these coalitions was to organize them, help them track legislation, and prepare talking points for Hill visits or letters from their grassroots. Each coalition was an ally and extended the power of cooperatives since all were supportive of people-to-people assistance.

U.S. Global Leadership Coalition

Before the 1994 election, no Washington insiders thought that Newt Gingrich, his Contract with America, and Republicans would take over the House. The next day after the election we knew that they were coming to Washington with their hatch pins to cut government down to size. This was the beginning of highly partisan politics and the death null for civil discourse.

I decided to look at the minority budget by John Kasich (R-OH) and later governor of Ohio. It proposed to cut foreign aid from $20 million to $10 million over ten years, an easy target for cuts, especially from newly-elected Republicans, many of whom did not have a passport. I knew we were in real trouble.

I began to call around to see what we could do. I organized a meeting with Charlie Flickner, the new Republican staff director of the House Appropriations Subcommittee on Foreign Operations, who said, "I am not interested in hearing from the old gang. I am working with Enron and new players now." Before Enron collapsed in several accounting scandals, they wanted funds to flow through companies such as theirs.

To form this broad coalition, it was essential to recruit AIPAC – the American -- Israeli Political Action Committee. Since I knew AIPAC leaders over the years, and whether or not I agreed with their viewpoints, they were the most effective foreign aid supporters. They rate members not only for voting on Israeli-related provisions, but overall support for the foreign aid program.

I raised the idea of forming a coalition with Jeff Coleman, their budget expert, and he got the go ahead from Ester Kurz, the AIPAC legislative director. My next step was to call Vicky Markell of the Population Crisis Committee since I thought she might be able to tap one of her contributors for startup money. She thought that Bob Wallace, son of Vice President Henry Wallace and heir to the Pioneer Seed Company, might help.

Together, we wrote a $20,000 proposal. We formed a review committee which I chaired to select an executive director. We had three potential candidates: a couple of former Hill staffers from Senator James Exon (D-NB) who knew little about foreign assistance. Exon had never supported it. My old colleague Denis Neal who was about to be indicted came to tell us, "it could not be done."

Liz Schrayer came to the meeting with a plan that paralleled her work as AIPAC's field director. She knew the aid programs and had what I called "a triple A personality." She had her own lobbying firm and wanted to spend more time with her two young sons, and less on the road. We hired her on the spot.

With cuts looming in Congress, we initially called the organization, Campaign to Preserve U.S. Global Leadership. After our initial Washington Lobby Day, she wrote a note to me and said, "I am extremely grateful and I know this day could not have been a success without you."

After its initial successes in defeating cutting amendments, she later wrote me, "It is hard to believe how far we have come from our first meeting over one year ago. Today, the coalition includes 125 organizations and businesses, representing hundreds of thousands of individuals. Given the situation, it is terrific that for the past two years, nearly $1 billon of additional cuts were avoided. You should feel proud of your role in this successful effort."

The name was changed to the U.S. Global Leadership Coalition (GLC) and was linked to a non-profit education affiliate, the Center for U.S. Global Leadership, formed in 2004. In time, GLC has become a powerful lobby for the international 150 budget account with over 400 international companies, for-profit and non-profit organizations. In 2016, it had a budget of $14 million, 45 staff, and affiliates in 21 states.

I served on the GLC board and watched it grow. When we were able to attract the Export-Import Bank supporters most notably Boeing (Ex-Im has been called the bank for Boeing), I knew GLC had arrived. I had tried to work with these international businesses at the coalition at the Chamber of Commerce with no success.

GLC is organized with an advisory committee headed by General Colin Powell, Madeleine Albright, and Henry Kissinger which includes every living Secretary of State and National Security Advisor. It advocates *Smart Power* in which the administration – Democratic or Republican - should use all of the tools for global leadership: diplomacy and military and foreign assistance.

With funds from the Melinda and Bill Gates Foundation, GLC has carried out Impact Campaigns for each presidential election to encourage candidates and their key staff to understand and support international affairs.   There is a military counsel of 150 retired Four-Star Generals and Admirals who support diplomacy and USAID before the use of military force.

Its annual dinners have stellar speakers: President George W. Bush, Secretaries of State Colin Powell, Condoleezza Rice, Hillary Clinton and John Kerry, Secretary of Defense Bob Gates, Vice President Joe Biden, Chairmen of the Foreign Assistance Subcommittees, and senior congressional leaders.

Condoleezza Rice as featured speaker

The annual dinners are so successful that they moved into a larger space at the Washington convention center. It is a "must" event for leaders of businesses and organizations engaged in international affairs.

On the hill, GLC sends up a group to lobby for the 150 international affairs account which has grown from $20 billion to $50 billion over its 20-year lobbying efforts, literally saving or increasing this account by billions. GLC has defeated all major cutting amendments.

President Obama called for doubling the foreign aid accounts when he ran for office; his administration successful increased them – although a lot has gone to reconstruction in Iraq and Afghanistan. President Trump wants to cut foreign aid by 39% which is unlikely

189

given its support on the Hill. GLC is successfully fighting these proposed cuts.

The GLC calls itself the "coalition of strange bedfellows" with members from CARE to Caterpillar, Lockheed Martin to Land O'Lakes, and Boeing to Better World Campaign because of its diverse mix of prominent international corporations, military contractors, and relief agencies. The groups do not see "eye to eye" on most issues but are united behind a stronger international affairs budget that stands at about 1% of the entire U.S. budget, and promotes American leadership and engagement.

I recall one meeting with a Congressman who said, "We must be having several meetings when he looked at the composition of our group." The dynamics of these Congressional visits are interesting. International corporations encourage support for development to build buyers and improve the business climate in poor countries where they want to expand sales. Development groups argue on behalf of US corporate investment and job creation for sustainable development.

In today's polarized politics, GLC is one of the few lobbying groups that maintains a bipartisan approach as the core to its effectiveness.

I addressed increasingly poisonous politics in a 1996 article for the League of Women Voters that was printed in the Voter by the Minneapolis League. In an article *Civil Discourse in a Democracy: Is it possible to disagree agreeably*, I tried to address the "politics of bickering, name-calling and abusive language that now permeates the halls of Congress."

"The League has been a civilizing force in local, state and national civic life through its consensus to action programs. Maybe it's time for the League to teach our politicians, as we have done for so many citizens, how to run a meeting without rancor and how to find ways to a consensus from differing points of view. The League should teach our politicians to take and live a pledge of civility."

I still hold these values despite today's raucous politics which disrespects democratic institutions and the presidency. As I was nearing retirement, I served as a GLC board representative from Land O'Lakes. Chris Policinski, the CEO of Land O'Lakes, joined the board, and it became clear that while I could stay as long as I wished, it made sense to resign since I was moving to Sarasota, Florida and was no longer engaged in foreign assistance lobbying.

Chris Policinski wrote to me, "While I was in Washington DC to attend the speech by President Bush at the U.S. Global Leadership event, I couldn't help but be struck by how much you personally contributed to Land O'Lakes and, more broadly, to global development over the years. What you've done is truly impressive and all of us at Land O'Lakes owe you our gratitude."

I remain active in the GLC Florida State Committee and organized a visit to the senior staff of Congressman Vern Buchanan (R-FL) with two prominent Sarasota business leaders: Richard Carver and Pete Kujawaski to demonstrate grassroots support for international funding and engagement.

GLC is an example of the importance in picking the right leader, Liz Schrayer, supporting her vision and obtaining significant financial resources, then knowing when to withdraw and move on. For me, GLC perpetuates American values of international leadership and support for diplomacy and foreign assistance as alternatives to military interventions.

Timothy Moley (left), formerly of TCHO, George Ingram (center), GLC President Emeritus, and me (right)

Chapter 10: Farmer-to-Farmer Volunteers

Volunteerism has been an important part of my life, and a key value.

From 1985 to 2010, the Farmer-to-Farmer Program sent more than 30,000 volunteers overseas. The title is a misnomer since most assignments match agribusinesses, rather than individual farmers. But the name stuck and the program remains hugely popular. It was not always so. How volunteer technical advisors became as successful and popular as the Peace Corps is part of my story.

Unlike foreign aid dollars, the Farmer-to-Farmer Program offers only technical assistance from the 1954 Food for Peace Act. The idea dates back to Harry Truman. In his inaugural speech after his election in 1948, President Harry S Truman launched the Four Point Program. He said, "Point Four is not an aid program in the sense the Marshall Plan and Mutual Defense Program are. It is a plan to furnish 'know-how' from our experience in the fabulous development of our own resources."

Truman said, "Point Four will be our greatest contribution to world peace." I researched the origins of the Point Four program while in the Air Force in Missouri where I visited the Truman Library frequently and read the early drafts of the program. I believe it is the origins of people-to-people assistance within USAID and the sharing of our U.S. cooperative experience.

The current Farmer-to-Farmer Program is closely identified with former Congressman Doug Bereuter (R-NB). He was an independent-minded Republican from a mostly rural Nebraska. We had in common, membership in the American Society of Planning Officials, an association of mostly planning boards.

Congressman Doug Bereuter

In April 2003, he was inducted into the Cooperative Hall of Fame for his sponsorship of several cooperative development provisions. He left Congress early to become president of the Asia Foundation in San Francisco. On retiring from Congress, he sent a blistering letter to his constituents opposing the invasion of Iraq.

In 1984, Congressman Bereuter was assigned to the House Foreign Affairs Committee, the only member from a predominantly farm district. He championed agricultural assistance and land grant universities including Title XII for the presidentially-appointed Board for International Food and Agricultural Development (BIFAD) within USAID.

As Doug Bereuter often said, he got the idea for the Farmer-to-Farmer program while traveling to Central America during the conflicts associated with the Contras in the early 1980s. The trip was to El Salvador and Guatemala with a delegation that included Congressmen Henry Hyde (R-IL), Robert Lagomasino (R-CA) and Gerald Solomon (R-NY).

He thought about how much his Nebraska farmers could help poor farmers with improved agricultural techniques. His original vision was to send groups of US farmers to developing countries in the off season (winter months) through their churches and other volunteer groups.

On his return, he spotted the Farmer to-Farmer provision in the Food for Peace Act. It was a dormant authorization since it had never been funded. Chairman Jamie Whitten (D-MS), and the longest serving member of Congress at that time, held a tight grip on the House Appropriations Subcommittee on Agriculture. He never favored the program, nor did any administration ask for its funding.

Origins of program

The original provision dates to the early 1960s under the Kennedy Administration when former Minnesota Governor, Orville Freeman was Secretary of Agriculture. Freeman was a strong advocate of the Food for Peace programs.

India was the largest recipient of government-to-government food assistance while undergoing its famous Green Revolution. Millions of rupees had built up in local accounts controlled by the U.S. Embassy and Indian government. These local currencies funded sending US agricultural volunteers to India from two farmer organizations which were the predecessors of Agriculture Cooperative Development International (ACDI).

When Patrick Moynihan (later US Senator) was appointed US Ambassador to India, he decided to return the rupees to the Indian government which, in effect, closed down this volunteer program.

Farmers Union and other groups turned to Congress. Senator Robert Dole (R-KS) placed the Farmer-to-Farmer Program in the Food for Peace Act (PL 480) with an authorization of $12 million.

Over the years, extraneous language was added, such as support for tropical agriculture, though it retained its core volunteer--sending approach.

Congressman Bereuter came up with a novel funding approach. He "earmarked" two tenths of a percent of the PL 480 resources or about $400,000 annually out of the billion-dollar food aid program. This sidestepped the appropriations process.

In the early 1980s, during markup of the foreign assistance authorization bill, he tried to move the provision through the House Foreign Affairs Committee which had joint jurisdiction on PL 480 with the House Agriculture Committee. USAID Administrator Peter McPherson tried to talk Bereuter out of pushing the legislation. McPherson suggested a two-year, $400,000 pilot program.

I will never forget the large meeting in the State Department with representatives from land grant universities and private voluntary organizations. These folks -- as well as senior USAID staff -- "dissed" the program and said that volunteers would be ineffective compared to "professional" technical advisors.

None showed any interest, except, Volunteers in Cooperative Assistance (VOCA), earlier known as the Volunteer Development Corps, or VD Corp, not an attractive acronym. As USAID's cooperative advisor, I inherited the pilot project with VOCA.

VOCA had a small staff sending about 25 volunteers overseas annually. It substantially increased its volunteer assignments with these additional resources.

Towards the end of the Carter Administration, Mike Snoddy carried out a study to determine if VOCA was effective and whether it had received private matching funds by US cooperatives as required in its initial grants. There was never any matching funding. I quietly buried this de-funding effort that was supported by three outgoing

USAID assistant administrators as I left the agency. In my new role at OCDC, my Job was to protect and expand VOCA as the volunteering sending arm of U.S. cooperatives. VOCA was later merged into Agricultural Cooperative Development International (ACDI).

Farmer-to-Farmer Program enacted

The pilot program was run exclusively through VOCA, and I tried to keep it that way. It became extremely popular as volunteers came back from their assignments and visited their members of Congress, and almost always Congressman Bereuter. He did not give up and went ahead with his original Farmer-to-Farmer funding mechanism, enacted in 1985.

Don Cohen, president of VOCA, wanted to expand the program into Poland, the USAID mission was not interested. Jim Phippard, on loan from USAID to the Senate Appropriations Committee and I, encouraged Senator Pat Leahy (D-VT) to earmark $2 million in USAID funds for sending volunteers to Poland.

The Poland program became an instant hit, especially drawing on volunteers from agricultural regions, such as Wisconsin with many Polish descendants. In one case, a group of Wisconsin volunteers helped form a machinery cooperative so farmers could share harvesting equipment. It worked for a year, after which farmers were unwilling to share the equipment due to the lack of trust among them, so prevalent in the former Eastern bloc countries. Trust undergirds cooperatives.

As a member of the newly formed Select Committee on Hunger, Bereuter's focus was helping poor developing countries. He resisted expanding the program to newly emerging democracies in Eastern Europe and the former Soviet Union.

Members of the House Agriculture Committee saw the program as a way to transform agricultural systems from collectives to private farms and to build US markets. Eventually Bereuter agreed to expand the program but only by adding another "two tenths of a percent" or another $400,000 for these "transitional countries," a euphemism for former socialist countries.

With additional USAID funding and its growing popularity, new implementers emerged through open competition including Land O'Lakes, Agricultural Cooperative Development International, Winrock International, and Partners of America.

Our major concern was to keep the program under USAID, not USDA where we feared it would be used to fund USDA international programs that rely mostly on former agricultural extension agents as volunteers. I made sure that report language and floor remarks from supportive members indicated that the program must be operated only by USAID and, where possible, in conjunction with USAID agricultural assistance programs.

Program expansion

There was pressure from various development groups to expand the program to "two way" farmer exchanges, but Bereuter resisted these changes. USAID did, however, separately fund some "star" recipients of Farmer to-Farmer assistance to participate in US agricultural and study tours including to the farms and agribusinesses of their U.S. volunteers.

This complementary program, initiated by Land O'Lakes, involved six-month farm stays. The assistant administrator who encouraged this reverse Farmer-to-Farmer program refused to sign off on an Action Memorandum to send US volunteers overseas. He opposed the concept of volunteers as technical advisors. What he did not know was that former staff director for Doug Bereuter, Helen

Sramek, was a senior advisor to USAID Administrator, Ron Ruskin. He was fired for his refusal to sign the memorandum.

Another major break-through occurred with the fall of the Soviet Union. President George W. Bush and his senior staff initially opposed foreign assistance to Russia and former Soviet Republics. The U.S. sent planeloads of agricultural commodities as a humanitarian gesture which was only politely received.

The Bush Administration decided to launch its first major assistance program to Russia through the Farmer-to-Farmer Program by increasing the "minimum" requirement in the legislation by an additional $10 million annually. American farmers were sent as "Ambassadors for Democracy."

Updating the legislation

In 1989, the Farm Bill was being re-authorized, and Senator Leahy's staff wanted to reform the Food for Peace Programs (PL 480) to provide clear authority over Title 1 government-to-government surplus food programs that would reside in USDA, and Title 2 humanitarian programs in USAID.

I had served on the Food Aid Coordinating Committee during the Carter Administration, and each agency (USAID, State, USDA and OMB) basically had veto power. It was classic inefficient bureaucracy in which any agency could veto the actions of the other.

Senator Leahy's staff indicated an interest in updating the Farmer-to-Farmer legislation and putting it into a separate title. I debated with its supporters whether to simply extend the program. I consulted with Congressman Bereuter and, with his concurrence, drafted the legislation placed in the 1990 Farm Bill that conforms to the current program. It focuses volunteer assignments on different agricultural sectors and strongly promotes agricultural cooperatives.

What I wrote better defines and broadens the program to recruit volunteers from:

"Agricultural producers, agriculturalists, colleges and universities (including land grant colleges or universities, and foundations maintained by colleges or universities), private agribusinesses, private organizations (including grassroots organizations with an established and demonstrated capacity to carry out such a bilateral exchange program), private corporations, and nonprofit farm organizations to work in conjunction with agricultural producers and farm organizations in those countries, on a voluntary basis.

To improve agricultural and agribusiness operations and agricultural systems in those countries, including improving—

(i)	*Animal care and health;*
(ii)	*Field crop cultivation;*
(iii)	*Fruit and vegetable growing;*
(iv)	*Livestock operations;*
(v)	*Food processing and packaging;*
(vi)	*Farm credit;*
(vii)	*Marketing;*
(viii)	*Inputs; and*
(ix)	*Agricultural extension.*

To strengthen cooperatives and other agricultural groups in those countries; transfer the knowledge and expertise of United States agricultural producers and businesses, on an individual basis, to those countries while enhancing the democratic process by supporting private and public agriculturally related organizations that request and support technical assistance activities through cash and in-kind services."

Doug Bereuter thanked me for these efforts on behalf of this legislation and he made sure the revisions were adopted in the conference with the House (S. 2830, Title XV) in September 1990.

In subsequent Farm Acts, the Farmer-to-Farmer provision was revised, but essentially operates the same way. In 2002, Congresswoman Eva Clayton (D-NC) wrote an African agricultural bill that would support historically black colleges to assist farmers in Africa and the Caribbean. Her bill was merged into the Farmer-to-Farmer provision. Another "tenth of a percent" was added for these programs. Traditional Africa-American, Indian and other minority colleges proved difficult to work with and had a poor record in recruiting strong volunteers.

On September 11, 2001, the Farmer-to-Farmer program was renamed for John Ogonowski, the pilot of one of the planes that crashed into the World Trade Center to honor his extensive work with immigrant Southeast Asian farmers. Later, Congressman Doug Bereuter's name was added.

What are the lessons about volunteer power?

Because of its grassroots nature, the program remains highly popular. Through evaluation after evaluation (and I have done at least eight), the program was proven effective. It is premised on people-to-people assistance to agribusinesses (small and large), cooperatives, cooperative banks and farmer associations.

I carried out an extensive evaluation of the program, volunteer by volunteer, and assignment by assignment. I concluded that 60 percent of assignments had some impact, 20 percent, strong impact and 20 percent, no impact at all.

In some cases, the program was linked with weak institutions, or had ineffective local project managers. I carried out evaluations of the programs in Jamaica and the Philippines. They were initiated by Land O'Lakes, which asked me to assess and strengthen them.

In Jamaica, the partner was the Jamaican Agricultural Foundation (JADF) that Land O'Lakes had established to provide loans through the monetization of US surplus butter. I found that JADF stopped providing loans and used the local currencies from the butter sales to pay staff who had little agricultural expertise. It was JADF's only program and the subject of weekly discussions by its board of directors, which I saw as mostly social meetings. The US volunteers had been intended to provide technical assistance to accompany JADF loans. Three projects I visited were either too small to be profitable, such as a shrimp pond, or had non-functioning equipment in this case for Sea Island cotton.

Rather than rely on JADF, I encouraged Land O'Lakes to hire Wes Moses, a local American, who turned the program around. In a subsequent evaluation, he refocused the work of volunteers to assist specialty products, such as hot pepper sauces for the U.S. Jamaican market, family-operated mushroom production, organic foods for restaurants and an association of farmers who produced fresh vegetables and papayas for the tourist markets.

Will Bullock (left), Farmer-to-Farmer project manager in Jamaica

In the second evaluation, the Philippine program with the Federation of Cattle Raisers (FCRAP) targeted large breeders, rather than small farmers. The manager brought volunteers to help her sister's small ice cream shop and a pig farmer, inefficient given that each volunteer costs at least $15,000 for recruitment, travel, local staff and overhead costs. The most outrageous assignment was to bring an American horseman to teach them Western saddle riding.

The project manager hired her husband as a driver and bought a Japanese car against USAID regulations which requires purchasing American cars. FCRAP had no financial records or annual reports. I told the USAID mission there was no malfeasance, it was just ineffective. My recommendation to terminate the program caused a row at Land O'Lakes when the Philippine staff disputed my findings.

I shifted this Farmer-to-Farmer program to Palestine where volunteers initially proved effective in the dairy, sheep and goat livestock sectors in dealing with diseases, proper animal rations and milking techniques. Volunteers strengthened a network of existing small dairies, but assignments were cutback with the Intifada (uprising).

Later, I was able to shift it again to South Africa where I designed a Land O'Lakes project to increase rural incomes and job creation in the livestock sector for emerging Black farmers. Apartheid pushed Blacks off productive farmland. The South Africa government under Nelson Mandela began to assist Black farmers by buying less productive farms through trusts. I visited several of them which operated similar to coops. My proposal focused on value-added dairy and sheep cheeses that could be sold in Cape Town. It helped that I had the support of a former VOCA staffer who had joined USAID as its agricultural officer.

My evaluations show that important results come through informal discussions across the dinner table, not necessarily the formal assignments. Volunteers are housed with farmers or at nearby local institutions to provide opportunities for these informal exchanges.

The local farm groups or agribusinesses aren't exactly sure what they need. They see volunteers as sounding boards--many times confirming their own plans with greater confidence in new ventures. Sometimes USAID's expectations are too grandiose and do not fully grasp many of the program's intangible benefits. Volunteers are motivated differently than technical advisors -- they can be more objective, draw on practical lifetime experience, establish long-term relationships, and follow up assignments with additional help -- sometimes cash, donated equipment and/or instructional materials.

Early in the program, some U.S. farmers asked: "Why should we help our future competitors?" When volunteers return to their communities, they share their experiences at service clubs, churches and local cooperatives. As a result, there is a broader understanding of the benefits of the Farmer-to-Farmer program in rural America.

The program is not just providing humanitarian benefits, but assists US agricultural exports, for example, the sale of U.S. tractors in Bulgaria, quality inputs like improved U.S. wheat seeds in Georgia, and bull semen for artificial insemination in Africa.

The program builds public understanding at the most fundamental, people-to-people level where they share common family and agricultural concerns. And, nearly every volunteer says that the experience is life changing and has given them an appreciation for other cultures and ways of life.

My visit to a Farmer-to-Farmer-assisted greenhouse

Chapter 11: Untold Story of Chile's Return to Democracy

In the spring of 1993, I was invited to a book signing party for Paul Sigmund's *The United States and Democracy in Chile* at the Hay-Adams Hotel across from the White House, where you could stay at $2,000 a night for the Inauguration. The Italian Renaissance hotel is named for the razed estates of John Hay, secretary to Abraham Lincoln and Henry Adams, descendant of two presidents.

As a professor at Princeton University, Paul Sigmund was the authority on the US and Chile. He dedicated his book to his wife, Barbara Boggs Sigmund, the mayor of Princeton who died of eye cancer while running for the US Senate. Present at the signing were his wife's sister, well-known journalist, Cokie Roberts and her equally famous journalist-husband, Steve Roberts. The late Tommy Boggs Jr, a Washington icon, lobbyist and dealmaker, was there too. It was a heady event for me.

Only Paul Sigmund and I knew the unreported and secret story of how Chile's return to democracy almost failed. In my copy of his book, he wrote: "To Ted, who was a key player in the successful effort to defeat Pinochet."

Sigmund began his fascination with Chile while studying Allende's Unidad Popular coalition government. A coalition of leftist, socialists and communists with 36 percent of the national electorate, Allende tried to steer Chile to socialism. The result was land seized by squatters, radical labor unions taking over industries, and a trucking strike that crippled the country.

The state visit by Cuba's Castro was the spark after which Henry Kissinger invoked the CIA to covertly support the putsch to fight communism in the hemisphere. Many Chilean democrats thought the military coup would be temporary. General Augusto Pinochet had a different idea for the next 17 years. These events were depicted in Paul Sigmund's first book about Chile and the US role in the overthrow of democratic governance.

After the coup, a quickly adopted public referendum on a constitution required another plebiscite to continue Pinochet's rule. He thought he was sure to win since he presented stability and opponents were divided into 22 squabbling political parties.

Paul Sigmund revealed in this book that Mónica Jimenez and her Civic Crusade was discreetly funded by our government. He wrote:

"As registrations lagged, and as the government began a massive spending program in the poorer areas under the auspices of the Pinochet-appointed mayors, many felt that Pinochet would get a "Yes" vote in the plebiscite, which according to the constitution had to be held in the last part of the year.

In early 1988, however, U.S. money began to flow into Chile in ways that, although legally nonpartisan in character, substantially assisted the opposition. The Agency for International Development had a Democratic Initiatives budget item in support of the promotion of democracy. In late 1987, it allocated $1.2 million from that program in support of the promotion of democracy.

The grant went through the OAS Commission for the Promotion of Free Elections (COPEL) in Costa Rica, which in turn channeled it to Civitas, a small private Chilean foundation with links to the Catholic Church.

Under the leadership of Mónica Jimenez, former dean of the School of Social Service of the Catholic University, Civitas created the Cruzada for Citizen Participation, usually referred to as the Civic Cruzada. As a result of the Civic Cruzada, the number of registrants

207

rose to an astonishing 7.2 million, or 92 percent of the potential registrants of voting age.

The Civic Cruzada registered 4 million of these 7.2 million, and while early registrations through the mayors and Pinochet supporters were heavily in favor of the "Yes" vote to continue Pinochet in power, the late registrations by Cruzada heavily favored the "No" vote. It is no exaggeration that the Cruzada was a major factor in the return to democracy in Chile. "

In April 2014, Paul E. Sigmund died at age 85. He was awarded the Bernardo O'Higgins (founder of Chile) Order of Merit for his book on the U.S. and Chile which remains the most significant book on Chile's return to democracy.

For Mónica Jimenez and her Civic Cruzada, I was proud to be a behind-the-scenes contributor. I designed, wrote and got the funding for this hidden US supported voter education and registration movement, critical to the defeat of Pinochet.

Cooperatives in Chile

How Civic Cruzada came about is partly my story. The following describes how I become the "right person at the right time."

Prior to the 1973 coup, Walter Sommerhoff, the dean of Chilean cooperatives, built the most successful consumer movement in the hemisphere with 17 cooperative grocery stores and home building outlets throughout the length of Chile. Walter's new son-in-law, Miguel Kast, was the senior "Chicago Boy." He was an adherent of Milton Freeman's rugged individualistic capitalism that was adopted by the military government. Miguel closed down Walter's prosperous consumer stores by unnecessarily recalling government credits. Miguel died as a young man of a brain tumor and, on his deathbed, apologized to Walter.

Walter (right) at low income housing cooperative

Walter Sommerhoff shifted his work to housing cooperatives and became so well known that, as I walked along the Santiago streets with him, strangers pulled on his sleeves to thank him.

Walter had a unique connection with US cooperatives. He gave a tour of Chilean cooperatives to Senator Hubert H. Humphrey on his visit in 1960. Walter picked up Senator Humphrey at the airport in his old beat-up car and drove him through the roughest sections of Santiago to introduce him to cooperatives and visit a very poor salvagers' cooperative at the city dump. It nearly caused a diplomatic crisis when he dropped off the Senator at the US Embassy because the officials thought he had been kidnapped.

Walter's connection with Senator Humphry went even deeper. Walter testified at a hearing chaired by Humphrey before the Senate Foreign Relations Committee for the inclusion of cooperatives in the Foreign Assistance Act of 1961. Among its early projects in the late 60s, the Cooperative Housing Foundation obtained US government guarantees to finance Chilean housing cooperatives.

Walter Sommerhoff was tall and a little stooped with an aristocratic bearing. He was grandson of the German composer Robert Schumann. His Spanish had a deep German accent. His parents sent him to Chile as a teenager because they saw World War II coming, and Chile had been neutral and far away in the First World War.

He told me about his mother's visits. She would bring several trunks of clothes, always wore white gloves, and expected to be treated like royalty even when she could see that Walter and his devoted wife, Ariana, lived in a modest home.

Founder of Cooperatives for American Relief Everywhere (better known as CARE), Wallace Campbell (everyone called him Wally) had a love affair with Chile from his first international housing conference there in the early 1960s. He and Walter Sommerhoff were soul mates with equal lifelong commitments to housing cooperatives that intensified when Wally became president of the Cooperative Housing Foundation.

Wally Campbell was the most persistent person I have ever known. He never really retired and remained devoted to cooperatives until his death in 1998. He founded CARE where he served as its volunteer president for decades. He wrote the *History of CARE: A Personal Account* which included his favorite story about meeting Pinochet.

Wally Campbell was at a meeting to discuss CARE but added that he worked for cooperatives. Pinochet was fascinated and didn't want to hear about CARE. Instead he grilled Wally about cooperatives. He said that he was surprised that a *capitalist country* like the United States would encourage cooperatives. The general just could not believe that cooperatives were supported by both Republicans and Democrats, nor that they could attract good management compared to private companies.

Wally Campbell at Chilean cooperative named for him

National Endowment for Democracy

My involvement in Chile began with a speech that President Reagan gave to the British parliament on June 8, 1982 in which he announced a new democratic initiative to combat communism. Dante Fascell (D-FL), chairman of the House Foreign Affairs Committee, hijacked the president's idea to create the National Endowment for Democracy (NED).

During the Vietnam War, the CIA had secretly funded various democratic groups and when it became known, there was an enormous scandal. Fascell wanted to fund these groups openly and that is what the foundation was designed to do.

On behalf of OCDC, I lobbied for passage of the NED legislation and the inclusion of cooperatives because, by their nature, they are *schools for economic democracy*. NED was modeled after German political party-related foundations that have long supported cooperatives overseas, including in Chile.

As it was being organized, I inserted cooperative language in Principles and Objectives for Strengthening Democracy Abroad (1984):

"Another significant private-sector economic organization is the cooperative. Groups of people uniting in cooperatives to carry out economic enterprises can acquire an invaluable grass-roots experience in democratic decision making. The Endowment will consider funding programs that reinforce the democratic character of cooperatives and enhance their contribution to the democratization of developing countries."

Despite this language, Carl Gershman, the new NED president, wasn't interested in cooperatives. So, I approached Dante Fascell, author of the legislation and first chairman of its board. I was on his fund-raising committee and had a close Arlington friend in his office. I had lobbied for anti-discrimination provisions in Revenue Sharing reforms which he championed when I was at the League.

Dante Fascell was a transplanted New Yorker and Congressman from Miami which was rapidly becoming Hispanic. He tried his best to learn Spanish but spoke it with an Italian accent. At the initial NED board meeting, Fascell took me by the hand to see Carl and introduced us saying, "Carl, you should consider funding cooperatives as part of NED's programs." Gershman got the message; and, as a result, U.S. cooperatives became one of its first grantees.

With the door now open, I asked members of my group where we could be helpful in promoting democracy. Wally Campbell instantly spoke up and said, "If you really want a challenge, what about Chile?" It was definitely a challenge given that Chile was controlled by a dictator, but those who know me, know I love a challenge.

Based on Wally's comment, I wrote a proposal and it was funded by NED. Iniltially it called for an exchange of cooperative leaders. Wally called his friend, Walter Sommerhoff, who arranged for Wally and me to tour Chilean cooperatives and plan for the exchange.

On this first of many visits to Chile, I experienced a volcano, riots, a declaration of a state of emergency with a 10 PM curfew, and a minor earthquake tremor that rattled my drinking glass while I was talking to my wife back home on the phone. I understood why our Chilean house guests always kept their bedroom door open to be able to escape in the event of an earthquake.

We were near Walter's summer home in Villarrica where he had created a vacation housing cooperative on this mountain and lake region of southern Chile. As I was sitting on a bench at a lakeshore hotel, a volcano erupted right in front of me. I began taking some of the first pictures of the unexpected event as white plumes shot up and lava darkened the snow top. Walter came speeding up in his car (he was a notoriously poor driver) and said that "his" volcano had erupted. It was the first eruption in 40 years.

I learned about the state of emergency while visiting Punta Arenas in the far south of Chile. As a sailor, I was always intrigued by the Straits of Magellan where Captain Joshua Slocum in *Sailing Alone Around the World* put tacks on the deck to ward off barefoot Fuegian savages. Here was my chance to see the straits for myself so I asked Walter to arrange a visit for me. He had two assistants pick me up at the airport; they were building cooperative housing for the military in Punta Arenas.

On the weekend tour, I passed the harbor with four sunken steel clipper ships now used as a breakwater. We drove 40 miles along the straits where the williwaw winds build to 40 knots during the day – where beech and cypress trees permanently lean over from the prevailing Westerlies.

213

They took me past a tall white marker which said "The Center of Chile," it was half way to the South Pole. We visited the grave of Darwin's first commander of HMS Beagle; Pringle Stokes who in 1828 committed suicide with these words, the weather was such that "the soul of man dies in him."

We stopped by a garrison at historic 1818 Fort Bulnes where the Chileans claimed and fortified the straits. I wanted to learn what a State of Emergency meant and here was my opportunity. I asked the soldier stationed there, "What does it mean exactly?" He responded, "I can shoot any terrorist who endangers the peace." "Are there any terrorists around here?" I asked, and, emphatically, he said, "Oh, no."

After this initial trip to familiarize me with Chilean cooperatives, I selected a five-person US cooperative delegation. We travelled the length of Chile, a 2,600-mile-long narrow sliver of land, only 221 miles at its widest point. It is twice the length of the US Eastern seaboard. In several towns, we were greeted as human rights investigators because the Chilean Federation of Cooperatives had put out a press release to that effect.

I drafted a statement of our observations, and our delegation held a press conference in Santiago. Wally Campbell, as our leader, said that smaller, peasant coops needed more support and encouragement by the government which overregulated them. Larger agricultural cooperatives were healthy but facing challenges from low import tariffs.

El Cooperativismo norteamericano está dispuesto a iniciar un programa de intercambio con su homologo chileno. Así lo indicó Ted Weihe.

② EE.UU.: clima favorable

uando la gente no puede acudir al Gobierno, el Cooperativismo crece" dice Ted Weihe, Director Ejecutivo del Comité Norteamericano de Desarrollo Cooperativo de Ultramar, para quién esta regla se confirma en el caso norteamericano, donde se desarrolló en una época de intensas necesidades, como fué la gran depresión de los años 30.

Sin embargo, en el sector donde mayor crecimiento ha logrado este tipo de organización fué en el sector rural, gracias a que el Estado entregó créditos a los agricultores que fueron finalmente la base de un sistema crediticio propio. "Es el único país del mundo que yo conozca —señala Ted Weihe— en que los agricultores controlan el crédito agrícola, o la mayor parte de él, a través de un sistema cooperativo". Junto con ser las primeras, las cooperativas rurales son las fuertes y poderosas en el gran país del Norte. El agricultor norteamericano medio está afiliado a unas tres o cuatro cooperativas y los agricultores suman casi cuatro millones de personas.

"Estimamos que hay unas 40.000 cooperativas establecidas en diversas comunidades rurales señala Weihe, añadiendo que —este número no dice mucho porque de ahí están excluídas las 17 a 19 mil cooperativas de ahorro y crédito, que cuentan nada menos que con 47 millones de socios y las eléc-

Article about the press conference

That is not what the reporters wanted to hear. They asked, "What are your impressions of the situation in Chile?" We tried to stay as neutral as possible and responded that we hope that cooperatives can promote grassroots democracy here.

At the press conference, I was introduced as having worked for the Carter Administration. A woman reporter took me aside and said she wanted to show me the National Stadium where Pinochet held prisoners including the American who died featured in the movie, *Missing*. Then, she drove me straight to her home to meet her husband, Juan Hamilton, who had been the Minister of Housing in the Allende government.

He wanted to thank me, because he was imprisoned with other ministers in the windswept, remote island of Dawson in Tierra del Fuego. He said, "Jimmy Carter saved his life," with an early release because of his human rights effort. It made me proud to be a Carter political appointee. Later, Juan Hamilton founded the La Diario La Epica, an opposition newspaper.

The Chilean exchange delegation was carefully chosen to represent cooperatives from all political views. A key leader was Elsa Gardeweg, vice president of the Confederation of Farmers Associations and personal advisor to Pinochet. Educated at Immaculate College, a small university near Philadelphia, she spoke five languages. Elsa was a true believer in coops in Los Angeles, where Germans settled on the frontier to contain the Mapuchi Indians, one of the last tribes subdued by Westerners.

From a trading family that reaches back to the Hanseatic League, she ran a successful asparagus farm. As matriarch, she put each of her five children into businesses. She set her son Werner up in an export business when she discovered a German businessman wondering around near her home who wanted to import wild mushrooms, plentiful in the region.

The purpose of the exchange was to get Chilean cooperative leaders who were hardly on speaking terms to work together to revive cooperatives and reform heavy-handed cooperative laws. By visiting similar US cooperatives, they could see how we operate in a bipartisan way despite strong political differences. These efforts failed. The conservative cooperatives would only attend meetings and conferences that I personally organized, but did not attend joint activities with leftist coops on their own. Chilean cooperatives were split between opponents and supporters of Pinochet.

Elsie and me at Chilean Fair

One of their housing delegates asked me to arrange an interview with the *Washington Post*. I told him that our papers are different from yours where I had been interviewed. Then, he almost went home on the next flight because he promised his wife to call every night and couldn't figure out how to make a long-distance call.

Unexpectedly after arriving in Washington, I sent Jorge Valenzuela, leader of small fishing cooperatives, to Alaska since there are not many in the US. He rushed out and bought warm clothing.

On my next visit, I asked Walter Sommerhoff to set up meetings with political leaders to understand the political dynamics. We met with Ricardo Lagos (later president) of the Socialist Party at his home, Jaime Guzman of the rightwing Independent Democratic Union (UDI) in a heavily guarded storm trooper office (he was later assassinated) and Sergio Molina, head of the Coordinating Council for Free Elections.

We met with retired Cardinal Raul Silva Henriquez, who led Roman Catholics for more than two decades, championed human rights, and reached out to the families of the missing. Our conversation centered on cooperatives which the Church promoted to serve the poor.

Cooperative workshops

I obtained a second NED grant to carry out workshops throughout Chile to support young leaders to revive the cooperative movement. During the Pinochet years, cooperatives declined by 44 percent.

The idea was to train a new generation of leaders in cooperative development and, then, provide them with seed funds for follow-up workshops. Each attendee was committed to training others in their organization. I ran the project through ICECOOP, a national federation of mostly agrarian reform, consumer, and worker coops.

I met with the new Ambassador Harry Barnes to discuss the cooperative workshops and invited him to participate. Harry had been picked by Secretary of State George Shultz though he had no Latin American experience. He was charged to modify U.S. policy away from Pinochet and toward support for human rights and democracy.

Born in Minnesota, he grew up knowing cooperatives and saw them as a way to identify with democracy. When we first met, he said, "Just call me Harry." Pinochet loyalists called him "Dirty Harry."

The workshop format was based on the training of trainers. The goal was to help trainers design their workshops and to role play one of the sessions as practice. My colleague Lee Rosner meticulously led the workshops. At them, he met and soon married Maria Eugenia. The two of them formed a lifelong friendship with Mario Radrigan, a Chilean trainer at the workshops.

Ambassador Harry Barnes took advantage of role-playing opportunities to demonstrate the U.S. commitment to democratic groups. He played a poor woman in one session and a youth in another. He had a grand time and had "everyone in stitches."

After each of the four workshops and accompanied by his body guards, he visited nearby cooperatives and talked about the importance of democracy. Harry Barnes translated for me at a workshop; others at the luncheon were aghast, but it was typical of the gracious ambassador who spoke 14 languages.

Informal lobbyist for Chile

Through the workshops, I became Harry's informal advisor and agent. He wanted to open up new programs and introduce the Peace Corps to Chile. I told him about the American Schools and Hospitals Program; brought the application documents with me on my next visit; and, met with officials of Santiago College, a bilingual English-Spanish High School, founded by American Methodists in 1880. They were successful in obtaining a USAID grant to build a computer wing.

After another visit and after discussions with Harry, I returned to Washington D.C. and, the next week, watched as a House Appropriations Foreign Operations Subcommittee wrote language that would cut off all US assistance to Chile.

I called the Chilean desk at the State Department and they said, "It didn't matter much." So, I faxed Harry and the next day, "all hell broke out" at the State Department. Harry and I strategized on the phone and got the decision reversed in full committee. Harry was political too, so we made a formidable team.

The ambassador pressed me to identity other organizations and funding sources. Wally and Walter dearly wanted to obtain a USAID housing guarantee program for low-income cooperative housing.

They raised the idea directly with Harry. I was skeptical and didn't think it was possible because the host government must guarantee the loan against currency risk, thus, identifying the U.S. with a repressive government. I mentally dropped the idea.

Walter Sommerhoff escorted me to various housing coops to help make the case for USAID housing guarantees. He showed me a cooperative for poor residents whose homes were destroyed by an earthquake. Each new house was expandable, had a tree out front and a garden in back. A priest built an entire village to replace housing destroyed in another earthquake. The students built their own schools. It was not mandatory, but everyone went to the Catholic Church.

In a tough neighborhood with heavy police presence, Walter showed me a labor union-formed coop where all of the streets were named for pacifists, like Martin Luther King and Mahatma Gandhi -- at one house, a couple pointed out the stray bullet holes in their ceiling as a result of nearby riots.

A few weeks later, Harry Barnes came to D.C., called me up, and asked: "How are we coming along with the housing guarantee fund?" A common trait I learned from Harry, Wally, and Walter is perseverance.

I directed him to the key USAID office headed by Peter Kim and told him that Peter's wife was Chilean and he was against any programs in Chile. Peter Kim put him off by saying, "USAID could never get Congressional approval for such a program." That set up a real challenge. So, Harry and I teamed up and got report language introduced by Doug Bereuter (R-NB) into the upcoming foreign aid bill.

The legislation said, "Private sector cooperatives play important roles in keeping alive the spirit and practice of democracy in Chile;

and the United States government wants to support democratic processes in Chile by establishing a foreign assistance presence"

As a result, Walter Sommerhoff put together a complex cooperative housing program that did not rely on the Chilean government but worked with Citibank as the guarantor for the loan. Through using the debt swap window, Walter covered the administrative costs and currency risks to Citibank by increasing the guaranteed loans from $5 to $8 million dollars.

I vividly recall the huge stacks of official documents as they were signed in a law office overlooking a corner of the White House. Harry had his wish, and he visited the newly-funded housing cooperatives as another sign of U.S. support for democratic groups. The guarantees went to four cooperative housing organizations under an umbrella association, Corporacion de las Vivienda Popular (COVIP), that provided for renewable loans of up to 10 years to finance 6,000 houses for residents who were below 50% of median income.

At the signing ceremony, Harry Barnes said, "During my career in the Foreign Service, housing problems have been my highest interest." "Over the two years since I came to Chile," he said, "he had analyzed cooperatives as an alternative way to address the housing shortage. They encourage people to solve their problems instead of waiting for paternalistic solutions."

Harry Barnes (middle) signing guarantee documents

He thanked everyone involved and "Ted Weihe of the U.S. Overseas Cooperative Development Council who made possible the signing of this agreement." Walter Sommerhoff sent me photos and press reports saying, "You may have 'heard your ears ringing.' I absolutely agree with the Ambassador and I want to personally thank you heartily."

On the next trip, they honored my wife and me at a Friday dinner where I mentioned to Hugo Yaconi, President of the INVICA Foundation, an industrialist that volunteered one day a week at the Catholic charity, that I was a sailor.

He invited me to a Saturday race the next day on his 34-foot Freres. Sailboat races are neither cooperative nor democratic with the helmsman in control, but I asked "Could I offer some suggestions?" On the upwind leg, I said, "Go to the shore, there is a lift there." He did, and we led. At the downwind leg, I said, "Let me take the chute and steady it," and our lead increased. At the leeward mark, the fleet was catching up. Nervously, he said, "take the helm." We got the gun and he excitedly told me "that is the first race I have ever won."

International conference

The final NED grant I wrote was to hold an international conference still trying to get Chilean cooperatives to work together and encourage the government to make changes in cooperative laws. Credit unions, for example, could be shut down if they didn't get their monthly financial statements to the key government officials precisely on time.

Cooperatives in Chile were especially controversial because peasants formed many of them during land reform efforts under President Kennedy's Alliance for Progress, and later through land seizures during Allende's rule. They were associated with the Christian Democratic Party or leftists, including Marxists and communists. At one large farm I visited, the owner was buying back the peasant plots which he called "his children." Judy and I stayed at his farm house and were aghast to see swarms of flies surrounding the vats where workers were making cheese.

After the 1973 coup, Pinochet repressed most cooperatives, many cooperative managers fled the country, and the government emphasized rugged individualism over cooperation. There had not been a single government pronouncement favorable to cooperatives.

In planning for the international conference, Ricardo Garcia, president of INVICA, invited Wally, Walter and me to dinner. I got into a heated argument with Ricardo on how to describe the Pinochet government. He said it was a constitutional government, and I said it was a military dictatorship. The conversation was abruptly ended when we noticed it was ten minutes to 11:00 when the curfew was to go into effect. As I rushed back to my hotel passing military soldiers at intersections, their presence clearly making my case for Chile as a dictatorship.

Little did we know that Ricardo would soon and unexpectedly be appointed Minister of Interior, the most powerful post in government which included oversight of the Carabineros, the national police.

On our next trip to plan the conference, Wally, Walter and I met with Ricardo at his offices in the Moneda, the Chilean White House. This was where former President Allende died after being strafed with bombs as the US Ambassador looked on. Despite our earlier conversation, Ricardo Garcia agreed to speak at our conference as a favor to Walter Sommerhoff. His remarks were the first kind words about cooperatives by a senior government official in the Pinochet government.

Walter Sommerhoff, Harry Barnes and cooperative leaders spoke at the conference which had to be held at the United Nations facility in Santiago because there were still restrictions on any public assemblies of more than five people.

The week before the conference, members of the Civil Alliance, who had carried out an illegal demonstration, were arrested. Only because of this conference did several cooperative leaders, who were Alliance members, stay out of jail. One of them pointedly did not shake the Interior Minister's hand.

In the dialogue, the cooperative leaders knew next to nothing about each other, and it would not occur to them to work together. In fact, a worker's coop leader claimed that electric coops where not even coops – which was not true. I had visited most of them, they had been formed in the late 1940s, and US electric coops had assisted them since the late 1960s. His comment demonstrated the gap between the left and right views of cooperatives.

In August 1986, I asked Congressman Doug Bereuter to insert into the Congressional Record this "historic" conference because Chilean cooperative leaders from diverse economic sectors and competing political ideologies sat down together for the first time.

The statement read that attendees agreed *"to get on with the business of creating cooperatives in the private sector. Twice as many Chilean cooperatives were represented at the session as had been expected."* It noted that *"U.S. cooperatives can intervene successfully under the most trying political circumstances, and in a totally private-sector approach, create and strengthen democratic institutions."*

I was told a Chilean idiom at the conference, "You arrived like a winter white horse." When I asked for a translation, they said: "You helped us to do things we couldn't have done on our own."

Walter Sommerhoff continued to work for Habitacoop until his death in 2001. He and his wife, Adriana died within a month of each other. He wrote two books about cooperatives, *Inflation and Cooperatives*, 1978 and *Dynamism of Cooperatives*, 1965.

Voter registration and education

Becoming involved in the plebiscite in Chile is somewhat complicated.

Pinochet called for a referendum on continuation of his rule for October 5, 1988. After the coup, all voter registration records were destroyed. To vote, Chileans required an identity card that cost about $1.50 in US dollars if they could find the right place to register.

It was similar to our "poll tax" system in Virginia designed to excluded African Americans from voting. Only the US and now Chile require voter registration. Most countries allow you to vote with identification or by just showing up. So, the expertise in voter registration drives is uniquely American.

I had become Harry's "go to guy" in Washington because after the conference, he asked me what organizations could help with voter registration. I told him that the League of Women Voters is the best non-partisan group to carry out such efforts.

During the Johnson campaign, my mother and I had worked the Glebe precinct, a former Freeman's Village from the Civil War. We would go up and down the waiting line of voters and ask them if they had paid their state poll tax. If they did, we told them "Don't forget to vote for both President Johnson, and Gus Johnson," a Democrat for Congress.

Because many Afro-Americans had not paid their poll taxes, Gus Johnson narrowly lost. I was there at 2 AM when he went on TV but would not concede the election until the next morning. Voter suppression is the reason he lost, while, at the same time, President Johnson defeated Goldwater in a landslide. Voter restriction efforts have taken a new guise by today's Republicans to discourage minority voting.

From my personal and League experience, I knew that voter education campaigns relied on face-to-face meetings, registration tables and door-to-door efforts to get people to register. The League provided non-partisan candidate guides which, in this case, meant objective views about the plebiscite.

My mother and I registering African Americans

Mónica Jimenez, human rights advocate

I told Harry Barnes about the League, and he turned to me and said, "There is only one person who could do this and it's Mónica Jimenez." He set up a meeting for us at the Hostal del Parque hotel. When I first met Mónica, I thought she was like my mother, but younger. She and Mónica had similar visions as nonpartisan activists.

Mónica was a member of the 14-person National Committee for Fair Elections that was formed to try to change the constitution and make elections honest and fair. She said she was willing to explore our ideas. Later, she cites our meeting as the inception of the new voter education organization – Civic Cruzada.

Mónica Jimenez served on the Pope's Peace and Justice Commission and was a leading human rights leader. She headed the School of Social Work at Catholic University. She graduated as a social worker from the Universidad Catholica de Chile. In 1981, she

227

obtained a Fulbright scholarship that allowed her to complete a postgraduate degree in Social Work Education at the Catholic University of America in Washington D.C. But, she always worried about her English which was really quite good.

Mónica's father, Oscar Jiménez, served briefly as Minister of Health under President Salvador Allende. At the age of 10, she vaccinated neighbors against deadly diseases alongside her father. She said he was a public health physician who "dedicated his life not to making money, but to serve others." Mónica had the same values as her father.

Her father became ambassador to Hungary at the same time that her husband, Juan, lost his job when the Allende government nationalized the metallurgic industry where he was the general manager. They took their savings and toured Eastern Europe to see what a "socialist" society would be like if Allende succeeded with his Marxist-inspired reforms.

Mónica is reasoned, gentle and thoughtful. A mother of five grown children, she was the center of her family and devoted to her husband, Juan. Her involvement with the Catholic Church and its human rights efforts under Pinochet were her focus. Her deep faith was obvious by looking at pictures of her with four Popes on the wall of her office. Her passion, somewhat like mine, was in development and poverty alleviation but with a social science perspective. She was a natural leader and her enthusiasm was contagious and nearly boundless.

In a small interconnected capital, it was probably not much of a coincidence that Mónica had once worked for Minister of Interior, Ricardo Garcia, at the Catholic charity INVICA that funded cooperative housing for the poor. Nor that Ricardo's brother headed the office of voter registration that proved steadfastly honest throughout the highly charged national registration process.

Voter registration drive begins

Harry Barnes arranged with his assistant, Marilyn MacAfee and me to design a United States Information Agency (USIA) travel study tour so she could quickly learn about voter education programs since the plebiscite was only a year away and time was short. Non-partisan voter education organizations had never existed in Chile, and, in fact, almost every civic organization was identified with one of the 22 political parties.

I arranged for Mónica to meet at the Civil and Political Rights Training Center, School of Social Work at Columbia University. She said, "It was there where I first linked my profession with what would become my future work in the Cruzada." I arranged for her to meet with my mother's League colleague, Mary Marshall, to discuss registration efforts while staying at my home.

At my suggestion, Mónica came to Washington with a proposal. It was modest at $50,000 sponsored by a well-known Jesuit organization. I said, "Let's make it meaningful so it could really have impact." I revised the proposal and scaled it up to $1.8 million. The idea was to use the same train-the-trainer methodology to recruit young cooperative leaders we used under the NED grant. The difference was it had three layers of trainers to reach the entire country with a sufficient number of voter election volunteers

I knew we needed an organization with an existing USAID grant to pass the money through to a Chilean non-profit organization. I talked to friends in USAID, especially Roma Knee, a deputy in the Latin American office, who became my secret agent, and she said only one organization was possible.

After working on our draft, Mónica changed her return flight and flew to Costa Rica to seek support from the Institute of Human Rights and its Center for Electoral Counseling (Capel). She didn't have a visa but called a Chilean friend who worked for the Costa Rican president picked her up at the airport.

When Mónica returned to Chile with our rewritten proposal and support from the Institute in Costa Rica, she met with the original Jesuit sponsoring organization. They were unwilling to let her run the program and thought it was too much money. She was discouraged but I did not want to give up.

On a subsequent trip to Chile, I called her up in Peru where she was carrying out a U.N. assignment on women in development. I told her we needed another sponsoring group, and she directed me to Christian Wood Armas, a cooperative housing lawyer whom I had met earlier. He suggested CIVITAS, an Italian Catholic group. With his introduction, I got the background information about CIVITAS and put it into the revised proposal.

With Harry Barnes' backing the proposal was on a fast track. I was asked to represent Mónica and CIVITAS at the internal USAID meeting on the proposal. The room was jammed full of officials, all of whom strongly opposed the idea.

The Deputy Assistant Administrator, Malcolm Butler, walked into the room and said, "I have a meeting with the Administrator and must leave immediately. This proposal will be funded. Find a way to do it." then he walked out. The room was stunned. There was a stony silence as the meeting broke up. Harry Barnes had done his magic backstage.

Senior USAID officials in the Latin American Bureau thought the voter education and registration drive would fail, the plebiscite was a fraud, and it would reinforce Pinochet and anti-democratic forces. They tried to kill it administratively by first sending auditors to Chile to prove that CIVITAS could not handle the complicated bookkeeping requirements. The auditors found that CIVITAS had a solid financial background. CIVITAS agreed to use the US auditing firm, Arthur Anderson, so that ploy failed.

As USAID continued to stall and time was running out, I called friends on the Hill who intervened to get the proposal moving. They traced the calls to me, so I became persona non-grata to the staff processing the grant.

Key USAID staff were instructed not to talk to me. But I continued "backdoor" discussions with Roma Knee, who believed in the effort and let me know when to intervene. A specific provision was put into the CIVITAS grant not to use US consultants, designed to keep me at a distance from the program. Instead, I relied on my NED funding to help Mónica carry out the voter education program.

As part of the delaying tactics, USAID asked for an extensive work plan prior to funding the proposal. Mónica and I met in Costa Rica and went to the Human Rights Institute to write what, in effect, was a completely new proposal. The day we arrived, the head of the voter education department left to go on vacation. The two of us wrote the work plan. We incorporated registration materials produced by Peter Hart, a well-known political consultant whom NED had sent as a volunteer to Chile. We were told the proposal should be written in Spanish, so I dictated and Mónica wrote.

On returning to the U.S., USAID staff changed their minds again and said the proposal had to be in English. That same week, the NRECA building where I worked caught fire so I was sent home. I had the proposal translated back into English by a friend of Mónica's at the Chilean Embassy and expanded it over the Christmas holidays. As a bonus, I learned to use my wife's computer. I submitted the work plan on behalf of CIVITAS on the first work day in January 1987.

Now the Institute for Human Right's board had to formally approve it – which resulted in more delay. Harry Barnes and Mónica weighed in again and got the Institute to become the principle sponsor. The campaign was on track.

Civitas project launched

With time running out and before the proposal was formally signed, Mónica and CIVITAS leaders announced the new program. We kept up the fiction that the funding was from the Institute, not the US. The Chilean Ambassador to Costa Rica visited the Institute to check out the source of funding where they said, "We get money from lots of governments including from Europe and the US." While it was publicly acknowledged that the US had provided $1 million in NED funding to opposition parties, the USAID funds were under the radar.

Mónica Jimenez said, "Harry was close to this whole process. We had breakfast together frequently. He would read our brochures, would encourage us, and got us to persist in the face of a multitude of difficulties."

Later in the year, the grant was increased to cover TV and radio advertising costs on voter education, but only a few stations like Radio Cooperativa were willing to broadcast their messages. Other TV and radio stations said it was "too political." Judy and I were thrilled when we heard Mónica on the radio as we drove on an overnight bus to Antofagasta to tour the Atacama Desert in the North.

The organization became known as the Civic Cruzada and used a cross and the papal colors of gold and blue with the slogan, "My Voice, My Vote." The previous year, the Pope had visited the length of Chile to encourage reconciliation and thousands of volunteers had arranged for his visit. These volunteers became the hub of what became the first non-partisan voter education organization in Chile. Information was evenly provided on what a "Yes" and "No" vote meant. "Yes" continued Pinochet's rule, "No" required new elections in a year.

Only the Catholic Church had true moral authority in Chile, and the military and political parties were mostly discredited. Mónica said, "The true beauty of the campaign was that it included hundreds of people who at that time did not have other ways to participate in the advancement of Chilean democracy."

To cover the entire nation, Mónica created a base of regional supervisors who organized groups of volunteers from different communities, often the poorest. She set up three levels of volunteers, trained over 600 people in national seminars using participatory group activities and reflection that resulted in cohesion between the volunteers. These volunteers were the backbone of the Cruzada's work.

At the conclusion of each training session, there was a solemn ceremony in which each volunteer pledged (*"compromiso"*) to work for the Cruzada. Volunteers agreed to be nonpartisan and not to take the pledge if they wanted to work within the political parties. Less than a dozen decided they could not take the pledge. The ceremony itself involved lighting candles and formally putting on a scarf with a Cruzada button.

La Cruzada volunteers

I visited with a regional group's volunteers in the South; they were highly motivated, non-political and committed to reaching out to their communities. They gave me a recording of traditional Chilean music. I ask them to play it at a bar, and everyone burst out into song. As they set up card tables in a shopping mall, it reminded me of my League efforts in doing the same thing back home.

In turn, these regional leaders organized coordinators at the community level to man booths and go door-to-door with literature that presented both sides of a "Yes" or "No" response. The pro-Pinochet groups so liked their description of the "Yes" vote that they duplicated it and sent it to their supporters.

The level one volunteers organized 517 seminars at which 7,352 committed themselves to the Cruzada. The challenge was to reach 40% of Chileans who had never cast a vote. The Cruzada printed millions of flyers, booklets on citizen participation and legal analysis of the Pinochet flawed constitution. I brought home a lot of their colorful posters. The Cruzada generated newspaper and radio news but had little success in getting on state-controlled TV.

Data on registration rates helped target their efforts with a statistician quietly working upstairs at their offices with print outs of each province and its registration rates. Pop singers, many of whom came back to Chile from exile, held concerts in which registration cards were the admission tickets. Chile had never seen anything like it before -- a grassroots volunteer movement.

I was present in one small village where the volunteers went door-to-door to meet with residents and urge them to vote. All the while, pro-Pinochet messages were blasting from speakers on the steps of the mayor's office.

On another occasion, I visited a Chilean electric cooperative near Ovalle in the central region which had just extended electric services to a small village. There was a great cheering with Chilean flags and announcing "How Pinochet had brought us electricity!" The government opened up its finances to local mayors to promote the "Yes" vote.

Man holds Pinochet photo at electrification ceremony

Suddenly, USAID was on board, and I arranged for Mónica to encourage Congress to provide additional financial support. In February 1989, I held a reception for her at my home with Congressman Matt McHugh and set up meetings with Hill staffers interested in Chile. Mónica reported back to Harry Barnes that, "All of these visits went extremely well with expressions of support from everyone."

Cover page of proposal for Cruzada

U.S. representative for Cruzada

With the Cruzada quickly running out of funds, I wrote a follow up proposal to the CAPEL in Costa Rica to pass along an additional $600,000 for educational materials to reach younger voters, and to train volunteers to monitor the plebiscite itself.

A week prior to the vote, Mónica got the idea to hold hands, pray and tie yellow ribbons around Santiago to urge a peaceful turnout calling it a "Human Chain for Peace." She was inspired by Hands across America for addressing hunger about which I had sent her press reports. The idea was a marriage of US and Chilean non-partisan activism.

The authorities did not know how to handle it but decided she needed a permit for a demonstration. She said, "It was not a demonstration but a prayer assembly for a peaceful plebiscite." She met with the general commanding the Garrison of Santiago who reluctantly agreed to allow the assembly and required Mónica to personally accept full responsibility for any damages. Without telling her husband, Mónica signed the document with some trepidation.

At the appointed hour, the organizers did not know if anyone would show up. The event was continuously broadcast on Radio Cooperativa, the voice of the Pinochet's opposition, which told people where to assemble at the given hour. And, did they - it was the largest "demonstration" in Chilean history with over 100,000 participants holding hands around the 68km (42 miles) of the Santiago circumferential.

Plebiscite results

The next week, the Chilean people elected to return to democracy with a 55% "No" against continuing Pinochet as President. Pinochet had misjudged the electorate. With backing from the military and his government officials, he expected to turn out the first wave of registrations. He knew that the second wave would come from the opposition, which unexpectedly united in a common campaign. He thought non-political Chileans would opt for stability over democracy. He was wrong, and Mónica and her volunteers helped Chileans choose democracy.

According to the U.S.-led Plebiscite Observers Delegation, the Cruzada's "volunteer network was essential for Chilean and international observers to determine whether or not the plebiscite was honest and without fraud."

La Cruzada trained the poll watchers and formed the volunteer network in place to assist the Committee for Free Elections. According to the international monitors, "Ten teams left Santiago for provincial capitals throughout the country. Upon arrival, the teams met with representatives of CIVITAS (the sponsor of the Cruzada).

"Events on the night of the plebiscite demonstrated the importance of the independent vote counts as the government delayed the release of the vote. Within La Cruzada, they carried out a "quick count" and had a strategy to provide the preliminary results, that clearly showed the "No" vote winning, and delivered the results to each member of the military Junta who then would give the results to Pinochet.

Later, Mónica Jimenez wrote me: "Volunteers visited each of the approximately two thousand voting tables to collect local results and forward them to central locations. This advance count made it possible to identify the trend toward the "No" vote early on, and relay that information to the government, political parties, international observers, ambassadors and other onlookers. The 'quick count' is credited with having played a historic role in curbing efforts by some Pinochet supporters to tamper with the election process. "

Betsey Barnes, the ambassador's wife and friend to Mónica, wrote::

"With many ups and downs, in Chile, Costa Rica, and the U.S., the program of work that became the Crusade for Citizenship took shape—an example in the world of citizen participation, which was able to motivate 4 million Chileans to register to vote."

The National Endowment for Democracy (NED) and the White House selected Mónica Jimenez as one of the first recipients of a Democracy Award. In March 1989, she received the award with Jacek Kuron at the George H.W. Bush White House. At the time, she said that she did not deserve it because Kuron had been jailed and persecuted for his opposition to Polish communists. They felt a kindship because both worked with the Catholic Church and organized democratic movements: Solidarity in Poland and Cruzada in Chile.

Mónica Jimenez, President Bush and Jacek Kuron

At the White House meeting, President Bush said, "Monica Jimenez de Barros founded and directed the Crusade for Citizen

Participation in Chile, a nonpartisan civic movement that registered and mobilized millions of Chileans to participate in the historic plebiscite of October 5, 1988. Her devotion to nonviolent political participation and democratic values helped preserve social peace and advance democracy at a decisive moment in her country's history."

While in Washington, we thought if she was going to get an award, why not ask NED for money to carry out candidate meetings for the upcoming free presidential election. All her funds had come from USAID yet NED was giving the honor. It was the easiest two-page proposal I ever wrote; I delivered it to Katie Kaufman who handled Latin America and later became an aide to Harry Barnes. The proposal went straight into the NED board book for approval.

With Pinochet defeated, the right wanted to become more legitimate and sought allies since the next election was for a new president. Mónica approached all of the major parties and got them to agree to League of Women Voter-style candidates' debates.

Participa

Mónica created a new incorporated group, known as Corporación Participa (Participa) which was formed to consolidate democracy. For direct USAID funding, it should not have an overtly religious affiliation such as the Cruzada with Vatican colors and a Christian cross.

Pollster Mata Lagos, a distant cousin of Mónica's, whom I met at an international social sciences conference in D.C., captured the mood of post-Pinochet Chileans. She found that public attitudes had changed little towards democracy. Growing up during the years of the dictatorship, she saw part of the democratic process as "assuring people get a piece of the cake." Participa was designed to change public attitudes.

Now, everyone in USAID wanted to take credit for Mónica's success, and directly fund her new organization. They sent evaluators to review the voter education and registration program, and secretly with my friend Roma Knee, I wrote their task order to make sure that it focused on the successes.

Mónica was surprised how "informed" the evaluators were. They recommended a $5 million program to be used over the next five years to promote civic discussion during the transition to multi-party elections. Participa retained a core volunteer network of over 900 Chileans in major regions while 15 coordinators in Santiago traveled, instructed and inspired the grassroots volunteers. Its goal was to teach democracy as a way of life.

After she received the funding, I went to Chile to discuss fund raising. I said, "Mónica, you have $5 million, but in five years there is a cliff with no new money. You must start a fund-raising effort now." In Chile, there was almost no history of charitable fundraising or giving except for some TV telethons for cancer and other diseases; and certainly not for civic causes.

A year later, Mónica said that she was really mad at me for telling her to raise money after she had just received a major USAID grant. Though, she heard my message and wrote in December 1994 that we now have a $240,000 endowment, "and you have been the key person in this challenge!"

I told her that you must bring your "development" person (euphuism for fundraiser), downstairs to office next to you, since "she is your future." Mónica accepted my advice and Andrea Sanheza not only raised funds, she became the next president.

About Participa, Mónica said that "In the United States I was inspired by the League of Women Voters, as well as by other university, church and union programs devoted to promoting citizen participation. These people guided me and still provide me with new ideas."

Participa became the most successful democratic organization in the hemisphere for the next 25 years and shared its experience with dozens of countries going through similar democratic transitions.

At a Democratic Revolution Conference in D.C. in 1989 on Capitol Hill, Monica said, "Life in a democracy requires each person to understand his or her personal attributes; be aware of his or her rights and responsibilities. They must be free, willing to participate, directed by values and respect, open to dialogue among diverse viewpoints, tolerant and uproot sectarian and fanatical attitudes contrary to democratic ideals."

The goal of Participa was to create a democratic culture, not only as a system of government, but as a way of life, and to reverse the prevailing oligarchical system that allowed a dictatorship to emerge in what had been a stable but not participatory democracy. In previous decades, the Chilean elected officials were chosen by parties. Leaders seldom went to their districts nor took their constituents views into consideration.

During the election year, Participa continued its nonpartisan work distributing informational voter guides, holding candidate forums, broadcasting voter information and training poll watchers. Mónica attributes the success of Participa to the "train the trainer" methodology reinforcing respect for pluralism, public service, peace and nonviolence.

President Aylwin sworn as president, next to General Pinochet

Mónica invited Judy and me as official guests to the March 1990 inauguration for Patricio Aylwin who won the election. We were treated like royalty when we arrived at the airport.

I decided to go to as many events as possible. Representing business cooperatives, I attended the luncheon, "Businessmen for Aylwin." I found an interesting person at one of the tables who spoke perfect English. The next day, our photo together was in the paper and I was told he was the most famous gun-runner in Chile, including selling arms to Saddam Hussein in Iraq. In another article in *La Segunda*, I said that "a democratic Chile will be more attractive to American investors.

We went to the celebration at the infamous Estadio Nacional where the military had imprisoned dissidents in the coup. The stadium was full and they sang patriotic songs and exchanged soccer chants from one end to the other. The mothers of the missing danced the

"Cueca" in colorful dresses holding white handkerchiefs. President Alywin gave an address, but most could not hear it. In fact, we were probably the only ones in the stadium that could not follow his Spanish.

Invitation to public ceremony

Afterwards, we tried to hail a cab and finally succeeded. The cabbie asked where to go, and we showed him our invitation to the Moneda, the Chilean White House. In disbelief, he raced us there. We met Mónica and her husband at this special event to celebrate the election of Aylwin.

Senator Ted Kennedy (D-MA) came to celebrate the inauguration and the return to democracy. He was scheduled to give a speech to the human rights advocates. Kennedy had taken his honeymoon in Chile. He held the first hearings on the demise of democracy after the Pinochet coup. He was a hero to many Chileans for his stance against U.S. pro-Pinochet policies and its human rights violations.

Nancy Soderberg of his staff asked Mónica to attend. Mónica responded that she was having her own dinner party with Harry Barnes, Judy, me and other supporters who helped create the

Cruzada and Participa. We agreed to go for dessert and hear his speech in which he, of course, praised Mónica and shook every hand in the room – the Kennedy touch.

Public health clinics

There was a reception at the American Embassy after the Kennedy speech. Harry Barnes who had been reassigned to lead a State Department taskforce on critical languages was there. I ask him what the US was going to do now that Chile was a democracy. The US appeared willing to help topple Pinochet, but nothing to help the new democratic government. Harry said it was bad etiquette for a former ambassador to interfere with the current one. But, he still wanted to be kept informed and up-to-date on my efforts.

I decided to act on my own. The easiest and most compelling proposal would be to support health clinics for the poor which had been underfunded by the military government. Two years earlier, when Judy and I were returning from Chile on a trip, we met Jorge Jimenez, Mónica's brother on the plane. Already a doctor, he was on his way to study for a Master's in Public Health from Johns Hopkins University in Baltimore. As fate would have it, and as he anticipated, he became the new Minister of Health.

I wrote up legislation to earmark $10 million for child health programs and called a friend in Senator Kennedy's office to sponsor it when the appropriations bill came to the floor. On March 18, 1989, I arranged for Jorge Jimenez to meet with Senator Tom Harkin, Congressman Matt Hugh and various congressional staff to discuss the funding request.

In talking points, I wrote, "while the upper and middle classes have benefits from the free market economy, 40 percent of the population suffers and expects immediate benefits from the return to democracy. In public opinion polls, 56% said heath care was

Chile's number one problem... Today, 20% of the population has no health care all. Infant mortality in poor areas is rising rapidly at 87 per 1,000 live births, four or five times the national average. The Ministry has a primary health care program ready to go."

With support from Senators Tom Harkin (D-IW) and Pat Leahy (D-VT), Kennedy said on the Senate floor.

"I recently had the honor of attending President Patricio Aylwin's inauguration in Chile. The new government has made it clear that their No. 1 social priority is health care, and they deserve our support.

Chile's primary public health care system was on the verge of collapse. Over the last 17 years of authoritarian rule, public sector spending for health care declined by 55 percent. Twenty percent of the population was without coverage of any sort—virtually all of whom live in impoverished communities. The health ministry has proposed to assist 158 clinics in poverty areas, support primary health education, and finance drug abuse and alcoholism prevention.

The people of Chile have suffered enormously over the last decade and a half – and all of us in Congress are well aware that the United States bears its share of responsibility for that suffering."

The measure passed unanimously, and Jorge Jimenez thanked me in a note for my help.

Accompanying health clinic funding, bill language provided "up to $5,000,000 to support democratic institution building including programs for nonpartisan democratic education, strengthening political participation in upcoming local elections and technical assistance to improve the operations of the new Congress." This language dovetailed with the five-million-dollar recommendation from the evaluators to support Participa.

Saving democracy

Mónica stayed at our home while attending a conference as an advisor to the Inter-American Foundation. Over the weekend, she told me this astonishing story about saving Chilean democracy as we drove along the scenic Skyline Drive in the Blue Ridge Mountains to Monticello, Jefferson's home.

Monica and me at Jefferson statue in UVA Rotunda

Democratic leaders feared that Pinochet would not accept the verdict of the plebiscite. There was an elaborate plan, that she devised, to deliver results of the "quick count" individually to members of the military junta. Each head of the military services then, in turn, would go to Pinochet and tell him that he'd lost even before the final votes were counted.

Two days before the election, there were rumors of a government plan to disrupt the plebiscite and blame the communists in order to call it off at the last minute. Harry Barnes and Mónica Jimenez teamed up for an international diplomatic and media initiative to head off such an attempt.

The fateful evening before the plebiscite is detailed by Harry's wife, Betsy Barnes in her account published in *American Diplomacy* in March and April, 2015. "I'm remembering my surprise when Zacarias interrupted our dinner that night – he had such strict rules for himself – that remarkable man who served as our butler, and in a more just world would himself have been served."

He said, "There are two people who would like to see you. They say, please, it is important." He was looking at both Harry and me. He added, "They are waiting at the bottom of the drive, by the guard house." It was unlike Zacarias to break into our evening meal, yet he offered no apology. It was a couple of days before the plebiscite and everything seemed a little out of sync. Our residence sat atop a hill and the walk down to the main road was a good way.

Mónica and Juan were standing just under the light by the guard's little house. We joined them there, but Mónica took my arm and steered us to the unlighted gatepost across the driveway. I had seen her face. Something serious had brought them. She spoke immediately, her voice quiet but distraught.

Betsey continued with details of the conversation in the article. When I shared the article with Mónica, she wanted to correct the record.

Mónica wrote to me what happened that day: "I visited with the general commanding the garrison of Santiago to ask for authorization to keep the La Cruzada House open on the day of the plebiscite, and to receive there the international observers. I was accompanied by a lawyer of La Cruzada that was also present during the conversation.

What I said to the general, after we finished the meeting and after we obtained authorization to keep our offices open, was: "It has been said, general, that there will be some public disturbances before and during the plebiscite ... What have you heard about that?"

He answered; "In fact, we also have that information. People will go on the streets equipped with shotguns: they will make bombs explode in the subway; they will try to begin fires ... but don't worry. As Armed Forces, we are prepared to repel these attacks. The population can be sure that we will be absolutely in control of the situation."

Mónica and her lawyer "evaluated this information as very delicate and risky." We informed Mr. Patricio Aylwin, who was head of the "No" campaign and he sent us to talk to Harry Barnes. Mónica continues, "The day after, every kind of political consultations were made, in different levels and with various groups including the most extremist ones: Nobody had planned any kind of disturbances of any nature. At that time, the population just wanted a plebiscite in peace.

Having this information and more certainty, it was thought that this could be a strategy of the government to "create conflict" and "repress it" in order to invalidate the plebiscite in case the results were averse to their interests.

After we contacted all of these political groups who promised not to carry out any disturbances, and they behaved in exemplar fashion on the day of the plebiscite. The citizens accomplished the goal. Everyone was in order.

After the nighttime meeting with Harry Barnes, Betsy Barnes wrote,

"His immediate cable to the Department of State urged them to call in the Chilean ambassador and report what we had been told. It was

249

a Sunday night in Washington, but the department, judging this the emergency that it was, forthwith summoned the ambassador. Nor was it an accident that when the Department's press spokesman routinely briefed the press the following day, the news of the Chilean ambassador's summons and its cause was leaked. In the blink of an eye the headlines reached Chile. The Chilean government was indignant."

More details have been reviled. In 2013, the National Security Archive filed a Freedom of Information request to obtain the classified cables about the plebiscite. They confirm the potential for a coup and the importance of the quick vote which Mónica organized.

The CIA station reported in a heavily censored cable, "The increasing resolve within the military to avoid a civilian government was the regime's record of terrorism and human rights violations. There was a great fear that a civilian government would cooperate with the United States Government in pursuing the case of the assassination of former foreign minister Orlando Letelier, as well as other abuses by the military, to the extreme detriment of the Chilean Army."

By late September, polls indicated that the NO campaign was surging ahead as the TV commercials gained a popular following and Chileans became confident that safeguards, including hundreds of international election observers, would insure a non-fraudulent election.

"Public perception of the `NO' is increasingly that of a winner," the Embassy reported on September 29, 1988. The next day, however, Ambassador Barnes sent the first "alerting" cable to Washington on information he had received from Mónica regarding an "imminent possibility of a government staged coup" if the vote went against Pinochet.

Both CIA and DIA intelligence indicate what Ambassador Barnes characterized as "a clear sense of Pinochet's determination to use violence on whatever scale is necessary to retain power."

In a secret report for Assistant Secretary Elliott Abrams, Barnes summarized Pinochet's scheme:

"Pinochet's plan is simple: A) if the 'Yes' is winning, fine: B) if the race is very close rely on fraud and coercion: C) If the 'NO' is likely to win clear then use violence and terror to stop the process. To help prepare the atmosphere the Center for National Intelligence (CNI) will have the job of providing adequate violence before and on 5 October. Since we know that Pinochet's closest advisors now realize he is likely to lose, we believe the third option is the one most likely to be put into effect with probable substantial loss of life."

Highly placed U.S. intelligence sources within the Chilean army command provided additional details. A Defense Intelligence Agency summary, classified *TOP SECRET*, reported,

"Close supporters of President Pinochet are said to have contingency plans to derail the plebiscite by encouraging and staging acts of violence. They hope that such violence will elicit further reprisals by the radical opposition and begin a cycle of rioting and disorder. The plans call for government security forces to intervene forcefully and, citing damage to the electoral process and balloting facilities, to declare a state of emergency. At that point, the elections would be suspended, declared invalid, and postponed indefinitely."

The Pinochet regime did try to implement its contingency plan to abort the plebiscite, announcing that evening that the 'Yes' votes were ahead and then halting hourly reports on the vote tally. "The GOC (Government of Chile) is obviously sitting on voting results," the Embassy cabled in a Security Situation Report.

251

These events were part of a Machiavellian plan worked out by Pinochet and his highest aides, a high-level military informant would tell a CIA agent, who would call the Interior Ministry to delay the announcement of voting results to agitate the opposition, announcing preliminary results favorable to the YES vote, and then call the YES voters to the streets to celebrate the alleged YES victory. This would then result in a strong opposition reaction, street clashes and the need to call in the army to restore order, thereby providing a handy excuse to suspend the plebiscite.

Pinochet's attempt to orchestrate chaos and violence in the streets failed, however, when the Carabineros (police) refused an order to lift the cordon against street demonstrations in the capital, according to the CIA informant.

In a dramatic last gasp to hold onto power, Pinochet called the members of the military Junta to his office at the Moneda palace at 1:00 AM. He was "nearly apoplectic" about the turn of events, one participant of the meeting noted.

"The Chilean President and CINC of the Army General Augusto Pinochet were prepared on the night of 5 Oct to overthrow the results of the plebiscite," an informant reported.

Pinochet was insistent that the Junta give him extraordinary powers to meet the crisis of the electoral defeat. "He had a document prepared for their signatures authorizing this .... Pinochet spoke of using the extraordinary powers to have the armed forces seize the capital.

At this point, armed with the results of the Cruzada-led quick count, Air Force Commander Fernando Matthei stood up to be counted. Matthei told Pinochet he would under no circumstances agree to such a thing ... he had had his chance as the official candidate and lost. Pinochet then turned to the others and made the same request and was turned down ...."

Without the Junta's support to overthrow the "NO" vote, Pinochet was left with no alternative but to accept defeat at the hands of Chile's democratic forces.

The point is that Mónica really did deserve the White House Democracy Award because she, along with Harry Barnes, saved democracy in Chile.

Postscript

Harry Barnes retired from the Foreign Service in 1988. We stayed in touch while he was working at the Carter Center on its democracy building projects. His obituary in the *New York Times* on April 17, 2012, said his highest career achievement was bringing democracy to Chile. He died at age 86.

Mónica Jimenez was appointed a member of the National Commission for Truth and Reconciliation which was an "effort to establish the truth and achieve justice, reparations and prevention with regard to serious violations of human rights perpetrated during the previous regime and thus achieve reconciliation among all Chileans."

The commission investigated human rights abuses resulting in death or disappearance that occurred in Chile during the years of military rule under General Augusto Pinochet. The commission created a list of individuals who had perpetuated or otherwise carried out human rights crimes. These cases are still going on some 25 years later.

The *New York Times* on February 29, 2016 reported, "Under successive civilian governments, Chile has been investigating human rights abuses under military rule. But progress has been slow.

More than 1,370 military, police and civilian agents have been indicted, charged or sentenced for human rights crimes. Of those, only 117 people have been imprisoned according to a report released in December by the Interior Ministry's Human Rights Program."

Mónica's husband, Juan Barros died in 2002. Maybe because of his death, she took a position as president of the Catholic University of Temuco in southern Chile. In 2010 she became the executive director of AEQUALIS (Forum for Higher Education). She served as Minister of Education for two years working on reforming the university system to implement the results of the report, "Dialogues for Education." She followed the guidelines as given, but they became unpopular with students who wanted free college education.

In 2014, Mónica was appointed to the Vatican as Chile's first woman ambassador to the Holy See. Recently, she observed that in a world where women make up half of humanity, "men have to share with us the family roles and we women have to share with them the public role in society and, of course, in the Church." She continues as a voice to advance women in the Catholic Church.

In the summer of 2015, we stayed at her official residence in Rome. She was a gracious hostess and seemed totally unchanged from when we last saw her some 24 years ago. She arranged for us to have dinner with her English-speaking friends, a monk, a priest and an American-Italian she called "her street friend" whom she had met while practicing her Italian on a bus.

Our discussions circled back to cooperatives. She was scheduled to hear Pope Francis First Encyclical Letter, Laudato SI in a Vatican conference room for 500 ambassadors and other guests. I asked her to bring me a copy in English since we knew that he would be addressing concerns about the environment and global warming. I watched the presentations about the encyclical on Vatican TV by different advocates: An Orthodox priest, German scientist and leader of Caritas, the Catholic Charity.

When she handed me the encyclical, I read it and found it very personal and moving. Then, I came upon a passage that said, "Liberation from the dominant technocratic paradigm does in fact happen sometimes, for example, when cooperatives of small producers adopt less polluting means of production, and opt for a non-consumerist model of life, recreation and community."

Francis acknowledged that he had no new "recipe" to quickly change the world. Instead, he spoke about a "process of change" undertaken at the grassroots level by priests, NGOs and community organizers. That has been my life's career.

Chapter 12: Micro-Insurance for the Poor

I wanted to see the impact of insurance firsthand.

In September 1989, I read about Hurricane Hugo in my sailing newsletter which devastated Culebra, a small island off Puerto Rico. The island sustained losses of 80% of its houses and displaced 2,000 residents who fled into the mangroves. The hurricane winds, recorded at over 200 miles an hour, destroyed over 200 boats anchored in what had always been considered the safest *hurricane hole* in the Caribbean. It has tall hills all around to deflect the wind shifts as a hurricane passes, and an excellent holding bottom for ground tackle with mangroves as tie downs for lines ashore.

Sailboats wrecked against bridge

Pictures showed boats strung all over, piled up against a bridge, and scattered and capsized in the mangroves. These were not ordinary boats but some of the most expensive million-dollar craft, charter fleets and cruisers. I had to see it for myself.

In October 1989, Dennis Reinmuth and I were on a swing around the Caribbean to design a cooperative insurance project for an upcoming RFA on cooperative development. We had a Sunday free, so we took a bus north and a ferry to the island. There were still sunken sailboats with only masts showing, and dozens of cruisers repairing their broken boats along the mangroves.

Most of the badly battered boats had been removed. There are no repair facilities on the island, and electricity was just being restored. Lloyds of London sent a barge to pick up all of the insured boats and took them to Miami to be repaired or written off.

The Dinghy Doc Bar-B-Q was the only open bar at the harbor where I met several survivors. They said the wind was like a freight train, sailboats capsized just with bare masts; once boats went adrift, they had a cascading effect, dragging all of the other boats with them downwind into the mangroves or worse against the bulkheads. Of the more than 200 boats in the bay, only five were left at anchor in the wake of Hurricane Hugo. At least 136 either sunk or were badly damaged.

I had been thinking about not renewing my hull insurance for my Ericson 35 in the Chesapeake Bay where I remember as a kid the 1954 Hurricane Hazel that passed over our home and miraculously my father's sailboat survived with only a 25-pound Danforth anchor holding it. This changed my mind.

Insurance is supposed to cover catastrophic events. We pay our premiums for peace of mind and to protect our property. Insurance only works when there are many people paying premiums and only a few claims.

Learning about insurance

Before this insurance exploration trip, I knew a little about insurance from my grandfather.

257

As a youngster, I loved him. He was larger than life, picking his teeth with a penknife and pushing the table away with his belly after a meal. He grew up in Harden County, one of the poorest in Kentucky. He became a recovered alcoholic. My mother, known as Sissy, basically raised her younger siblings. My grandmother worked and rented rooms while grandfather was getting sober.

My grandfather was a natural salesman and successful district and state manager of the Woodman of the World, a fraternal Christian life insurance company. He would sell life insurance door to door. When he was let in, he would walk over and turn off the radio or TV and tell the man of the house "with a stroke of this pen, I will make you rich." Pointing to his wife and kids, he would ask, "Who will take care of them if you are gone?" Of course, to become rich, you had to die.

JB as he was called wrote *Monday Morning Refreshers* that he sent out as motivators to his insurance salesmen. I wrote them up for a family reunion. His most memorable expression: "It takes guts, gumption and spizzerinktum to be successful." He used spizzerinktum because "I can't think of a more appropriate word to use for the purpose I have in mind." He meant "get off your fanny and go to work in earnest."

Insurance for development

My task was difficult. What does insurance have to do with helping the poor in developing countries? Nowhere in development literature is there a mention of insurance. No USAID programs had ever promoted insurance except for the very modest people-to-people and company-to-company programs of the North American Association of International Cooperative Insurance Federation funded through the Cooperative Development Program.

Insurance is an intangible benefit, unless needed. It provides "peace of mind" to the insured. There must be trust among the insured that, if and when you need it, the company will pay for your claims. It is easy for many of us in the West to take insurance for granted, but for those in most developing countries, their only insurance is meager savings or property that they must sell off when tragedy or adversity strikes. Cooperative-based group insurance may be their only option.

Insurance is particularly important on the death of a credit union or cooperative member since these coops reach the poorest segments of the population.

I learned about cooperative insurance from Bob Vanderbeek who headed the League Insurance Company and was active in the National Cooperative Business Association (NCBA, formerly CLUSA). He put me in touch with Dennis Reinmuth, a professor at the University of Michigan on insurance. Dennis led efforts in Michigan for no fault car insurance, worked for the League Insurance Companies, and staffed the Americas Association of Cooperative/Mutual Insurance Societies (AAC/MIS).

AAC/MIS projects helped existing cooperative insurance companies in Latin American with management advice on a coop-to-coop basis. The association itself was headed by Harvey Sigelbaum who at the time was president of the New York Garment Workers insurance company.

Harvey Sigelbaum and me

AAC/MIS carried out exchanges and seminars as a program of NCBA. To become an independent cooperative development organization (CDO), their program should focus on technical assistance for struggling and start-up insurance companies. The purpose of the trip was to make this shift as they prepared for an upcoming request for proposals and create a development methodology.

As Dennis and I traveled to the Dominican Republic, Belize, and Barbados, I picked his brain and we wrote the first document, *Insuring Development Through Popular-Based Insurance,* that made the case of why insurance is important for economic development and helps the poor. Carol James edited and produced it.

Poor people face more risks than the rich, so they need insurance to "provide relief from the financial consequences of uncertainty." The document described the evolution of insurance from informal economies, intra-lending among families, to more formal economies with insurance companies.

The document laid out the relative risks of insurance compared to administrative complications – group life insurance has the least risk and is easiest to manage. The document discussed the insurance development process and different stages of insurance from an agency representing an insurance company, a risk bearing department where the company accepts some of the risks and collects some of the premiums, to an independent insurance company.

The document discussed the importance of credit unions (savings and credit cooperatives) which provide insurance, known as group life savings and loan protection. It is not new. The founders of credit unions – Feline and Desjardin – in 1908 said credit unions should not pass debt to the families of the deceased, and their savings should be insured, providing twice or three times the amount to help the family when a wage-earner died. They said, "Debts should die with the debtor."

Few in USAID had any idea that insurance related to poverty alleviation, nor that many Latin American countries had cooperative-based insurance companies that help some of the poorest in their societies. Since we take insurance for granted, require it for mortgages and cars, few development types even think about it, or think it is relevant.

While insurance is second to banking for capital formation in the West, it is designed only for the wealthy or middle class in Latin America. The exceptions are credit unions or cooperative insurance companies.

USAID Administrator Peter McPherson read the document and said, "It was excellent to see your report on insurance companies. I suspect that this is one of the more important ways to help people and increase growth – not in the short run but over a decade or two – that could be pursued."

Where to start an insurance company

We had to find a suitable country. Dennis and I visited Belize which had credit unions but no independent insurance programs for its members. We went to the capital – Belmopan – in the center of the country which had been relocated from Belize City because of several hurricanes. The town had few residents and looked like a university campus.

We tried to find the commissioner of insurance. He had many hats including finance and banking. We asked him to show us the regulations. He went to a dusty bookshelf and picked up a well-worn book of its 1922 English code. Dennis and I concluded that Belize which had recently gained independence was probably not a good candidate for an insurance company.

Insurance coop in Dominion Republic

We stopped by the Cooperativa Nacional De Seguros in the Dominican Republic that nearly failed because of poor management, and was bailed out by the successful Puerto Rican company, Cooperativa de Seguros Multiples. It had injected some finances into the company, put its own representative on the board, and provided management consulting.

Insurance companies are complex organizations that need technical assistance in collection systems, actuary data, product design, claims processing, etc.

Initially, we wanted to work with the Caribbean Confederation of Credit Unions (CCCU) but it was sponsored by the CUNA Mutual Insurance Company in the US, which provided savings and loan insurance (LS/LP) to CCCU credit unions. CCCU was not interested in forming a separate Caribbean regional insurance company.

Cooperativa Nacional Seguros

Still searching, our final visit was to the Barbados Cooperative Credit Union (BCCU) which had ten strong credit unions as members. While there were 18 foreign-owned insurance companies in Barbados, and was the center of insurance in the region, none were owned by residents of the Caribbean. BCCU had accumulated a surplus of its savings and loan insurance through its self-financed insurance department. We suggested using this surplus as well as financial support from their member credit unions to form a company.

There was one hitch: Barbados was not an eligible USAID country because of its high average incomes (GDP). We encouraged BCCU to form a company with other English-speaking countries of CARICOM. We suggested outreaching to credit unions in St. Lucia and St. Vincent and the Grenadines to form a regional company, but these efforts were not successful.

Based on our publication on the importance of cooperative Insurance, I wrote the proposal to USAID that averaged about $100,000 a year from 1990 to 1993 for technical assistance to cooperative insurance companies on a coop-to-coop basis, largely in Barbados.

AAC/MIS sent experts to set up the insurance company, most significantly Pat Roberts of Nationwide Insurance. Roberts had been CEO of a Nationwide Insurance affiliate in Germany that was sold. Later he headed Nationwide's international department. He was blunt with the organizers of BCCU, emphasized keeping staff small and operationally efficient as it started up.

In 1925, Nationwide was formed by Murray Lincoln with $5,000 from the Ohio Farm Bureau. My father always called it the Ohio Farm Bureau Insurance Company though it changed its name to Nationwide in 1943 to recruit farm bureaus all over the nation. Farm bureaus sponsored the startup of many agricultural cooperatives.

Now, 86 years later, Nationwide had grown from a small mutual auto insurer owned by policyholders to one of the largest insurance and financial services companies in the world, with more than $158 billion in assets. At the time, Nationwide provided technical assistance and training in its Columbus offices to emerging cooperative insurance companies in developing countries.

Barbados project

In early 1991, AAC/MIS designed and BCCU conducted a survey of the credit union member market in Barbados, listing the number of homes and automobiles owned by members and indications of their willingness to shift or acquire insurance from the new firm. It demonstrated a clear statistical basis for a viable company.

In August 1992, Dennis and I carried out an initial evaluation. We found that the credit union league had sufficient management and financial skills for the complex task. It already operated a risk-bearing, mutual benefit life insurance program for its members. The project was to shift from an agency of the US-based CUNA Mutual that backstopped the credit union insurance to its own independent company.

AAC/MIS experts helped the league develop a business plan, meet registration and capitalization requirements, and acquire reinsurance (insurance for insurance companies).

Pat Roberts and his wife, me, Nationwide advisor and Dennis Reinmuth (left to right)

AAC/MIS representatives met with the supervisor of insurance to ascertain regulatory requirements and required capitalization of US $500,000. They prepared a three-year business plan that included reinsurance, management staff, and indications of the sources of business. Because the company would be the first indigenous company to be registered, it received greater than normal regulatory scrutiny.

Because of recent hurricanes, reinsurance was difficult and expensive. AAC/MIS initiated discussions with the International Cooperative Reinsurance Bureau {ICRB) under the leadership of the Co-operators of Canada, an AAC/MIS member. The Co-operators became the lead reinsurer as well as Nationwide.

Peat Marwick generated projections of cash flow statements, projected earnings, balance sheets, and impact on capital accumulation. The model tested assumptions on reinsurance programs and the volume of business which can be written safely. From this data, the business plan projected a gradual buildup of business beginning in the initial year with 750 auto insurance policies and 470 property policies.

Denis Reinmuth and Pat Roberts refined the model that was submitted to the supervisor of insurance. The model was used as an educational tool in seminars to train staff in insurance operations.

The application documents were prepared and informally discussed with the supervisor of insurance, then formally submitted March 27, 1992. The supervisor requested clarification of several items and wanted a more qualified insurance manager to run the company.

There was infighting among the credit unions about who should be on the board of directors, and the largest credit union refused to join initially. AAC/MIS held workshops for the credit union leaders, trained the nine members of the board of directors, installed computer systems, and organized its management structure.

Co-operators General Insurance of Barbados began operations in 1993 for loan protection and life savings, property, motor, and other lines. The company was eventually owned by 28 credit unions.

Using its private jet, Nationwide flew its entire board to Barbados for the opening. I was proud to attend knowing that Dennis, Pat and I had helped create this company. Today, it remains a strong company and recently completed construction of its own headquarters.

The project was a complex undertaking and involved a lot of technical assistance from AAC/MIS members. Factors for success were the leadership and commitment of BCCU, support by the larger Barbados credit unions and their ability to raise significant capital.

New General Co-operators building in 2016

How insurance helps the poor

No one had ever asked how survivors or beneficiaries of insurance claims use the funds after a death or loss.

Pat Roberts and I designed a project that would find out in Colombia, Bolivia and Guatemala. No study to my knowledge has ever analyzed these payments, recently or in the past. I put together a team to do the analysis: Nicole Dubois, a Canadian insurance analyst living in Bolivia, and Karen Schwartz and myself for Colombia and Guatemala.

In all three countries, we asked the managers of cooperative insurance companies to identify recent claimants and asked if we could meet with them at local credit unions. It was awkward because the people we were interviewing assumed we wanted to know about the death or loss in their family. After listening to their woes, I asked, "How did you use the insurance money?"

We interviewed 125 beneficiaries with total claims of $250,000. We found that the companies reached low income members for loan life insurance because it is simple to automatically add to the costs of the loan. Life insurance helped survivors pay for funerals, maintain living standards, and reopen microenterprises when the bread earner died. Most beneficiaries were women.

Because they receive their insurance through group-based programs by credit unions and cooperatives, the claimants often were not aware of the cooperative-owned insurance company which provides the coverage. Working through mostly credit unions and some other types of cooperatives, we found that these insurance companies are a significant source of funds to continue family-owned microenterprises.

While not among the largest insurance companies, the cooperative insurance companies reached the largest numbers of low income people: five million in Colombia and 600,000 in Guatemala. Most of the credit unions in Latin American insure savings and loans. Many offer group life, individual life, and special insurance for funerals.

I was surprised that most of claims were for violent deaths: a son collected after the shooting deaths in separate incidents of his father and mother who owned a bar; an industrial accident killed a husband when a limestone rock exploded; and another husband died when a bus went off a cliff. Most of the deaths were relatively young men in their mid-thirties.

All of the payments were modest, usually a few hundred dollars. About 25% helped continue small family enterprises and the rest paid for funerals or living expenses of widows and children.

Guatemala

In Guatemala, I interviewed the son and daughter of a credit union founder who died at 62. She had just enough savings ($10) to maintain her credit union membership and to qualify for a special life insurance policy of $1,666. This policy was sufficient to cover the costs of her funeral. Her son, who worked at the credit union in the agricultural town of Gualan, told me, "Our mother taught us the importance of life insurance."

In the highlands, Maria's husband died three months earlier. She had four children who were 16, 10, 6 and 2 years old. Angela, the eldest, told us how her father was ill for nine months. He was a tailor, who made traditional Mayan jackets and aprons. He had a small shop which he started up with a credit union loan. When he got sick, he taught his daughter about his business and its finances. He took her to the market place to show her where he sold his goods and to whom, since he often marketed through other sellers. He used his credit union savings to keep his loan current so that it was fully insured and paid off upon his death. Angela planned to reopen the small store with the insurance payment and obtain a new loan to expand the business so she can increase the family's income. I bought one of her traditional aprons.

In another example, Manuela planned to use the insurance from her husband's death to continue his microenterprise which crushed rocks for whitewash and sold it at construction sites. Very poor, neither she nor her husband had a loan. Since his death was an accident, insurance paid twice the amount of his savings. Fortunately, her husband taught her about the business so she had a livelihood as a widow.

Leoncio, who was 46, had a loan to repair his taxi. He died before it was paid off. His wife cared for their eight children and five additional relatives. She owned a small stand at an open-air market where she makes $100 a month. The insurance paid off her husband's loan and she sold the vehicle. The additional money allowed her to take a small loan of $900 to expand her business. Thanks to insurance, she now makes enough money to pay her family's living expenses.

Colombia

In Colombia, I interviewed the wife of a retired military sergeant who left her to work illegally in the Medellin drug trade. He told her he would send her money in three to six months. He never contacted her, so after eight years she sued the military for support. She went to her credit union for military retirees and asked for help. They directed her to go to Medellin and carry out her own search. By looking at mug shots at the police station, she learned he had been killed. As a result, the credit union provided her with her husband's insurance and helped arrange to receive his survivor's pension for the rest of her life. The life policy was worth $700 and the insured savings, $1,200.

Maria Antonio, a housewife with four children, was well informed about the insurance policies that her husband had at the Coop-Kennedy, near the Bogota airport, because he had been one of its founders. Her husband, Ernesto was killed while painting his small van. Because it was an accident, Maria Antonio got double benefits of $1,000, and the cooperative took care of all the funeral arrangements and costs. The cooperative is named for President

Kennedy who personally inaugurated the Alliance for Progress housing complex for workers in Bogota. The cooperative runs a small credit union for its 125 low income members, operates a dry-cleaning business, and provides funeral services and life insurance. Members pay $13 a month for these benefits.

Credit union and cooperative-based insurance companies are good at insuring individuals with group life, loan and savings insurance, but only indirectly support microenterprises of their members. I knew that I needed to recast the AAC/MIS insurance program to focus directly on microenterprises, a USAID priority.

Microenterprises and insurance

I wrote a proposal to Development Alternatives that managed the USAID program on microenterprise. We decided we needed to work with Seguros La Equidad in Colombia because it was the strongest cooperative-based insurer. Fifty percent of GDP in Colombia is generated by microenterprises and it has some of the strongest microenterprise organizations.

In 1996, Bogota was not a safe place. The manager of the insurance coop picked me up in his car with a body guard. While writing the report on the project, I walked to the Gold Museum downtown. A taxi driver stopped me and told me it was unsafe for Americans to be walking around the area. After his warning, I stayed pretty much in the hotel, or when travelling went only with an official of our insurance partner.

In preparing to write the proposal, I visited many microenterprises to ask them what they thought about insurance. Some I visited were totally unsafe: a kiln that regularly blacked out the neighborhood when operating. At a wood products firm, I found dust all over the floor, no masks for workers, and an empty fire extinguisher. There are no enforced safety standards in developing countries unless insurance companies require them for property insurance.

I found that there was definitely demand, but each business was so different. Some were small enterprises; others, family run. They needed all kinds of help – insurance was not their highest priority.

The staff of Seguros La Equidid designed the product. They hired a firm that held focus groups and interviews with 305 microenterprises. It validated there was a demand for a simple, combined insurance product that would be flexible to different types and sizes of microenterprises.

The policy would cover fire, theft, flood, hail, explosions, civil disorder, terrorism, and high winds. Additional policy options included earthquake, assault, liability, losses of internal equipment, and funeral expenses for family members and employees.

They called the product "Equienpresa" (business insurance) because the owners of microenterprises prefer to be called simply businesses. The staff designed the product and hired 10 women agents to sell it in October 1996. None of them sold any policies, and the agent approach was abandoned.

They tried to sell the product through microenterprise organizations with a 20% commission. This approach did not work; the product was too complicated and difficult to administer. They sold the product through their extensive 1,200 cooperative network, but it did not sell well.

We concluded early on that the pilot project was not going to be successful. It was run by junior staff who were not interested in any critiques since they were "experts." It was just too complicated, and partner networks were not equipped nor able to sell the product with sufficient returns for their efforts.

With Karen Schwartz, I wrote a monograph: *Insuring Microenterprises,* again the first in this budding field. Our conclusion was that while insuring microenterprises holds "great promise" and is an "untapped market," it is difficult to market property insurance for these small and diverse enterprises.

Micro-insurance

The focus on microenterprises led to a third proposal to the Microenterprise Best Practices program on how microenterprise organizations themselves offer member benefits such as loan forgiveness for death, or funeral benefits.

In 1998, Pat Roberts and I visited three microenterprise organizations in Guatemala that provide loans to groups of women who jointly pledge to repay the loans. All three had "solidarity" programs to pay back a loan if their fellow group members could not because of death or illness or refused to repay it. If there was a loan default, the entire group could be cut off from further loans.

In one case, clients in the groups paid off 35 loans from clients who died. Another one paid off loans to 13 clients who died and two with permanent disabilities. The third organization paid off loans for 16 clients who died.

What we found was that death or disability wipes out the ability to repay loans, often resulting in the family closing its business. Most microenterprise organizations that we visited shared risks among their borrowers with "solidarity funds." They did not grasp the advantage of transferring the risks to a credit union-based insurance company with similar low income clients.

We found that the microenterprise organizations did not see or understand that their group benefits were a form of insurance. They had not assessed the risks, nor evaluated the benefits based on standard insurance or actuarial data. Some collected too much money and others not enough to support loan losses. Poorly designed solidarity funds were in trouble when losses exceeded income. They either must terminate the plan or assess members to cover the deficit.

The resulting monograph was entitled *Insuring Microenterprise Loans: A Primer for Micro-Finance Institutions.* These documents were acknowledged as pioneering in subsequent publications by Warren Brown and Craig Church: *Insurance Provisions in Low Income Communities: Lessons Learned from Microenterprise Experiments of the Poor* (2000), and an International Labor Organization book by Craig Church entitled *Protecting the Poor: A Micro Insurance Compendium.* (2012).

I was flattered to learn that Craig Church included me "among the many pioneers in the field who have sought or are seeking the perfect balance of controls and costs, coverage and price, and accessibility and affordability to enable the poor to be insured."

Micro-insurance is now an established development field.

HealthPartners

Even more challenging is health care for the poor. Pre-paid health care – HMOs – are another form of insurance. It is expected that many people will pay for health care, but only a few will need it. It is the most risky and complicated type of insurance.

Since 1994, Land O'Lakes had been assisting dairy cooperatives in Uganda. They found that members were selling their cows to pay for family health emergencies. Land O' Lakes approached HealthPartners in Minnesota on the feasibility of setting up a health care cooperative in the Bushenji District near the border of Rwanda.

In 1997 under a Land O'Lakes sub-grant from USAID, HealthPartners began working with dairy cooperatives and expanded to cover other groups such as coffee and tea cooperatives, micro-finance organizations, and students at boarding schools. At its peak, they developed 53 group plans covering 5,600 members.

Uganda has a long history with international donor organizations. There is an expectation that money and resources should be provided for free to the community. HealthPartners attempted to overcome this legacy with Uganda Health Cooperative (UDC) because it is member-owned and requires commitment from providers, members, and community leaders.

By 2004, however, funding cuts as their sub grant funds ran out caused UHC to reduce staff and cut 17 plans (mostly older, larger plans) for 3,000 members. When they tried to get villages to adopt plans, their expenses went up and often the villages would drop out. Collecting funds through volunteers was a challenge.

In my 2004 evaluation and case study, it was clear that HealthPartners needed additional funding to succeed. I helped them become a cooperative development organization so they could carry out the project themselves, rather than through Land O'Lakes.

In helping them design the proposal, I visited several villages, talked with the UHC promoters, and met with doctors at the government-run Naguru General Hospital. There were about 15 doctors, 30 nurses, and five midwifes. At this public hospital, patients were on the floor with one or more relatives sleeping next to them. Outside, families prepared meals over open fires. Since President Yoweri Kaguta Museveni was to visit in two weeks, the staff was whitewashing the buildings and cleaning the property, rather than spending scarce resources on patients.

The three hospitals I visited appreciated pre-paid plans since they had a 40% non-payment rate for walk-in patients. Even if plans did not cover all of the costs, it represented revenues that they otherwise would not receive, just like here in the U.S.

In 2006, a board of directors was elected, the first annual general meeting held, and, in the following year, intensive capacity building took place for health providers and the board of directors. The project depended on local volunteers who helped manage and promote the prepayment plans between the insured groups and hospitals and reviewed the benefits and coverages which may differ among groups.

Child survival proposal

In my second evaluation, I was critical of the project since I felt that the pre-paid costs were too low to provide sufficient revenues so that the UHC could achieved self-sufficiency. The project needed more resources and staff to grow coverage, so I wrote a proposal for a Child Survival Grant which was one of the hardest I have ever written.

The criteria were tough to address since I was unfamiliar with child survival programs, and USAID used an outside evaluator who reviewed the proposal and asked difficult questions to which I had to respond. I focused on three activities: malaria (50%), control of diarrheal diseases (25%), and maternal and newborn care (25%). Much of the earlier cooperative health costs were for malaria pills or treatment, especially for children. HealthPartners had experience and staff in these areas including several expatriate African health experts.

With this grant in hand, I traveled to Uganda to gain the approval of the Ministry of Health which USAID required to start the project. Unlike in agriculture, I was impressed with the professionalism in the health ministry that insisted on collaboration among donor agencies and projects.

I came back with critical comments of the project manager who was not on site, had weak administration skills, and infrequent visits to the project site. While I write detailed evaluations, I provide US project managers with an oral assessment of their field staff. Eventually, she was replaced with local staff on site.

While the additional resources would build the health cooperative, it meant additional health services focused on children under five. A major advantage of the Child Survival Program is capacity building, team building by outside experts, on-going support, and up to five year's funding if UDC hit its annual targets.

From 2005 to 2010, UHC served 34,500 women and 15,500 children under five of which they were able to enroll 14,000 in pre-paid health plans. However, the final evaluation echoed my earlier concern that UDC's success "depends on expanding its membership." While pre-paid insurance suggests a solution to reaching the poor, the challenge remains sustainability without significant government subsidies and donor funding.

The US project manager is Jennifer Stockert at HealthPartners, the largest consumer-owned health care organization in the U.S. While I worked with her in 2003 to set up both the cooperative and child survival projects, it was not until 2016 at a cooperative development summit that I met her for the first time. With a background in traditional Chinese medicine, she had grown into an articulate and accomplished project manager. I was so pleased to meet her since launching international careers has been one of my passions.

In my mind, vision is to see opportunities, analyze underlying systems or approaches, fund pilot projects and set the stage for their replication. I have been lucky to find partners who appreciated and supported these ideas and made a difference in the lives of the poor.

Chapter 13: Electricity for Peace & Prosperity

Worlds apart, two different conflicts had similar impacts in bringing electricity to formerly embattled residents: Perquin – the home of the FLMN rebels in El Salvador, and Yei – the first liberated town in South Sudan. Both got electricity as a result of tangible American gestures of peace.

I evaluated the impacts at Perquin and put in motion the process that brought electricity to Yei.

In addition, I evaluated the impacts of electrification after Hurricane Mitch in Guatemala, and Hurricane Georges in the Dominican Republic. Throughout my career, promoting cooperative electricity held a special place for me. For 23 years, the National Rural Electric Cooperative Association (NRECA) was my business home. They provided OCDC with workspace and benefits for me and my assistant.

Switching on the electric lights for the first time is an event never forgotten. My mother remembers when TVA brought power to her home in rural Kentucky. Whether in rural America or a remote village, the joys are similar. There is a lighting ceremony, everyone turns on their lights and then smashes their oily and smelly kerosene lamps in a ditch. I witnessed these joyful celebrations in El Salvador, Guatemala, Chile, and the Philippines and vicariously in South Sudan.

Most of us think of electricity as a necessity for modern life. Rural electric projects are challenging because rural people have lower incomes, use less energy, and have fewer customers. The costs of electric grids and power lines are higher per mile. Overwhelming evidence shows that electricity is highly valued and rural people are willing to pay for it. Their costs are often less than kerosene, candles, and cell batteries.

The economic benefits are obvious: agricultural processing, lighted towns, businesses, and microenterprises. The social impacts are broader: electricity liberates women who have fewer babies and advances their education. It modernizes rural residents - now "connected" to the nation and world with radios and TVs. Electricity strengthens civil society in remote areas with lighted evening meetings, street lights, commercial activities, and evening public services.

Rural electric coops are more effective than commercial or privately-owned utilities because residents know that losses or electricity theft adversely affects their rates. Community peer pressure is effective. From the depths of the depression, US electric coops are an American success story that has been shared around the world.

In these efforts, Myk Manon of NRECA personally climbs the poles, directs the stringing of the power lines, trains local linemen using US volunteers, ships U. surplus electric equipment to the sites, and builds the electric grid systems. There is no one anywhere in the world who has lived in more dangerous and remote locations than Myk Manon who believes in the power of electricity and cooperatives. Myk is married to Lupe whom he courted by riding a donkey on his days off to her village while in the Peace Corps in Nicaragua.

He seldom came to NRECA headquarters, always needed a visitor's pass or access code, since he spent 40 years almost entirely overseas managing NRECA projects in Bolivia, Bangladesh, El

Salvador, the Dominican Republic, the Philippines, South Sudan, Nigeria and Haiti.

It was my privilege to support his heroic efforts. He brought electricity to some of the poorest and most isolated communities in dozens of countries – restoring the lights at Port of Prince four days after the devastating 7.0 Haiti earthquake. In 2016, his last assignment was to bring electricity to northern Haiti prior to retiring to Florida in 2017. One of his greatest joys is his Hummer which he saved for three years to buy, cherishes and took to every assignment if possible unless restricted as a military vehicle.

Living in dark places where few can afford a generator, and most rely on candles, kerosene or small wood or charcoal fires, residents flock to Myk Manon. From his former Peace Corps days in Nicaragua, he has one passion: to bring low cost electric systems to rural villages that generate more than light; electricity generates modernization, hope, and economic development.

Only because of the collapse of the Soviet Union, the Farbundo Marti National Liberation Front (FMLN) did not win the civil war in El Salvador after its final and nearly successful offensive in 1989. FMLN guerrillas gained support in the poor neighborhoods of San Salvador which led directly to the US.government pressuring the Salvadorian government to negotiate for peace after 12 years of civil war that claimed 75,000 victims. An accord was signed in 1992.

Beginning in 1988, Myk Manon and NRECA directly engaged in restoring power when the FLMN cut the lines or shot up the transformers. It was dangerous work, guards protected his supplies. As a USAID contractor, he could not carry a gun.

Initially, US Ambassador William White said the conflict was "a foreign inspired Marxist aggression." On two separate trips to meet with FMLN leaders in Santa Marta, near Perguin, the Ambassador built confidence on both sides in the civil war. As a *peace dividend*, he turned to Myk Manon to restore power in Perguin which was the site of major military operations as the hometown of the rebels.

As Myk and I drove to Perguin, we passed a downed bridge on the outskirts of San Salvador that the guerrillas had blown up on the last offensive to reach the capital. We approached the Honduran border and the conflict region around Perguin. Ambassador White wanted to make Perguin a showcase to demonstrate the US sincerity in the peace process.

Myk Manon assigned a full-time construction staff to rebuild the distribution lines to Santa Marta Province and surrounding towns. He showed me how he optimized line design and construction methods expanding projected electrical coverage at reduced costs. The project reach 40% more consumers with service than the original design by the San Salvadorian government. Rather than supervise work by the national utility, he found it was quicker and more efficient to have NRECA carry out extensions from the main grid to nearby unlighted villages.

Myk Manon built 92 kilometers (57 miles) of line to eight former rebel towns with 56,000 residents. While electric lights and appliances were greatly valued, about 60% of connections were to family-owned microenterprises.

In Perguin, Myk and his crew personally climbed the poles, strung the lines, and restored power to the small town. I could see where transformers had been shot up and buildings still damaged.

Initially, power was provided through a diesel generator. By May 1994, the town was connected to the national grid.

A great believer in the power of cooperatives, Myk organized the Perguin electric cooperative with a seven-person board. Forty-two of its 65 members attended its first general assembly. I interviewed Sandra Medrano, who was president of the board and a former guerrilla leader along with her FLMN commander husband. She said that she made sure that the board was composed of ex-combatants and non-combatants. She said, "The cooperative is a democratic institution where residents can learn and practice democratic decision-making with direct relevance to their lives."

The cooperative had ten employees who installed house wiring, read meters, and provided line extensions and maintenance. The board and staff were trained by NRECA which arranged and placed a US Peace Corps volunteer, Dan Beckley, for administrative and accounting support to the coop. He lived in a primitive house, there was a sheet above his bed to catch droppings of rats in the rafters and a cow outside on a tether for milk. He said, "The town is very conservative, and when I go to buy beer, I am careful to keep it out of sight."

In gathering information for my report, I walked around the town and counted the electric connections to 80 small stores, five restaurants, three carpentry stores, a pharmacy, hardware store, tailor and stationary store. The cooperative provided electricity to four schools, a day-care center, five mayor's offices, two police stations, three Justices of the Peace, a telephone company office, two health clinics, four community centers, and 21 public/security lights.

Lights and refrigeration were the heaviest loads. Women benefited through labor saving devices including an estimated 75 electric irons that replaced coal irons, 15 refrigerators, 100 TVs, and 190 radios.

Electricity generated substantial savings in the cost of kerosene and candles. I interviewed a woman who was sewing a dress on an antique Singer sewing machine while her son watched TV. She came from a nearby village without power to use her sister's machine. An electric sewing machine is 1,000% more efficient than a paddle driven one.

I interviewed residents on the street; they said that they felt safer with public lighting, and the police told me that there were fewer thefts. Refugees and former combatants were returning from Honduras and opening up small businesses. A women's center held evening classes. Restaurants opened in the evening and offered cold drinks and hot meals. Electricity directly resulted in a 40% increase in municipal growth.

I asked the rebel leader, Sandra Medrano, to give me a tour of the Museum of the Guerrillas. She showed me documents, photos and weapons including homages to heroes and martyrs. There were tents showing guerrilla life, and radio equipment for Radio Venceremos that broadcast during the civil war. I was particularly impressed with the wreckage of an American helicopter. The guerrillas had shot it down killing an El Salvadorian general on board.

Museum for guerrilla heroes and martyrs

The advantage of doing an evaluation with Myk Manon is that you can ask a question, and he goes to his computer and comes up with answers and figures. Since he did surveys of unlighted and lighted villages, he had statistics on the impacts of electricity.

The NRECA El Salvador project reached 180,000 rural consumers; generated $79 million in economic development; and created 12,000 micro-enterprises. I wanted to know the impact on women. Myk calculated that the introduction of electric grist mills for tamales saved 937,000 women days, and electric sewing machines generated 30,000 more garments per year. Grinding and mixing corn and mulch for cattle saved 156,000 hours a year.

His innovations in routing of electric lines saved 14,000 trees and produced 1,000 metric tons of fewer carbon emissions by substituting electricity for kerosene, candles, and firewood for cooking.

In El Salvador, Myk Manon was able to get generous donations from US electric coops in substations, hardware, meters, and utility trucks, worth over $320,000. He not only solicited donations from American rural electric coops, he would drive there, pick them up and take a convoy to a port or overland to El Salvador. It is a great example of rural America helping the less fortunate.

He exceeded all of the project impacts in the project by factors of two or three. He trained over 2,400 local electricity staff in design, linemen qualifications, operations, material management, and energy efficiencies. Throughout the civil war since electric systems were often attacked by guerrillas, USAID was providing poles, hardware, insulators, meters, and other equipment to the national utility to replace them. NRECA was overseeing these US procurements. The warehouses were still full of this equipment.

When I debriefed Carl Lenard, the USAID mission director, I looked directly at him and said, "You had better not terminate the project immediately, otherwise, this equipment will disappear, be stolen or put on the black market." He extended the project another year for an orderly close out.

The project in El Salvador benefited from $35 million in earmarks over five years as part of Reagan's Caribbean Basin Initiative. USAID is reluctant to support rural electricity because of its costs and lack an appreciation for its impact on poverty.

Dominican Republic

When I was in USAID, I was assigned to the Disaster Office when there was a major earthquake or hurricane. My job was to respond to calls from Capitol Hill. In 1979, Hurricane David, Category 5, was the worst to hit the Dominican Republic in a century.

Claude Pepper, the oldest member of Congress, called and said he had asked his Miami constituents to collect water in Coke bottles.

He wanted USAID to fly them to the Dominican Republic. I explained to him that we want people to send money, not supplies which are often useless, and certainly were in this case with water in Coke bottles. He was not deterred, called the White House, and got the water bottles sent on an Air Guard flight.

As a sailor, hurricanes fascinate me, and now I had another opportunity to see their devastating impacts. Hurricane Georges passed over the Dominican Republic on September 22, 1998, as a category 4 hurricane with winds reaching 130 miles per hour. The eye of the hurricane entered the southeast portion of the country where it destroyed housing, uprooted trees, and demolished crops. The impacts completely destroyed the electrical grid and the distribution systems to the towns of Boca del Yuma and San Rafael.

From August 1999 to December 2001, USAID funded a $2 million project for NRECA to rehabilitate the rural electric systems in the region. Myk Manon and his team restored electricity to 2,175 homes, 350 small shops, 15 elementary schools, 13 drinking water systems, a 25-bed hospital, and a high school.

Myk began by restoring the basic grid and again providing new extensions to nearby homes and businesses. Many of these homes, including the one I visited where five Haitian families lived in a tiny rental house, never before had electricity.

Crowded rental house for Haitian workers (Myk on right)

The downed electrical systems had been poorly designed with low voltage and frequent outages prior to the hurricane; most homes and businesses received less than six hours of electricity daily.

Myk Manon pointed out that the concrete poles were set in the former raised sea bed in which the hurricane winds broke them at the bases. He brought in better wind resistant wooden poles and properly set them.

I saw the impacts of reliable electricity with the creation of many new businesses including auto mechanics, car washing, restaurants, and a furniture plant. I visited the fishing village of Boca del Yuma where he electrified cold storage. Now, they could serve seafood to locals and tourists who took day trips to the village. While I was there, a colorful tour bus passed by that was full of young tourists, blaring music, and plenty of booze for lunch there.

Manon restored electricity to Boca del Yuma and San Rafael in less than 90 days. These town systems have the best service in the country. I watched him teach a class about cooperatives which he helped form. The coop would facilitate residents of the towns so they could deposit their electric bills at the cooperative, rather than each homeowner and business individually traveling 20 miles to pay their bills at a larger town where the utility had its offices.

Myk Manon with board of directors

Based on US rural electric standards, the project utilized conductors, pole spacing, and transformer sizing that allows for further low cost expansion to outlying communities and farms adjacent to the project areas. One project that I visited used electric pumps for drip irrigation to grow vegetables.

The town of Benerito had been by-passed when the original transmission line was constructed between La Romana (a major resort area) and Higuey because it was too costly to put in a substation. Myk Manon arranged for a donated transformer from the Electric Cooperative of New Mexico and powered the town.

Donated transformer

I visited the families in the Haitian workers' village of Padre Nuestro where they had been relocated because they had formerly lived on top of the aquifer and were contaminating the water supply for local hotels and resorts.

These industrious hotel laborers had constructed a shantytown from corrugated roofs that came off the hotels in the hurricane. Myk Manon worked with the Cooperative Housing Foundation (CHF) to help build new homes for the workers. The residents constructed a level playing field where I observed young people playing soccer.

Under the grant, NRECA purchased $502,539 in US transformers, lines, poles, equipment, and regulators from companies such as Coopers, North Pacific, and ERMICO. AES (US electric holding company) contributed over half million dollars in meters and metering materials, power lines, conductors, poles, and other equipment.

NRECA sent 18 lineman volunteers for construction of the electric systems. Three US electric coops donated three vehicles: two cherry pickers and a line truck.

There are three characteristics of a Myk Manon project. He is hands-on and enjoys doing the wiring especially lines to poor villages and homes beyond the requirements of the project. He brings in volunteer lineman from rural America, many of whom have never travelled outside of the US. For them, it is a life changing experience. He finds, organizes and personally delivers donated surplus rural electric cooperative equipment.

Guatemala electrification

As the funding from USAID dried up, I told the new NRECA international administrator, Jim Durnil, that an alternative source of funding was the US Department of Agriculture Food for Progress program. I wrote the next proposal to tap these funds in which US surplus wheat is sold and the local funds used for development.

In Guatemala, NRECA arranged for 20,000 tons of wheat to be sent to seven flour mills that generated local currencies for a trust fund jointly administered by NRECA and BanRural. In 2000, I visited four sites to evaluate the Guatemala project in which NRECA staff reviewed the applications, provided fee-based technical assistance, and the trust funded these activities.

The project was managed by David Kittison, an expert in renewable energy, productive uses, and designs for rural electrification. He had extensive experience in organizing and supervising fieldwork to determine clients' willingness to pay, economic benefits, demand studies, electric line design and construction.

I visited the Pulberizadora El Terreadero, a privately-owned crushing plant that produces calcium for soil improvement of melon, coffee, and chicken production and cement for ceramic floors. The plant had 15 fulltime employees with a capacity of 500 100-lb bags per day from a 32-horsepower crusher.

The project installed a new, higher voltage line and three transformers that increased power by a factor of five. A second, larger parallel crushing operation increased employees from 15 to 30 and produced 2,500 100-lb bags per day. The additional crusher produces phosphate for fertilizer. On the road, I saw the old method of producing lime without electric crushers in which workers "cooked rocks" by burning old tires and splashing water on them to "explode" the rocks. I recalled the wife who lost her husband to this dangerous process while evaluating an insurance program.

Village of Manabique

I took a high-speed boat with twin 100 horse power motors to Manabique and Quetzalito villages, two remote fishing villages on a peninsula situated by the Refugio de Vida Silvestre, a wildlife nature preserve. The villages can only be reached from Port Ban'ios by boat.

The project provided 43 solar home units, each of which consisted of a photovoltaic panel, pole, regulator, battery and three lamps per house. In addition to lighting, there was sufficient power for a television and a radio that most villagers now owned. Homes were self-constructed either with sand floors or on stilts.

The project cost $30,000 in which each family contributed $130, the Ministry of Energy provided a grant of $13,000 and the municipality, a loan of $10,000. The installation of solar electricity replaced candles--with a flip of a switch the villagers entered the 21st century.

I interviewed several villagers. One of them said, "The lighting gave him a feeling of greater security just like the city." A woman said that electric lights extended hours for socializing and her children can study in the evenings. A fisherman said that he can repair his nets at night. There were electric lights at a small rustic hotel.

All of the villagers were trained in using the system using a chart beside each battery listing "dos and don'ts." Solar power is appropriately nonpolluting to this natural reserve area with rare species of plants and wildlife. The fishermen could now use a solar phone to check prices at the market place for their catch, but there was insufficient power for refrigeration.

I visited a furniture factory, Maderar Milpas Altas, where NRECA upgraded its power system, raised the plant's roof for better ventilation, and added translucent roof panels for natural lighting to improve working conditions. The plant produced high quality furniture (e.g., armoires, mantels, tables, chests and dressers) for export to the U.S. (about 290 containers a year). With 400 employees, the factory turned raw wood into finished product with annual revenues of about $5 million. The project resulted in 25% energy savings.

I wondered what Jesse Helms, chairman of the Senate Foreign Relations Committee, would think about this project that imports furniture and competes against North Carolina manufacturers.

The final project I visited was a municipal sewage treatment plant in Frijanes in which the project installed a three-phase power system for $29,000 (12% of the cost matched by municipal funds). The new sewage water treatment plant had major environmental and health benefits since current septic tanks were inadequate and overflowed onto streets. The wastewater was polluting streams and resulted in Dengue Fever for children. Water from the plant is now used for irrigation to grow tomatoes and other vegetables and provides water for the municipal soccer field. Water is metered at each house for water conservation.

At the NRECA local office, I interviewed beneficiaries of the project. It funded three coffee farms in Santa Cecilia, Los Angeles and La Providencia. This resulted in increased productive capacities through upgrading coffee drying and sorting with improved incomes.

The project provided grid extension for new low-income housing in San Pedro, Ayampuc, and the municipality of Santa Maria. Several microenterprises got together for a line extension for their woodworking and metal operations as well as a line of credit for electricity to an association of cooperatives in Huehuetenango, located in the so-called Peace Zone, after 36 years of war with the Contras.

Two new villages, where refugees from Hurricane Mitch had been resettled lived in new homes with roofs, floors, water and sanitation. With separate funds, NRECA provided grid extension to these 40 families.

I met with the Minister of Energy and Mining to discuss the challenges of rural electrification now that the power system had been sold to a Spanish firm. Under the sale, the energy company is supposed to provide extensions to villages from a set aside fund.

Visit with Minister of Energy

I indicated to him that trying to force private electric companies to make unprofitable line extensions to rural villages was unlikely to be successful given the US experience with the Rural Electrification Administration (REA) during the Roosevelt administration.

I strongly believe bilateral U.S. foreign aid should reflect and share positive examples where we were able to reduce poverty. None are more successful that REA. Although 90 percent of urban dwellers in the US had electricity by the 1930s, only ten percent of rural dwellers did. Private utility companies, who supplied electric power to most of the nation's consumers, argued that it was too expensive to string electric lines to isolated rural farmsteads. Anyway, they said, most farmers, were too poor to be able to afford electricity.

Conventional wisdom was wrong and today nearly 900 rural electric cooperatives serve rural America, bringing light and economic development to these families and communities.

Charter 14: Sudan & Yei Electric Coop

Sudan's size, strategic location, and oil reserves made it a Cold War target of superpower intervention. Massive injections of US and Soviet arms kept a bitter civil war raging between north and south for nearly a half century. In 1996, the US designated Sudan a "rogue state" and broke relations with the current regime for harboring Islamist terrorists including Osama bin Laden and in fomenting genocide in Darfur. Formal relations were re-established in 2002.

An estimated two million people lost their lives and more than four million were displaced in the guerrilla warfare between north and south. Large numbers of South Sudanese fled the fighting, either to the north or south to neighboring countries. Many were in refugee camps.

For South Sudan, I arranged for a cooperative delegation to introduce cooperatives as a transition from relief to development and to support the emerging new country and leadership. About one-quarter of USAID's African funds were flowing into Sudan, mostly for relief and capacity building by religious groups and other NGOs. Sudan was especially important to the Bush Administration because of strong support by evangelical Christians for the south against the attacks by the Moslem-led north Sudan.

As we took our delegation to South Sudan, peace talks were underway that culminated in a 2005 Peace Agreement and 2011 referendum for independence. All infrastructure that we saw such as roads, utilities and many buildings were damaged or destroyed often by north Sudanese bombers.

Though the economy is based on subsistence agriculture, South Sudan has the potential to be a major agricultural producer with a rainy season and good soils to the west (equatorial Sudan), and mostly desert to the east and north. It enjoys major revenues from its oil reserves shared with the north.

Among its conflicts are border disputes and cattle-raiding feuds between rival ethnic groups which have left hundreds of people dead and some 100,000 displaced. Outside of Haiti, South Sudan is the poorest country that I have visited but it had the potential to adopt cooperatives as an engine for economic development.

I approached Roger Winter, the USAID Assistant Administrator, who had a long involvement with South Sudan, to engage U.S. cooperatives in the transition from relief to development. He formed a taskforce led by Brian D'Silva who had a similar commitment especially for Yei, the first town liberated by the Sudan People's Liberation Movement (SPLM).

I hired Stella Kenyi, as an intern, to make contacts with the SPLM and plan a trip for the cooperative delegation to Sudan. Stella was a young and bright refugee who escaped from Sudan with her mother and brother, when it was overrun by SPLM, since her father was an official of north Sudan.

Her family was "adopted" by Ruth Buckley, a USAID officer in Nairobi who sponsored them to the U.S. Stella graduated from Davidson University in North Carolina and later obtained a Masters from Cornell in Ithaca, New York. She set up meetings for us with Steven Wondu, the SPLM U.S. representative as well as other officials from the rebel movement when they visited D.C.

As part of their college credit, Davidson University offered financial support for students to travel abroad. Stella approached me and suggested carrying out cooperative training in Yei for her college credit. I agreed and USAID cooperative project manager Tom Carter and I trained her in cooperative development. We knew that anything about cooperatives would be very basic and she could teach the fundamentals.

Stella Kenyi spoke three local languages as well as Arabic so the plan was to hold training workshops for officials and businessmen in Yei on how to form a cooperative. It was not easy to get across the Ugandan border as she was stopped by armed rebels and forced to take several of them to Yei. Later, she worked at NRECA in electrifying Yei, undertaking a survey on the costs and benefits of replacing small diesel generators with an electric grid.

With Stella's help, our mission to South Sudan was to assess local conditions with an emphasis on economic development, resettlement of refugees from the north and basic electric and internet services as *peace dividends*. The team assembled near the Entebbe airport in Uganda, made famous by the successful Israeli rescue of Ethiopian Jews, the so called "lost tribe." As we were about to fly with Mission Air, the pilot asked us to hold hands and pray. Not a good omen before taking off.

Since I had taken two weeks of flight classes in the Air Force, I was designated as co-pilot. Prior to entering Sudan air space, the pilot reached up and turned off the transponder. I told him, "You just turned off the device that my father invented, why?" He said that it was best to fly low, avoid flying over towns, and use coded communications with the ground. All these precautions were to avoid being a target for the Sudanese Russian-supplied air force that frequently bombed the south.

As we landed in Yei, there was an anti-aircraft battery near the dirt runway and a destroyed tank on the road that we had to drive around, as we drove into town. Yei is a market town, near the border of Uganda and the main transit for trucks for relief or supplies to the interior. The only other accesses were from the Nile that was blocked and mined from the north, or across the desert to and from Kenya.

We met with SPLM leaders including the head for cooperatives who knew little about cooperatives but supported them as a basis for development. He was missing one lens in his eye glasses and was looking through it as he held it with his hand, getting new glasses was expensive and hard to import. At the time, it was thought that Yei may become the capital of the new country, but that did not occur when Juba, a garrison town at the time, located on the Nile was selected.

Our hotel in Yei

We had a good meal at a small restaurant and stayed in a cluster of adobe houses that was the only "hotel" run by a women's empowerment group. The next day, the group split up. Don Crane took the agricultural group in a four-wheel drive Land Rover to look at agriculture in the west. They visited two agricultural towns of Marie and Yambio. They drove over heavily eroded dirt roads and often had to pull the vehicle out of water holes with their winch. Sudan is not accessible by road or planes during the rainy season.

Our group focused on infrastructure and refugees. We were lucky to travel east by air to Lobone, a refugee resettlement camp and the Bor region where a massacre had occurred and which was to be a prime location for refugees returning from the north.

We met with the Catholic Relief Services staff and 40 chiefs of the sprawling camp made of sticks and adobe. We visited a Catholic church on Sunday morning where two young people walked down the aisle singing and holding Bibles. It was a long building built with logs and a thatched roof. It was like no Catholic service I had ever attended with neither communion nor reading catechism.

Each of us as visitors was expected to speak to the assembly about why we were there. Most of the communications in South Sudan were done through churches – a combination of animist and Christian believers. In the afternoon, we visited several projects supported by Norway and the US for medical care and elementary education. Most Sudanese are uneducated; 90 per cent have less than a fifth-grade education.

Catholic Church at Refugee Camp in Lobone

On Monday, we flew to Panyagor in the Bor region of the Dinke. It was a tiny town, like an island along the Nile with flood water around it. We flew up the White Nile, a meandering river that I read about in high school. *The White Nile* by Alan Moorhead is a classic bestseller describing the daring exploration by Stanley Livingston and Richard Burton in the late nineteenth century as they discovered the most mysterious and impenetrable region on earth. It still is.

As we flew high over the Nile basin on a crystal-clear day, what impressed me most was the spatial pattern of huts below that were clustered in small hamlets. I guessed most of these residents had never seen a Westerner or knew anything about the "modern" world. I ask a colleague at Samaritans Purse how they could put a hospital in a small town in South Sudan. He said "Villagers are typically willing to walk five days to get medical care."

As we arrived looking down over Panyagor, we could see huts with a few cows surrounded by dykes. There was a small market where there had been a solar system, now defunct.

Most of the American and foreign NGOs offices were staffed by Kenyans or Ugandans since living at these sites was difficult and isolated with supplies flown in, limited electricity by small generators and battery-operated phones.

We stayed at a CARE office, ate canned food, and slept in huts. For a shower, you poured water over your head. There was an outhouse. A huge problem is poisonous snakes who want to come into your hut for warmth. The major USAID project in Panyagor was drilling boreholes for water wells to accommodate thousands of refugees who were to be barged down from Khartoum.

For the next leg of the trip, we waited for the supply plane – a Buffalo aircraft formerly used by the Canadian paratroopers which was delayed. It had rained in the night, and we were told if the runway was slick, we could be stuck there for days. A member of our delegation had been trapped in the town for 10 days because of the slippery runway. When the late-arriving plane landed, we rushed to get our bags and with great relief got onboard.

Don Craine's half of the team was secretly flown to what was called "New Site" where they met with most of the SPLM leadership and future ministers for industry, mines, agriculture, cooperatives, finance, customs, and natural resources. All of them were supportive of moving from relief to development. They saw cooperatives as important to these efforts. They placed a priority on electricity and telecommunications.

The two groups rejoined at Rumbek, the UN center for relief with a concrete runway. Several planes had been pushed off the runway since they had mechanical problems with little likelihood of repairs anytime soon.

Our USAID colleagues selected Rumbek, the last stop as a reward, the only town in Sudan with cold beer and 24-hour electricity. The tent city was run by AFEX, an English company out of Kenya. In front of each tent, we had our own fox hole.

Cooperative delegation at Rumbek

Here I visited a cattle camp which helped me understand the challenges of marketing cattle. I used the experience to write a proposal for Land O'Lakes. Sudan is mostly a pastoral society where cattle are owned for prestige and sold when needed for ceremonies or other economic needs. The proposal was to develop more formalized cattle markets, trek them to the border and sell them to Uganda.

USAID relocated the project near Juba, the capital, and refocused it on creating a dairy cooperative. The challenge for Sudan is that while they have agricultural abundance, they compete with Uganda for the same crops. Most trade to the north was difficult because of the 22-year conflict and repressive government.

We flew back to Entebbe where I spent the day sailing a Laser on Lake Victoria, got a terrible sunburn on my exposed feet, and gladly got on a plane home.

Yei Electric Cooperative

Not a single town we visited had an electric grid, and those that had earlier ones were destroyed. Small generators where the only power, and diesel fuel was expensive and trucked in by barrels.

Jim Willis of NRECA did an analysis of the costs of kerosene, batteries, charcoal, wood, and diesel on a monthly basis, compared to the costs of a large, more efficient diesel generator and town grid. I added a section on how to form an electric cooperative, recommending that NRECA electrify Yei which I knew was the favorite town of Brian D'Silva, head of the Sudan Task Force.

Yei had significant small industries and a well-organized business association with the capacity to pay for the electric service. It was close to Uganda for getting diesel supplies, the most significant cost. As in many of my initiatives, I set the stage for both projects. The Land O'Lakes proposal for dairy development was highly supported by the mission director in Khartoum who grew up in Minnesota and was a relative of the Land O'Lakes international director.

Dan Waddle of NRECA traveled to Kenya and met with James Walsh, the USAID project manager and later employee of NRECA who approved a $5 million, three-year project with an 18-month deadline to provide street lights in Yei to celebrate South Sudan's independence from the north.

With the project in hand, Dan turned to Myk Manon to manage the project. Myk called me to get some background on Yei. I told him that living there would be difficult, but at least it was near the Uganda border and the best location for an electric cooperative. I believe that only Manon would be willing to undertake such a project where he had to build his own house, construct the basic grid, import all of the equipment, train the local staff, and negotiate the many challenges with local authorities.

He said that he was periodically "arrested" for some minor issue as a shakedown – but resisted any bribes. He said that when he needed electricity at his home, he walked to the powerhouse and turned on the generator. He had the first refrigerator in town; no one there had seen one. He offered a cube of ice to his staff who said, "It burns."

NRECA had been trying to develop projects in Africa for dozens of years without success – but mostly just electrification studies. The Yei Electric Cooperative is the first and among the few electric cooperatives in Africa to my knowledge. It is still struggling.

Myk Manon said, "USAID saw the electric coop as part of the peace dividend and post-war reconstruction. The project had been an interesting experience. For our customers to pay for electricity involves a change of mindset as they are not used to paying for services. The Yei cooperative was powered by 1.3 MW generators and 40 km of distribution lines to 1,200 sites. Thirty of the connections were businesses initially with nine hours of service."

He provided electricity to the Yei Civil Hospital which now has X-ray and ultra sound equipment, pump systems, and computers. At the ceremony turning on the system in October 2009, he said "Yei is a business town. This means that the business people will go into mechanization and make Yei what it used to be called, Little London."

NRECA volunteer training Yei lineman

Myk Manon was required to put in electric lights as part of the initial contract which he accomplished in less than 18 months - erecting 87 poles and 25 street lights with 20 NRECA volunteers. With the lighting ceremony at Freedom Square, Yei became the first town in South Sudan with a public power grid.

In February 2010, Yei Electric Cooperative held its first general assembly where the initial board of directors was elected in front of 300 community members and officials. Yei Electric Cooperative received donations from NRECA, expanded significantly and collects regular bills from customers.

Unfortunately, a USAID evaluation in May 2008 predicted that the cooperative would not be viable with 72% of its costs for importation of fuel. The evaluators recommended alternative options such as solar power or micro-hydro. This is typical of development professionals who want to assign Africa to their preferences for solar cookers, solar or wind power, rather than a central grid system that exists in every Western country.

We expect to just turn on a switch for electric power, and alternative systems such as solar are inadequate for industrial power uses. NRECA has created electric cooperatives in dozens of countries and with the exception of Nicaragua where dictator Anastasio Somoza politicized them, all or nearly all are still in existence in some cases for over 50 years. Entire countries, such as the Philippines and Bangladesh, have replicated the US REI model with over 200 operational rural electric cooperatives.

The Yei Electric Cooperative continues to function as South Sudan plunged into genocidal conflict in Dinkes and Nuer tribal warfare with hundreds of thousands killed, driven into swamps and facing starvation. The NRECA staff was withdrawn from Yei in July 2016 due to the violence.

Some of the worst human right violations are taking place there, rape, and unheard-of brutality. The conflict ranks among the most devastating on the planet in 2016-17. When the last war ended, there were high hopes that there would no longer be bloodshed and war. Peace and reconciliation appear remote.

Chapter 15: Telephone Coops in Poland

When I was a student at Georgetown University in the early 60s, the Cold War was hot: Mutual Assured Destruction, the Bay of Pigs, Soviets ring Berlin, Ich bin ein Berliner, Cuban Missile Crisis, and Operation Rolling Thunder over North Vietnam.

During the Bay of Pigs, my brother, Dean, sat at the end of a runway at Ramstein Air Force Base ready to take off in his nuclear-armed F-100 for a one-way mission to the Soviet Union. Later, I sat in command of 10 Minuteman ICBMs in rural Missouri aimed at the USSR, flight time: 24 minutes on target.

The Cold War began to thaw first in Poland.

After a period of martial law, the Polish people discovered that if everyone dissented and did not follow the Communist line, political liberation was possible. This time the Soviet Union did not invade though they had many of their Warsaw Pact troops throughout the countryside.

The rise of Solidarity was a mass movement of democrats led by courageous intellectuals, labor unions and the Catholic Church. Poland was the first former Soviet bloc country that I visited. I tried to help in their transformation to a market economy.

Jan Karski, often voted by students as the best teacher at Georgetown, was a Polish resistance fighter. He reported to Churchill and Roosevelt about the Holocaust, encouraging them to bomb the rolling death trains to Auschwitz. With an incredible presence, lanky, well-dressed and dignified, he spoke English with a heavy Polish accent. He assumed the persona of a communist and with dry humor explained its interworking, always without notes.

Professor Karski

Karski risked his life to bear witness to Nazi atrocities against Jews, Catholics and Polish dissidents. In disguise, he snuck into the Warsaw Ghetto and a Nazi transfer camp. He reported his terrifying observations of the Holocaust to the civilized world.

I remember he said, "A good government rules well," whatever its form – not acceptable to me as an idealistic student who believed that democracy was the only acceptable form of government. In hindsight, I realize he was pretending to be a Soviet communist.

On my first trip to Poland in 1990 right after the Solidarity government come to power, I walked over to the Warsaw uprising site. There was a marker and earthen mound where the last Jewish resisters fought the Nazis. In an open field sat a card table with two young Polish men selling souvenirs such as spent German bullets. On the table, I spotted two papers by Jan Karski where he described the suffering in the Warsaw Ghetto. I told them, "He was my professor at Georgetown" to their astonishment and disbelief that I knew this Polish hero.

Jan Karski was the courier from Poland and leader of the underground. Unlike other occupied countries, the Polish Resistance Movement did not confine itself to military activities. It created a network of clandestine organizations in culture, education, propaganda, justice and economics to undermine the social control of German forces, which he depicted in his 1944 best seller, *Story of a Secret State*.

On June 2, 1982, Yad Vashem, the holocaust museum in Jerusalem, recognized Jan Karski as *Righteous Among the Nations.* Although he had not saved individual Jews, the Commission for the Designation of the Righteous decided that he had risked his life in order to alert the world to their extermination. He had incurred enormous risk in penetrating into the Warsaw ghetto and a camp, and then committed himself to rescuing the Jews.

On April 13, 2012, President Obama posthumously awarded Karski the Presidential Medal of Freedom. Today, many students sit on a bench next to a bronze statue of him on the campus. As my professor, he never mentioned his clandestine life.

It never occurred to me that I would be travelling to the countries behind the Iron Curtain and engaging in their transition from socialism to free market capitalism. Those early days in Warsaw were depressing, drunks outside of the historic town plaza and well-dressed prostitutes at the Victoria Hotel where the Polish soldiers were housed during martial law. I could walk over to the nearby Opera House and with a couple of dollars get the best seats to the Magic Flute and Aida.

There was only one private restaurant, reportedly run by the mafia. I bought a blue sheep skin coat for $1 million zloty; a stack of money was transferred from one window to the other – the cashiers pretending to count it. It was the equivalent of about $100 dollars, cash only, they gave me a chit to take to another counter to pick it up.

I flew on Polish Lot's first 737 with only a few passengers, and an attractive female stewardess hovered over me and wanted my comments, "Is our service up to international standards?"

In some ten trips to Poland from 1990 to 2002, it looked like a different country every six month – modern hotels replaced old Soviet-style rundown ones, new restaurants with expansive menus popped up, fashionable shops advertised Benetton sweaters, and recently elected local mayors had refreshing ideas on how to spur economic projects. Yet, my first trip was the most memorable.

Agricultural mission

I was a member of an agricultural delegation to develop projects to submit to USAID which operated the programs out of Washington D.C. We visited a fruit and greenhouse operation near Warsaw, then the teams broke into groups of two or three to assess potential project sites in four agricultural regions.

I was assigned to Jim Salisbury, a Farm Credit banker from California. We went to Radom, an early site of the Solidarity uprising and a tough workers' town where, under our windows, the police broke up fights after the bar closed.

We walked into the local cooperative bank and immediately knew it was not a bank at all, but a dispensary of top-down government credits. We met the "Red Chicken King," his own description, at the branch office where he had no problem getting credit for his sprawling operations.

In a briefing with several Solidarity Congressmen, they had set up foundations to focus on the need for rural telephones. Under communism, rural areas usually had only two phones – one for the priest, another for the communist party chief.

Rural communities were organizing self-help efforts to build telephone services and, once they put up the poles, strung wires to their homes and built an operational office in a central location, the state monopoly (PTSA) provided outdated analog and very noisy exchanges. They installed modern digital equipment in the cities.

Polish farmers courageously resisted Communist collectivization and retained their family farms. As a consequence, they were denied physical infrastructure, fewer than ten percent had telephones. Even with the collapse of communism, it was less profitable to bring telephone service to rural areas – the same situation as rural American in the 1940s.

Jim and I asked to visit one of these telephone committees. I immediately thought they should really be formed into telephone cooperatives where the community would own the system rather than do all of the work and turn it over to the state monopoly.

When I raised the idea of telephone coops, Ron Gollehon, who headed our delegation, said, "That is not the purpose of the mission, we are an ag group." Gollehon was president of the Agricultural Cooperative Development International.

At the end of our field trips, we debriefed Josef Slisz, the founder and head of Rural Solidarity. He was both a Senator and Vice Marshall of the Sejm (Senate). He represented Southeastern Poland where individual farmers were very numerous and the Roman Catholic Church was the strongest.   In early 1981, the main center of farmers' protests was Rzeszów. The rural farmers' movement began in his town.

He organized the Trade Union of Individual Farmers and participated in the Round Table talks that led to the Solidarity government. He told us that he always opposed Communism and saw cooperatives as a means to organize small farmers. He had been arrested many times by security forces and refused to sign a loyalty oath.

Poland had vibrant cooperatives before World War II. The discredited old Peasant Party supported an economy based on cooperatives. In its return to democracy, Josef Slisz wanted to recreate independent cooperatives and convert top-down Communist-style collectives into member-owned coops. He formed the Christian-Peasant Party to politically support independent farmers.

I quietly mentioned to Josef Slisz that telephone cooperatives would be a means to bring services to rural areas. He was interested and I told him that I would get back to him about the idea.

In the old system, farmers were independent but monopolies controlled everything else – fertilizers and seed, and they could only sell to the state. To gauge how backward the Polish countryside was when I went there, the way to get supplies or sell your crop was to carry it on a horse-drawn cart.

Typical way to get inputs and sell farmer products in 1990

When I returned to Washington, I suggested that the National Rural Electric Cooperative Association (NRECA) could apply for a grant to help form rural Polish telephone coops. The head of NRECA international programs, Sam Bunker said, "You need to ask the National Rural Telephone Association (NTCA) to sponsor the project."

Most telephone coops in the US began at the rural electrics and were spun off – though a few cooperatives still provide both electric and phone service. Rural electric cooperatives were created mostly in the 1930s and 40s. These communities did not have good or any telephone service at all. I recall the 17 families on my telephone while in the Air Force in rural Missouri. Many of the rural electric cooperative founders who created telephone cooperatives, were still alive and could be tapped for this Polish project.

I knew its president Mike Bruner, who was a Republican member of the Arlington County Board. To the chagrin of my Democratic friends, I had supported his election because he had helped us when he served on the School Board and our daughter was having problems in school.

NTCA agreed to operate the project, and Mike appointed his speech writer, Marlee Norton, to manage it. In August 1990, I wrote a $173,000 grant to help establish two telephone cooperatives.

I returned to Poland and told Josef Slisz to his great surprise that I had a grant to start telephone coops. He said, "Take my driver and car, go to my village where my mother lives without a phone, and start your telephone cooperative there."

Meeting with telephone coop founders

On the trip, I met with mayors at two villages outside Rzeszow near the Ukraine border who were interested in the idea. I saw some of the 100 manually-operated phone exchanges which reminded me of Lily Tomlin as the chatty telephone operator.

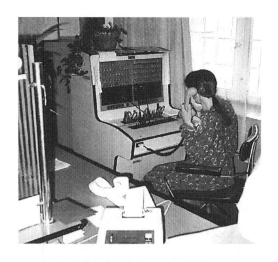

Local telephone exchange

When I returned to Warsaw, I told Slisz that I thought it was possible but he needed to come to the US to see for himself. "Seeing is believing," I said. I told him that he would stay in my home and visit telephone and other cooperatives to better understand them in a capitalist system.

As a farmer representative, Slisz refused to wear a tie, dressed in plaid shirts and had never travelled abroad. He had turned down dozens of trips, but he accepted mine because I assured him that I would take care of him. I arranged for Adriy Trzeciakowski, the English-speaking son of the Solidarity Ministry for the Economy, to come with him so he would have no language problems.

Minister Trzeciakowski was a hero of Solidarity. He came back voluntarily from Switzerland to be arrested during martial law. His son, Andriy, worked at the US-supported Foundation for the Development of Polish Agriculture which was formed by Norman Borlaug and J.B. Penn to support agricultural scientists during the martial law period. It was the first foundation formed in Poland, and our counterpart for our initial trip and programs there.

I arranged his tour. We drove to West Virginia to visit the Hardy Electric Coop. It is an agriculturally poor region. Slisz said "If you can build a telephone coop here, it would be easy to do it in my rich farmland."

Josef Slisz and Marlee Norton of NTCA

I took him to an electric coop in Harrisburg Virginia where there was a large display that looked like a Star Wars board for managing its power connections. We visited a rural credit union and farm supply coop. His passion became telephone coops when he returned to Poland.

Marlee Norton and I had a hard time finding a good project manager – several candidates knew a lot about telephones since they had worked for Telkommunickacja Polska (TPSA) but did not speak English and were more interested in technical than organizational issues. They wanted job security like in the old system which was not possible in our three-year grant. An applicant that I interviewed thought that reporting to a supervisor was like communism. Under capitalism, he said," Everyone should do as they want with no need to report to bosses."

Finally, Marlee selected Janusz Lato, a computer guru and national skeet champion. He tracked every shot as a skeet shooter and was taught sports psychology in Russia. He knew little about telecommunications but was a quick learner, organized training sessions using NTCA volunteers, and brought the leaders of the local organizing committees to the US to learn about telephone cooperatives. It was a totally people-to-people effort.

New telecommunications law

The major impediment to independent telephone companies and cooperatives was that they were not authorized by law. A new telecommunications bill was coming before the Sejm. Slisz asked me to write the amendment to authorize them. I looked up the Rural Electrification Act that is the basis for the US telephone cooperatives revolving fund and paraphrased it.

The Telecommunications Act of 1990 privatized TPSA under a duopoly in which they could continue to operate local service but maintained a monopoly for international calls. The new law allowed local carriers to compete with TPSA in the provision of telephone services in local markets.

I have written lots of amendments or speeches in our Congress but had no idea how to address the "chair" in a parliamentary system. In any event, Slisz got the amendment approved that authorized telephone cooperatives and established a Plenipotentiary for Rural Communications who was supposed to champion rural telephone coops within the Ministry of Telecommunications. Unfortunately, with frequent turnover, none of them were effective.

TPSA was one of the most powerful government entities with employees throughout the country. TPSA tried to frustrate any local carriers. At a meeting of a telephone committee with TPSA officials, I asked, "Why should local telephone committees do all of the work and then turn the system over to you?" My question resulted in a heated discussion.

At every step of the process, Slisz had to intervene with TPSA to get the systems hooked up to the national grid, work out revenue sharing arrangements and get international service. The major regulatory challenge was shared revenues with TPSA in which a NTCA advisor provided the formula based on the origins of calls.

Building the system

The key to a telephone system is the "digital switch" in which all of the telephone lines come into a central location and calls are sent out or received. We promoted Nortel DS 10s, a system geared to rural communities.

Marlee and I visited the plant in North Carolina that was building them. Both telephone coops were able to get loans to buy the equipment, and all of the construction was done by local volunteers. Villagers had to pay for their own phones and connections to their houses.

I included a line item for equipment in the grant for small items related to the switches. Marlee called me and asked, "Do you think we can use the equipment line for developing the first telephone books in Poland?" I responded, "It sounds like equipment to me."

In the first year of the grant, local residents at WIST and Tyczyn were trained by NTCA in how a cooperative operates and is managed. Their decision-making process within the cooperative was deeply democratic in which over 1,000 members attended their twice annual assemblies.

The villagers paid for 70% of the costs in cash and in kind, while loans and donors paid the balance. The founders initially took out loans from equipment companies and were able to obtain a foreign currency guarantee from the US Export-Import Bank to purchase the initial Nortel DMS 10 central switches.

Within a year, both cooperatives were profitable, and all of the start-up loans were repaid within three years. WIST was the first independent operator in Poland and was officially switched to the national network in May 1992.

Testimony

Before the Senate Appropriations Committee in 1992 with Senator Lautenberg in the chair, I reported,

"I came back from Poland last week and there is progress. The progress you won't find in Warsaw. You'd have to go out to rural areas, where you have the newly elected mayors who are really implementing the changes.

The sort of help that we are providing is we are sending volunteers. We have sent over 50 volunteers to Poland alone. We will be sending another 215 volunteers, mostly in the agricultural sector, trying first of all, to make their cooperatives real cooperatives.

In Poland, of course, the farmers were independent. But everything around the farmer was controlled by state entities. We are trying, essentially, to give the power to the farmers to take over the process in their transportation and marketing functions that we kind of accept in our country, but which is not possible there.

We are having great progress. We are either taking old cooperatives and making them real, democratic, farmer-owned cooperatives, or we are starting from grassroots.

For example, we are trying to create model telephone cooperatives. In Poland, there are only 2.3 phones per 100 residents in rural areas. Of course, 40 percent of the population is in rural areas. The communists did not really like telephones too much.

I think that we can make profitable small telephone cooperatives work in Poland as a way of bringing telephones through self-help action. There are 1,500 social telephone committees that want telephones and, quite frankly, have the money. Working with one of the major U.S. suppliers of telephone equipment, we are going to be able to set up some model systems there."

Early success

By the second year, the two coops were serving over 1,800 members. An incentive to join the coop was free service within the local net because it did not cost anything and was automatic with the digital equipment. The two coops were the only private operators with this service. Customers had a choice with TPSA but chose the cooperatives which offered cheaper and better services.

I wrote the next grant of $259,750 that ran through March 1994. In total, NTCA provided less than $1 million for the project over six years in which two successful telephone companies were formed, but we failed to expand the model to other rural communities because of ongoing resistance by TPSA and outside investors who promoted private companies as highly profitable businesses.

WIST staff

I conducted two evaluations of the project. Progress was staggering. No USAID program that I had ever been associated with had succeeded so quickly. The $173,000 initial grants leveraged $2.7 million in U.S telecommunications equipment – a multiplier effect of 16 to 1.

I interviewed the manager and chairman of WIST. His cooperative competed with the TPSA since the coop was located near Rzeszow. He told me, "If one of our lines is down, we fix it in a day. If it is TPSA, it takes a month, if the customer is lucky."

I ask him to call some new subscribers randomly for me, so I could ask them questions about getting telephones. A farmer said, "It made buying supplies and selling my crops easier because I can call different stores and buyers." We estimated that farmers saved eight hours a week in obtaining supplies or selling products by using their phones. Another caller responded, "My son's life was saved when he became ill one night, and a doctor was immediately summoned by phone."

I asked the cooperative manager about the pattern of calls. He said, "When they got their phones, they immediately called all of their neighbors and it was free. Next, they called their friends around Poland and it was more expensive. Then, they called their relatives overseas, got a whopping bill and stopped making those calls."

On my third trip, we were trying to expand the project beyond the two model sites. I visited the local governor of Kielce and noted that the officials of the TPSA monopoly had formed their own import company. The officials were basically buying the equipment and profiting personally from the sales that they arranged. The governor responded, "That is the way it is, and the only way I can get things done."

To get import licenses for telecommunications equipment, companies such as Siemens and Ericsson bribed officials, usually through contributions to the members' foundations. Nortel was unwilling to use bribery but did give free "training" switches to TPSA. Ironically, these switches became available and were bought at a heavy discount to build out the two model telephone coops.

USAID talks sustainability, but never really tests it. I did a retrospective of the two telecommunication coops after ten years of operations. From 1994 to 2003, revenues increased from 12% to 38%; and averaged 24% from 2000 to 2003. By 2003, WIST had 8,279 member/subscribers; Tyczyn had 6,749. They invested in new buildings and major facilities. They shared technicians in the installation of switches and lent construction equipment to each other.

They had relied on NTCA volunteers to build out their systems including the introduction of internet and broad band services. WIST provided telecommunications services to 933 businesses including the regional airport and a new swimming complex that I visited. Tyczyn served 40 villages, 65 public facilities, and 445 rural businesses, including 20 local cooperatives since it was more rural than WIST.

The telephone cooperatives were a catalyst for other successful enterprises. The founder of Tyczyn telecommunications coop and local mayor, Kazimierz Jaworski, created the Alfred Drinking Water Bottling plant that served 70,000 families who can order by phone or Internet. Jaworski led efforts to buy a biological sewage treatment facility from the US for his town. In 2016, he is a five-term Polish Senator. Jaworski said, "We were skeptical of forming a cooperative but when we saw successful telephone coops in the U.S., we knew it could be done here."

On my last trip to Poland in 2003, my greatest disappointment was not to be able to meet with Josef Slisz who had died a couple of years earlier from cancer. But, I did visit the church where he was buried and viewed the bronze fresco on its door that depicted Slisz and founders of Rural Solidarity.

**Tadeusz Slisz, WIST manager, Josef Slisz &
Mayor Kazimierz Jaworski**

In my retrospective study, I found key factors for success were: energetic recently elected local mayors, existing telephone committees, high demand, volunteer construction, success in obtaining grants and loans, ability to negotiate acceptable terms with TPSA and, most significantly, technical assistance and knowhow from the National Telephone Cooperative Association.

Twenty volunteers from NTCA gave practical advice on management and organizational and technical issues. Many of the U.S. volunteers had lifetimes of experience in telephone cooperatives and were involved in the initial start-up of their own systems. They carried out site surveys and assisted in the design, construction, operations, and technical training manuals.

Unfortunately, we were not able to take the cooperative model to other regions, though we tried. The Ministry of

Telecommunications offered 90 territorial concessions in which all of the applications for companies were investor-owned. NTCA worked with a World Bank-funded project to assist in the development of five private companies, but they later merged with larger regional companies.

The telecommunications cooperatives are the only ones in Poland and, I believe in Europe though earlier ones did exist in rural areas of Finland that were privatized. The US and Canada still have vibrant rural telephone (now telecommunications) cooperatives.

Exploring other countries

We tried to take the success to other former Eastern bloc countries. I worked with NTCA to explore the cooperative telephone model in Bulgaria. I visited two potential sites in Bulgaria – one rural forested area near the capital of Sofia, and another one in Ravda on the Black Sea.

In both cases, it was clear that the organizers were interested in obtaining free digital switches, but did not have the leadership, community support or legal environment to be successful. In fact, when they applied for licenses in 1996, the Bulgarian Telephone Company (a state monopoly) turned them down.

In the Ukraine, I visited two potential sites for telephone cooperatives, but again there was lack of leadership and a conducive financial and legal environment. Instead, I helped Michael Telelman of NTCA design another approach to create seven model telecenters (Business Internet Centers or BICs) in underserved areas.

Telecenters

This project received a USAID grant of $2.4 million over four years and I carried out a final evaluation in July 2005. They were really full service Kinkos, privately-owned and almost immediately successful and profitable within 18 months. The project provided startup capital and technical assistance.

In my evaluation, I found that each telecenter was different but all offered fee-based computer training, internet connections and business services, especially duplication of documents for required business permits for small enterprises.

Several served low income communities, others were suburban. Often, they trained government or business employees and served as billing centers for local businesses. One created commercial computer programming. The BICs trained 3,000 people in computers of which a third were in rural areas and served 50,000 clients in the initial three years of the project.

I concluded that the right leadership, the right timing, a strongly felt need by consumers, and energized US volunteers resulted in successful telecommunication projects.

Another conclusion that I have found true in many of my project designs is that too much aid money that must be spent quickly is unfortunately not helpful since you are paying for the services or infrastructure, rather than asking the recipients to raise the funds themselves. Cooperatives provide a means to do this.

Computer training at Ukraine TeleCenter

Chapter 16: Market Reforms in Eastern Europe

Poland became the platform for Land O'Lakes, a national butter cooperative, to become a successful overseas development company. Like NTCA, they had the right technology for the shift from communism to capitalism.

Similar to NTCA, I recruited Land O'Lakes as a member of the cooperative development association I ran and wrote most of their proposals in Eastern Europe. I arranged for two $5 million earmarks from Congressman David Obey (D-WS) who had more dairy cows in his Wisconsin district than people; and dairy report language for the next 20 years.

Earlier, USAID had done an internal study and decided not to support cattle or dairy projects. My earmarks and report changed that, and dairy projects became some of their most successful USAID projects.

Vern Freed, the first head of Land O'Lakes international programs, turned to me for help. He initiated two U.S. Department of Agriculture (USDA) projects in Jamaica and Indonesia – neither of which was successful. In Jamaica, he created a foundation to support agricultural investments, but most of the loans to projects failed. In Indonesia, he delivered quality Holstein cows in a "whole dairy buy-out program" through USDA. Under the program to increase American dairy prices, US cows were slaughtered or sold overseas. Without proper rations and infrastructure, local Indonesian farmers were unable provide them with sufficient feeds.

I helped realign the Land O'Lakes projects to focus on the formation of dairy cooperatives. In his memoir, *Child of The Prairie, Man of the World,* Vern Freed credited me with helping get the programs moving ahead. "It helps to have friends with connections."

Vern Freed told his life story from humble roots in North Dakota to promoting cooperatives around the world. After retiring from Land O'Lakes, he assisted the Russian Farm Community Project which was funded through the Food for Progress Program to share U.S. agricultural practices with Russian farmers.

Martha Cashman took over when Freeh was required to retire at 65 – company policy. At the time, there were only three staff in the international development office. Focusing on Eastern Europe and later Africa, Martha built the program to over $25 million in annual revenues, reaching some 80 countries. She was the spark that motivated employees including me in preparing proposals and carrying out evaluations.

From a large Minnesota family, she began her international career when she married Tom Winn in Gambia where they managed a ground nuts project (peanuts) with an emphasis on numeracy so small farmers were not cheated when delivering their crops for processing. She and Tom moved to Jamaica to run the Land O'Lakes butter monetization project through the Jamaican foundation as seed funds for emerging agribusinesses.

Her husband, Tom Winn, probably the best international cooperative trainer I've ever met, died of leukemia in 2006. They adopted two children, one from Gambia, and the other from Jamaica. For 14 years at Land O'Lakes until 2001, she considered herself a "brash woman" in a male-dominated agricultural field. For several years, Martha worked as outreach staff for the Mayo Clinic. She tragically died in 2017.

The final international director that I worked with at Land O'Lakes was Tom Verdoorn.   He spent 32 years in various positions there, including Vice President for Dairy Foods Finance and Administration. His initial involvement in international programs was closing down the unsuccessful Polish investments. He took a very business-like approach to development and linked projects to the Land O'Lakes management systems. Tom appreciated my representational role on behalf of Land O'Lakes on the Advisory Committee for Voluntary Foreign Aid and the Global Leadership Coalition.

At the urging of Land O'Lakes President Ralph Hofstad, an innovative cooperative leader, most of the training and the technical assistance was carried out by his employees. Their technology was appropriate since many of the Land O'Lakes dairy plants were 40 years old and constantly being upgraded. Their technicians knew how to modernize Communist-style dairies. He saw it as a way to prepare Land O'Lakes for entering international markets. Eventually, vice presidents and supervisors terminated these assignments. "If they have time to take these trips, they are not working hard enough," a vice president said.

Land O'Lakes did create a milk replacer firm in Poland, a feed supplement so heifers are fed while their mother cows continue to produce milk for the market. It did well for several years until the French and Dutch entered the market at lower costs. Land O'Lakes sold off its plant that at one time produced 90% of Poland's milk replacer which Land O'Lakes invented in the 1950s.

Initial projects focused on cooperative and marketing training throughout Eastern Europe. In the second round of USAID proposals, I wrote three of the four agribusiness proposals: Land O'Lakes in Poland, ACDI in Hungary, and Tri-Valley Growers in Bulgaria. I was able to evaluate each of these projects.

Prospective on evaluations

In October 2009, I lead an evaluation taskforce by the Advisory Committee on Voluntary Foreign Aid. It concluded that USAID should carry out more rigorous monitoring and evaluations, re-establish USAID as a leader in evaluation, better integrate evaluations with program design, and include more operational level evaluators within USAID. The report and workshop recommended more mid-term evaluations so project corrections can be made, and more post-project evaluations "to better assess sustainably several years after projects terminate." USAID talks sustainability but seldom tests it.

I have an unorthodox approach to evaluations. The goal is to strengthen implementers understanding and ability to deliver better results, not impress USAID with detailed and quantitative evaluations that are seldom read.

I endeavor to help staff think about their projects with workshops after the evaluation to internalize learning. Basically, I look at the methodologies. At an interactive workshop, I lead staff to think about and review their project activities – positive and negative. I tell them "build on success, and abandon failure." It sounds simple but I have seen projects that continue to push unsuccessful approaches such as an olive soap factory in Palestine where each new NGO took on this uneconomical project. The goal is to free up the mind, see a better path and take action (specific and time framed) for revisions. I do my best to help staff think conceptually and visually using line drawings and graphs to illustrate impacts.

Millstones Cooperative Farm to Market System

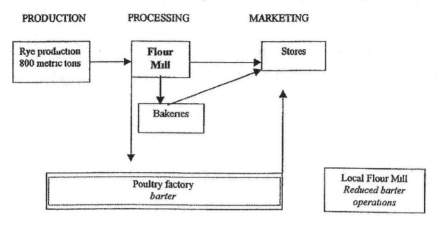

Because they are usually boring recitations of facts and figures, evaluations are almost never read by USAID staff. So rather than accumulate large qualities of data and analysis, my evaluations tell a story. Staff are able to communicate in storylines so both USAID and implementers understand and are proud of their achievements.

To carry out an evaluation, I read the project reports and have five key questions that I ask beneficiaries. I engage in a discussion without notes. For example, in Eastern Europe the questions might be: Tell me about your farm or business (to get a feel for it), what is different from now and during former communist times, and what do you think has been successful. Since they will always be complimentary, I want to delve deeper.

All of my questions are open ended, and I follow up on specifics based on their responses. For example, if a farmer says the advisor recommended shifting from rye to barley crops, I try to quantify it. How many acres were in rye compared to barley before and after the change? Give me a rough estimate on the per acre crop differences in costs? Thus, you do not ask them how much additional income they may have gained, rather deduce it with approximate figures. This interview approach is time consuming – up to an hour- rather than the usual ten-minute evaluation approach of reading them a checklist and recording answers.

Evaluations in Eastern Europe

Land O'Lakes conducted 111 training courses for 3,000 participants from five Eastern European countries in 14 subjects, including agribusiness management, marketing, cooperative development, and technical dairy topics such as milk collection and assembly, and plant maintenance.

I began the regional evaluation in Estonia which resembles Wisconsin as dairy country. In 1991, Estonia regained its independence in a quiet and successful struggle known as the "Singing Revolution." Large crowds gathered and sang their way to freedom.

Estonians are survivors from Nazi and Soviet occupation -- many were deported to Siberian camps. They are held together with folklore, wear traditional clothing, and a very difficult language. For the transition, they declared that they were a Scandinavia country and got lots of technical help from Finland across the Baltic.

At its capital, Tallin, I visited the Black Lutheran Church with German coats of arms on the wall, and our local manager railed against the Russian-speaking Estonians who made no efforts to integrate into Estonian society. At the time of independence, Estonia was populated by 40% Russians and they only spoke Russian, not Estonian.

During the transition, Estonia lowered their tariffs and faced competition from subsidized dairy products in Europe. With Land O'Lakes' help, the survivors in the dairy industry quickly adjusted to competition. I visited a model dairy plant that Gorbachev had praised. Two Land O'Lakes plant technicians were providing technical assistance in proper cleaning of the milk pipes that ran throughout the plant and in learning how to clean the milk trucks so no bacteria contaminated the milk. Previously the plant would not have met USDA safety inspections.

I visited five farms, and I knew instantly that all of them had poor sanitary practices since foul smelling barns introduce musty odors in raw milk. Many of these problems originated at the collective farms that were being privatized. Individual dairy farmers were trained in good sanitation and cow hygiene. Like Poland, Estonia was a quick success.

Evaluation workshop to review Land O' Lake's projects in Warsaw

Poland

A dozen of the 50 Polish interns, who had visited Land O'Lakes farms in the US, organized a Future Farmers of America (FFA)-type organization in which they created eight clubs at about 200 high schools in the Sielce region. From these models, they extended the program nationwide in conjunction with vocational educational schools and extension services. The organization intends to bring prestige to being a farmer, educate youth on modern farming practices, and tries to reverse the flow of young farmers to urban areas.

In Poland, a Land O'Lakes employee carried out six training courses for the manager and four employees of the Wloclawek Dairy Cooperative. The French company Dannon had entered their market. With this help, the manager responded to the new competition by creating a logo with a local milkmaid, made their yogurt cup a little taller, and encouraged local groceries to put their taller yogurt in front of Dannon. They shortened their 30-letter name to a five-letter acronym. Sales immediately increased by 20%.

I gave two sample yogurt cups from the cooperative – one plain and one with the dairy maid and one cup from Dannon to Jim Snell in USAID, and he would pull the three cups out to show visitors how effective Land O'Lakes projects were.

I interviewed a former biology teacher who had become a trader, bartering in fish meal, casein, and powdered milk from Belarus. He learned to write specifications into contracts to make sure the quality met the terms of the contract. As a result, his two-person firm saved $20,000 in three months on a volume of business of about $75,000 a year.

Bulgaria

In Bulgaria, I arrived at the same time as the first day of its new project manager – Manuela Russeva, who had been a teacher. I told her that she would have to shift her program from training to technical assistance for emerging private agribusinesses.

Later, she wrote me,

"I want to thank you for everything I learned from you – both professionally and personally. I still remember things like 'the history and origin of roof tile shapes' (which I learned from Chile) and boat terminology, evaluation techniques, proposal writing, lobbying and association development, coop member services, insurance, and regional trade. At times your ideas seemed 'impossible' and like 'science fiction' for our Balkan environment, economics, infrastructure and democratic stage of development, but at the end all of them worked and we all realized that your vision and ideas were well-positioned in the future."

I interviewed a dozen Bulgarian professors at the Agricultural University of Stara Zagora on a train-the-trainers program in agribusiness management to assist new private farmers. They were impressed by the interactive teaching techniques and how to do extension work. During the round-table discussion, a professor emeritus walked in and said, "What are you talking about, peasants are not farmers. We only deal with educated managers who tell the workers what to do."

In another interview, I talked with four participants who attended a course on cooperatives by Vern Moore, former vice president of Land O'Lakes: a Marxist professor, a state farm manager, a student who attended because her mother lived in the village, and a band leader who was there to set up the sound system for the lecture.

I asked the professor, "Why did Soviet-style cooperatives fail?" He replied, "There was nothing wrong with Marxist-Leninism, but Bulgarian leaders followed the flawed Stalin model of cooperatives." I asked the former cooperative manager, "Why had the cherry collective failed?" He said, "It was due to poor management."

Next, I asked the young student, "What did you learn in the lecture?" and she said, "The former state farms lacked any incentives for the farmers to operate the orchard."

I turned to the long-haired band leader. "What type of cooperative would you like to form?" He said, "Since sound equipment is expensive, my band could form a cooperative to buy it." The youths got the idea of cooperatives right away.

It was obvious from these evaluation interviews that cooperatives were not possible at these early stages of transition in Bulgaria. But, it was possible to boost emerging agribusinesses.

Land O'Lakes helped launch Milk Way, a new private processor of cheese, and the most modern in Bulgaria. The technical advisors helped the company prepare its business plan. It was classic marketing: initially capture the local markets with branded and superior traditional white brine cheese, expand into the Sofia market, then begin export to Lebanon.

The Milk Way manager said that the U.S. technical advisor was "sent from heaven and worked day and night for 15 days on the business and marketing plan," which was totally adopted. He said, "Land O'Lakes is the only foreign organization that is doing something real here in Bulgaria." Another training participant said he had been taught economics in school, but "not really." "It's another way of thinking: before someone made the decisions for us and we just obeyed."

A 17-member family enterprise got their land and title back in Bulgaria through restitution. They learned to capture the local market in cooking oil and wheat flour for bakeries. At the town, I talked with the former communist mayor who said he opposed privatization, but "that is the law." He said three additional small enterprises were formed as a result of the Land O'Lakes training.

My conclusion was that training had been effective in the early transition to the market economy, but now these struggling enterprises needed more intensive technical assistance to grow and prosper.

Agribusiness exchanges

In August 1993, I evaluated the Agribusiness Exchange Program by Agricultural Cooperative Development International (ACDI), a $7.1 million four-year project to strengthen private agriculture in Poland, Bulgaria, and Romania.

I interviewed a diverse ideological group of Polish parliamentarians who had come to the U.S. to learn about cooperatives and our legislation. ACDI worked with them to develop a consensus on a private sector cooperative law. They learned about cooperative principles, governance structures, the role of lobbying, and the farm credit system. The draft law would wrestle control away from the national cooperative unions and from the current managers who controlled the individual coops. Polish farmers were not interested in joining these top down coops still controlled by former communists.

The Polish legislators passed the new cooperative law, but it was vetoed by Lech Wałęsa because of opposition by the old line cooperative managers. These leaders of cooperative unions appealed to the International Cooperative Alliance, which had included communist-style, so-called cooperatives in its membership since 1945. The ICA president sent a letter to President Lech Wałęsa opposing the bill. I wrote a scathing letter to ICA on how ill-informed the ICA president had been in undercutting real member-owned and controlled cooperatives.

I interviewed an extension agent in Poland who told me that she had learned that "Everything before was top down and that now we must learn to serve farmers and meet their needs." Before I took orders and made presentations to farmers. We were to "shape small farmers to meet the ideas of the state."

Another agent said the training changed her entire way of doing her job. "I gained many new perspectives, for example, rather than start from production, I learned that you start from the customer and markets, and then work backwards."

A woman Minister of Agriculture was appointed and promptly fired a third of the extension agents – most of whom were totally incompetent with little motivation as government employees. The extension agents who were retained "got the message. "

A farmer who came to the US for training told me that, "I have changed my way of thinking. Before we thought that if you were a good producer, you would make money and it was easy to find a market. We had no idea how to survive in a free market economy."

Another U.S. trainee said, "I learned that American farmers calculate everything!"

In Bulgaria, the manager of a poultry plant echoed similar conclusions; the training had "changed his way of thinking." He said, "I now know the importance of a work ethic, quality controls, profit motivation and market information in decision making."

Another participant said that his ambition is "to penetrate the brains of people who are working around him and try to get them prepared to carry out change." A farmer said that he learned "the importance of reaching consensus in practical ways to persuade people to work together."

Dr. Verghese Kurien, founder of the Indian Amul dairy cooperatives, the largest in the world which organized 12 million poor women of the lowest castes, said, "Development is the development of the mind." I was present when he received the World Food Prize at the State Department. I have repeated his words often.

ACDI concentrated on reforming the farm credit systems in Poland, Romania, and Bulgaria. They brought bankers from the region to see how cooperative banks and credit should be provided to farmers. They learned about credit worthiness, business acumen, farming financial analysis, and cash flow analysis.

ACDI technical experts carried out extensive training to reform local farm banks, eliminate the central cooperative bank, and make regional banks freestanding and able to provide disciplined credit to farmers.

Early in the transition, I attended a meeting at the World Bank which signed an agreement to extend a line of credit to the national Polish "cooperative" bank. I warned them that it was a bad idea since the bank dispensed credit but had a poor record of repayments. In fact, none of the loans were repaid to the World

Bank, and they just disappeared into the corrupt system in which credit was used to buy loyalty and reward friends.

After ACDI trained 285 loan officers, the World Bank learned from its mistake and concluded: "The private cooperative banks are at present actively improving services, have set up a sound method for credit applications and financial analysis of investments to be financed, are a major participant in the banking sector for rural and agricultural credit and therefore are considered as important intermediaries for World Bank and other similar credit lines."

Given the rapid progress in Poland, a major recommendation was to shift Lee Rosner (a friend and colleague) as project manager from Warsaw to Bucharest. His new assignment was to train loan officers and strengthen the Romanian Bank for Development.

Lee Rosner and me in Romania

I welcomed a delegation of these bankers to my home during their Farm Credit observation tour.

With the exception of Poland, I concluded that the breakup of state collectives and state farms into small plot holders with diverse crops would not result in conditions conducive to successful cooperative formation. Slow land restitution and lack of titling made it difficult to form cooperatives as well as the reluctance of small farmers to join them and work together.

Poland ag-information

My final evaluation in Poland was a two-year, $1.5 million project by Land O'Lakes and Sparks Company Inc, a US family based agricultural information firm, to develop agribusiness market information systems. The project goal was to speed the shift from a command economy where government defines and directs state-owned enterprises to helping newly privatized firms in decision-making based on sound market information and risk management tools such as hedging. Hedging is a marketing devise to reduce the financial risk from changing prices by selling crops early and not taking a risk that they will decline.

I reviewed the Western-style commodity reports and outlooks in dairy, poultry meat, and grains that were issued quarterly. Marketing information plans were developed for 35 firms which were now heavily impacted by foreign firms buying up facilities and investing in their own plants.

In a feed grains plant, I visited, the French company, Louis Dreyfus had fired 120 employees and installed automatic systems to provide feed grains to customers. I visited a dairy cooperative where it was apparent that the project staff had visited a few days earlier to coach the manager in responding to my questions. He was not convincing in terms of project impact since he could not respond to simple questions in the project's commodity documents.

The project trained Polish staff in outlook and commodity reports by different sectors. They formed a company to try to continue the ag-information documents. In-fighting among staff and the unwillingness of firms to pay for the marketing information doomed the effort.

What I found was that managers lacked awareness of the importance of marketing information. They relied on word of mouth or informal information in making investment decisions. The managers tended to be copy cats in which they followed the actions of similar firms.

In a few cases, managers used market information such as a milling processing company that found through the commodity reports that purchasing Ukrainian grains was cheaper than Polish grains. Yet, a grain storage company filled their elevators and got stuck with excessive inventory as prices fell, as predicted in the commodity report. A meat processing firm developed a business plan and used marketing information to expand annually by 350%.

In my opinion, it was just too early to put in place a sophisticated private sector market information system. This point was confirmed when Sparks set up an information unit in Poland, but it was unprofitable. Polish agricultural firms were not willing to pay commercial prices for marketing information and consultants to assist them in investment decisions.

Finding the right partners

In designing projects, it is important to recruit and work with change agents. It was easy to identify the old guard communists. At one meeting, they thought we were US investors and said, "We can take care of any problems you have with the government."

Another tipoff was if they offered to start a meeting with vodka, early in the morning.

In Moldova, the village chairman and head of the wine collective "captured" us at his daughter's wedding, hid our coats, and expected us to drink and party all night. We had to make a scene with the drunken chairman to find and retrieve our coats before leaving.

On another occasion, we were stuck at a meeting in Poland where they intended to keep us for a long and leisurely lunch. I whispered to Kate Kaufman who accompanied me and had been an assistant to Ambassador Harry Barnes in Chile, "How can we get out of here?" She said that Harry instructed her that if she got caught at an endless meeting, to stand up and say, "we have an appointment with the U.S. Ambassador, and must leave." I did not have the nerve to do it, but Kate did.

Romania

In the winter of 1992, I visited Bucharest, Romania to evaluate the Land O'Lakes dairy project there. At one of the few restaurants, there was no power, we wore coats, and they only served a few items on their extensive menu.

The project helped modernize several dairy coops in Transylvania including at Hungarian villages where they offered me their version of "moonshine." We drove up mountains with lots of tiny Fiat-type Romanian cars that could barely go over 25 mph, visited what was called Dracula's Castle and next to it a Roman toll station. The Romanian language is descended from the Vulgar Latin dialects spoken when the country was part of the Roman Empire. Possibly because of this history, it was one of the most backward Eastern

European countries where changes towards a market system were slow.

It was clear that it would take years to restore land to farmers at this early stage in the transition. I found that little changed politically or economically in Romania with the same nomenklatura in charge. I visited old run-down factories that would not survive in a market economy. Yet, there was a bright spot.

In 1994, I led a delegation to develop a joint project in Romania. We saw the greatest opportunity in Timisoara, an ethnically diverse and progressive city on the border of Austria. It was where the so-called Romanian revolution took place.

Demonstrations began in Timisoara against the harassment of a dissident ethnic-Hungarian priest, Laszlo Tokes. It led to protests about a lack of basic food such as bread. The backlash from Ceausescu's harsh armed forces led to accusations that many people were massacred, though few were in reality.

After ten tumultuous days of violence and an upsurge of mass protests against Ceausescu's regime in 1989, the deposed Romanian president Nicolae Ceausescu and his wife Elena fled, were captured and executed after a secret military tribunal found them guilty of crimes against the state. They were convicted of genocide and undermining the national economy among a series of other offences, officials said.

Their deaths ended the dictator's 24 years as communist party leader, 21 of them as Romania's president during which he suppressed all opposition, using brutal force. The National Salvation Front came to power. The new government pledged to replace the tyranny of Ceausescu's rule and to allow free speech, free thought, and free enterprise in Romania.

There was no true revolution – just a power struggle between the army and the secret police. Communists relabeled themselves as social democrats. For the next 25 years, what they got was second-tier communist apparatchiks and corrupt government.

Despite the slow transition, an innovative proposal helped NGOs shift from state support to be independent in action and funding. The model NGO project in Timisoara ran from 1994 to 1999 with $2.4 million from USAID. It was managed by CHF International (CHF) the lead organization of a consortium of U.S. cooperatives. I conceived this project based on my own experience working with NGOs at home and abroad.

The concept was simple. Most NGOs under the communist system were controlled and funded by the national or local government. Now, they were cut loose to survive on their own. The project tried to find revenue generating activities to sustain them.

The program created a model for community-based economic development by developing, strengthening, and working through Romanian NGOs to provide enhanced services and credit to their members on a sound basis. CHF established a Technical Service Center to enable local NGOs to draw upon the collective expertise of US cooperatives.

CHF trained a variety of NGOs in capacity building from business, cultural, and social service sectors. They were given technical assistance and training through a task order system for short-term assignments. Assignments included developing business plans, market studies, and facilities development. In addition to short-term technical assistance, the program provided NGOs with institutional support grants and access to small loans for their members to carry out economic activities.

In 1993, I evaluated the project and visited many of its targeted NGOs. At the Opera House, we worked with management to create an income generating restaurant. At an art studio, we recommended adding a telecenter. I bought paintings from one of their artists which were recognized by the Romanian banking delegation when they visited my home.

For a youth hostel, they charged kids to use computers, mostly for games, and rented out their first level floor to a bakery. For a publishing company, we helped the participants develop a weekly advertising sheet.

In time, the project refocused its efforts to provide loans through the USAID-initiated Romanian-American Fund which was designed to provide loans to new and startup businesses.

The project demonstrated that NGO income generation could pay key staff who were taught proposal writing so that they could attract donor support. Like an accordion, it showed them that they could grow with contract staff when they had grants, and when grants ended, the core staff stayed in place, funded by their business activities. This was a model I borrowed from Monica Jimenez and Participa in Chile.

The Governor of Timisoara told me, "The CHF project changed the mindset of the Romanian people. They see its success as how community groups can organize and work together for their mutual benefit." More proof that changing minds is a way to help institute positive change and promote community values.

While progress has been dramatic at the enterprise and NGO level, the post-communist governments in Romania remain corrupt. Only in 2016 have the crimes against humanity in the Ceausescu regime begun to be prosecuted.

Evaluating projects in Romania

Chapter 17: Seal of Quality in Macedonia

I learned how complicated ethnic identity is with my next assignment in Macedonia in the Balkans with its history of conflicts. Tito had required Macedonians to alter their Turkish names given the long-standing opposition to Ottoman Turks. Albanians in Macedonia were persecuted as a Muslim minority in an Orthodox Christian country. Roma were persecuted even more harshly throughout the Balkans. They are still repressed as evidenced when I toured one of their shantytowns.

Greece opposed the creation of Macedonian as an independent Republic from Yugoslavia because of confusion over its name and the Greek province of Macedonia. The naming dispute goes back to the Balkan wars where Greece claimed the region of Alexander the Great of Macedonia.

In Lviv, Ukraine, I attended a Land O'Lakes workshop prior to going to Macedonia to write a proposal for an upcoming RFA. I got up in the middle of the night, wrote a concept paper on a paper napkin and slipped it under Martha Cashman's door. I was leaving early for Macedonia the next morning so wanted to give her a heads up on what I was thinking. I had been agonizing on how Land O'Lakes, a butter and cheese company, could compete for an agricultural RFA against agricultural organizations with wide membership, and longer and broader international experience in development.

Martha kept the paper napkin and showed it to me several years later. I always write highly focused proposals since "doing everything results in nothing." I came up with a novel idea. The project would create a "Seal of Quality" through testing and sampling of meat and dairy products. The seal would help local companies compete with imports then flooding the Macedonia market.

If sales to the companies that earned the seal increased, they would be motivated to help improve and support their supply farmers with higher quality production of meat and milk that the companies would process, package and sell.   In agricultural lingo, it is called backward and forward linkages from the company to its farmers (backwards) to its customers (forward).

The idea fit Land O'Lakes because that is how it was formed in 1923. It was organized by creameries that insisted on top quality raw milk (sweet not sour), bought refrigerated tanker cars, and shipped top quality butter to markets in New York City.

Unlike most cooperatives, the farmers wanted the coop to supply them with feeds and farm supplies too. More often, US agricultural coops either provide farm supplies, or processing and marketing of their products. Land O'Lakes does both, and today is the second largest U.S. cooperative with $14 billion in sales and is one of the top 500 companies in the U.S.

A key to Land O'Lakes success is its brand. At an annual meeting, I recall Julia Child who was promoting her new cook book and said, "I only use Land O'Lakes butter." The Land O'Lakes brand is known by 97% of American households for its high quality.

My competitors for the RFA would suggest the usual approach to strengthen the entire food chain from farmers to markets. A little here and there, but not much impact. My idea would be "revolutionary" in the development field.

Most projects are based on assessments and observations and determining how to respond to challenges with limited funds, time, and interventions. The vast majority of USAID projects are formulaic using a development organization's experience in similar types of projects, perceptive analysis, solid local partners, and quality staff, especially the chief of party.

In my career, there are few moments when you can propose an approach that has never been tried since USAID is risk averse. The Seal of Quality idea was truly inspirational. It became a new approach to agribusiness development as other development organizations grasped its strength in accelerating market-driven and consumer-based preferences for quality foods; easily identified, tested, and certified for quality.

When I arrived in Skopje, I visited several small Turkish-run grocery stores. I interviewed shoppers who confirmed that they bought Danish butter and European processed meats since they were of higher quality. I went to an open market to buy sheep cheese; a customer dipped her finger in a large container to sample it and decide if it was sufficiently tasty to buy. I learned that Macedonian food companies had a poor reputation for quality, consumer friendly packaging and marketing.

With the concept in mind, I designed a Seal of Quality which would prominently feature "Made in Macedonia" with a sense of pride by Macedonians, especially given Greek opposition to the name. I had help from Jeton Starova, an Albanian Macedonian and expert in agribusiness and sheep. He knew Macedonia and guided me in preparing the proposal with the names of prospective companies we would reach out to encourage them to adopt the seal. We outlined how we would carry out quality standards, best manufacturing practices, and sampling though taste panels to rate quality and consistency.

Yeton Starova

Balkan ethnicity

I wanted to better understand Macedonia as background in preparing the proposal. I asked Jeton why he called himself Albanian since he had always lived in what is today the Republic of Macedonia. He said, "Because in the Balkans you identify yourself by ethnicity. My family on my father's side is ethnically Albanian. My grandfather was born in the Ottoman Empire, as was my great and great-great grandfathers, and so on for 20 generations."

He said,

"My father was born in a country called Albania in 1933, 20 years after it got its independence. I was born in a country called Yugoslavia in 1964, 20 years after WWII. My daughter was born in a country called Macedonia four years after it got its independence. These four subsequent generations were all born in different countries although the family never moved more than 100 miles. So,

we see our identity in terms of ethnicity -- Ottoman, Albanian, Yugoslav or Macedonian."

He explained that countries came and collapsed or moved borders. Nations in a sense of "citizen-nation" are not yet a concept that has taken root here. Yugoslavia existed for about 90 years and at its peak only 7% of the citizens called themselves Yugoslav by nationality.

He said, "A lot of people that identify themselves as Macedonians by ethnicity would even object to me calling myself Macedonian. Not that I would want to call myself Macedonian." He identifies his wife as Turkish. I asked, "Is your wife really from Turkey? "No," he responded, "but her family is Muslim, and the Ottoman Empire treated all its Muslim subjects in the Balkans as Turks, whether they were Serbian, Albanian, Bulgarian, Greek or Romanian."

He told me,

"During the 500 years of Ottoman rule a lot of families whose ancestors converted to Islam and especially those that moved to urban areas, started speaking the Turkish language there as a language of education and administration. Some intermarried with Turkish settlers that moved to the Balkans from Anatolia and of course they got assimilated and they now, rightfully so, to a large degree feel they belong to the Turkish ethnicity and call themselves Turks."

In describing ethnicity vs. nationality issues, he said, "what it meant in the Balkans in the 20th century with empires falling new 'nations' and states emerging, then collapsing, shrinking, expanding resulted in how a person coped with their identity."

355

As confusing as it is, identity remains an issue among Macedonians and others I met in the region. In this small country of two million, about the geographic size of Sarasota County, Florida where I live, the official languages are Macedonian 66.5%, Albanian 25.1%, Turkish 3.5%, Roma 1.9%, Serbian 1.2%, and others 1.8% (2002 census). This presented a marketing challenge where a seal needed to convey consumer information across languages.

Seal of Quality

Since the project would target agribusinesses and middle-income citizens, I wanted to add a component for poor farmers. We came up with a similar seal for Albanians in a mountain area known for its quality sheep cheese.

Local residents would drive up the mountain where sheep feed on new spring grasses to get their cheese. We added a packaging and labeling machine to the proposal so that cheese could be sold in stores for a higher price. The semi-nomadic herders move their sheep flocks up the mountains in late May and produce sheep cheeses in small huts, known as "Badza" or "Bachilo." These herders get 60-70% of their income from lamb and 30-40% from cheese. These herders are less wealthy than the sedentary sheep farmers since they have less land and their only assets are their sheep.

The final challenge was how to hide the cost of all of the advertising that was essential to success. Basically, once an agribusiness got the seal, we would hold press conferences, put signs in stores, and advertise the award of the seal and company on the local TV. I knew USAID would be suspicious of a large advertising budget so I divided it up into different categories such as TV, radio, in-store and open markets.

After the proposal was submitted, the USAID mission decided to interview the top three ranked proposals. Later, I learned from an USAID friend, Frank Mertens, who was an evaluator, that ours had come in number three. USAID had never seen a proposal like it before.

For the "show and tell" interview, I devised a strategy in which the chosen team leader, John MacKillop, would start off with a power point of quick flashes of seals of quality, including an emphasis on the importance to Land O'Lakes. Jeton Starova followed this with how the project would work in Macedonia. They wowed the USAID staff.

Macedonian Seal of Quality

The project was suited to the current agricultural situation which was undergoing major transformation despite the country's strong agricultural heritage, the break-up of Yugoslavia. Not only had the former state-run farms and processing enterprises been cut off from government subsidies, many links with traditional market outlets within other Yugoslav republics had broken down. It was compounded by the fact that in Yugoslavia, Macedonia was primarily a raw material producer, supplying processing industries based in other republics.

As Macedonia liberalized its economy, an increasing variety of imported food products made their way onto local shelves to fill the void. Macedonian entrepreneurs began to build a domestic food processing industry. These new businesses created from privatized state enterprises suffered from inefficient and outdated equipment and were too large to be run profitably. Most of them failed.

At the same time, new facilities built from the ground up were small, fledgling operations, producing a limited number of products and marketing them in substandard packaging. Inconsistent quality, together with a lack of standardization and branding, made it difficult for consumers to differentiate between high and low quality domestic food products. As a result, consumers were increasingly attracted to the imported, reliable and branded products.

At the outset of the project, a survey indicated that consumers preferred to buy meat from Serbia and dairy from Croatia and Slovenia. At the end of three years, "85% of urban consumers purchased at least one Seal of Quality product regularly."

The project became a quick success in meat and dairy, and later with fruits and vegetables. Thirty-seven firms earned the Seal of Quality for 205 dairy and meat products and for 11 fruit and vegetable companies. The project helped four lamb and sheep facilities achieve European standards so that they could export to the EU.

Impacts

John MacKillop and Jeton Starova made a strong team as project managers. As chief of party, John knew every aspect of dairies and cheese making from his academic and hands-on work experience in Vermont; Jeton, his deputy, specialized in sheep cheese and lamb production. From 1998 to 2003, the project tripled the domestic meat processing industry. Forty- four percent of the dairy industry had significant sales increases every year.

Imports of European products declined as consumers bought good, cheaper, and well packaged domestic products. In "agriculture talk," they say "You should begin by knowing and responding to your customers." The Seal of Quality was the first USAID project to test and prove this axiom.

Given Land O'Lakes contacts among the rural residents through its Seal of Quality program, the State Department provided an additional $250,000 to encourage ethnic harmony to maintain multi-ethnic associations and business activities between Albanian and Macedonia producers. Participating sheep herder organizations wanted to establish ethnically separate associations. The project resisted these efforts.

I returned to Macedonia in July 1999 during the height of the Kosovo conflict that drove lots of Serbian tourists, unable to summer at the Croatian islands, to Lake Ohrid which was a transit place for Albanians who were trying to get to Europe by swimming or boating across the lake. It was home of the Monastery where the Cyrillic script originated. Here I interviewed some of the participants in the multi-ethnic associations.

Six multi-ethnic, local associations in western Macedonia were linked to an existing regional association with which Land O'Lakes had a close working relationship. In this region, there had been less discrimination and more trust among rural people, so the challenge was to keep external ethnic politics from adversely affecting the way producers live peacefully and do business. This is the essence of cooperation.

In 2017, the conflict between the Albanian ethnic minority and orthodox Macedonians continues to plague Macedonia, rooted in ethnically-based political parties and their difficulty in forming multi-party governance.

Economic progress in Macedonia has been slow since independence. Agriculture production and processing represents 18% of GDP. Produce quality suffers from lack of needed infrastructure especially in post-harvest treatment and packing as well as inefficient processing and marketing.

Despite lack of government support and appropriate policies, the Seal of Quality Project points the way to the future of agribusiness as Macedonia integrates into the European market.

Seal of Quality products at a grocery store

Chapter 18: Dairy Farmers of Albania

Albania was part of a larger Roman province. Statues of Skanderbeg on horseback were in the town square; he was considered the country's founder. An Albanian nobleman and military commander who served the Ottoman Empire in 1423–43, he led a Christian rebellion against the Ottoman Turks. I visited a mountain fortress where he tried to hold off the invading Turks, and a Christian Orthodox monastery that was being rebuilt.

With the collapse of the Ottoman Empire in the Balkan Wars, Albania became independent in 1912. The Kingdom of Albania was invaded by Italy in 1939 and became a Nazi German protectorate in 1943. I saw this Italian influence in its architecture. In 1944, the socialist People's Republic was established under Enver Hoxha. Albania became a democratic republic in 1991 and again was at the frontline in the conflict between Orthodox Christians and Kosovo Muslims.

Albania's Stalinist dictator, Enver Hoxha, who was totally paranoid, kept his people cut off from the rest of the world. His fallen statues littered the parks, and his odd shaped museum was used by kids as a slide for cardboard sleds. Later, it housed USAID in a bit of a twist.

Hoxha collectivized the entire countryside -- the only place in Europe where this happened. Collectivism was supposed to mold rural Albanians into a new society. Instead it brought down on them the scourges of hunger and scarcity.

He found that Stalin was not tough enough and turned to Mao and China for most of his country's assistance. His idea of agriculture was not only self-sufficiency but each region should be self-sufficient. So, there were duplicate facilities everywhere to process food.

He wrote 17 red books about the ideal life under communism that were delivered to every family who was ordered to read them. Most of these books that I saw were used as door stops or thrown away in a heap.

Albania was declared an "atheist state." The elite were very small in numbers, mostly family members of the ruling clique which meant that there were almost no houses to rent. Dissidents and often their family members were put to manual labor in mines which produced aluminum and other minerals which were bartered to China and communist countries for critical imports. Hoxha's followers retained power after his death in 1985, but the fall of communism brought reformers into power in April 1992. Most of them were young with little experience in how to run a country.

Albania was the last of the central and eastern European countries to embark on democratic and free market reforms. It started from a disadvantaged position due to the catastrophic repressive and economic policies. The democratically-elected government launched an ambitious economic reform program meant to reverse economic deterioration and put the country on the path toward a market economy.

Entering Albania

Getting into Albania was not easy after the reform government came to power. I called their consulate in D.C. for a visa. I got their representative on the line as he was cleaning out his apartment, fired by the new government. He could not help and was not sure if a visa was required.

I decided to chance it and scheduled a flight via London and Rome to Tirana. I found an English-speaking guide to meet me at the airport. On the flight, I observed Baptist missionaries arriving to convert the citizens of this so-called atheist state, but who were really conservative Muslims. Since English had been forbidden, the Albanians did not care if learning English included Jesus. On the plane, Texans in cowboy boots were there to check out the possibility of oil.

When I flew in, a half dozen MIG 17s were flying overhead, planes that we use as stunt planes at fairs, not of much military value. As we landed on an iron landing strip, probably put there after World War II, next to the tarmac was a T-33 trainer that wandered into their airspace in 1957. I recognized the plane, since at Air Force ROTC summer camp, I had flown in its back seat.

It was a challenge squeezing through the airport security with the crowd from the plane, no organization but luckily, I could see my guide waving to me. On the way to the only hotel in town, I noticed rusty spikes on top of poles in wine vineyards to repel the expected American paratroopers, and 700,000 pillboxes dotting the landscape. No one was allowed to live on the beaches since that is where US marines would land.

Outside the hotel, there were gypsy boys holding tiny malnourished babies begging for money. The hotel had only cold water, water stains on the walls, and breakfast that was uneatable, with lard covering the food. It was with good reason that I was advised to bring my own food.

Pillbox in a Christmas Card from Diane Blane

There was only one outdoor restaurant that served shrimp. Few private cars were on the roads since they had been outlawed, but there were antiquated Chinese trucks, knock offs of a 1940 Ford and motorized Chinese motor bikes with long arms attached the front wheel with a seat and a cart in the back.

As we travelled around it was like Benito Mussolini had reinvaded. Relief trucks flew the Albanian and Italian flags driven by the Italian army. Relief ships were off the port of Durres where desperate Albanians swam out to them to try to get on board. Riots had broken out around the Cuban Embassy with a crowd of Albanians trying to get visas.

During the Hoxha era, the only tourists permitted into the country were British on guided tours with Albanian minders to watch over them and make sure they did not talk to any "unauthorized" citizens. Today, I call my wife, "my Albanian minder" when she is overly directive in correcting my behavior. I was one of the first visitors to newly democratic Albania. I went to the national museum which had a temporary wall in front of a communist era and a statue of Hoxha lying on the floor.

Workers mural in city square

My assignment was to develop a quick dairy project with only 18 months remaining on its USAID grant to Land O'Lakes. In the previous three years, they held a single Albanian conference on dairy development, but no program activities.

It was easy to see that Albania was the poorest country in Europe, and the most rural. More than half the population of 3.2 million live in villages, practicing subsistence agriculture on an average of about three acres per family.

The typical Albanian family live in a stone house with electricity but no telephone, plumbing, or reliable source of safe drinking water. They use hand tools to coax vegetables and wheat from small plots of stony ground. Along the dirt tracks of Albania's villages, the scene hardly varied: chickens scratch in garbage heaps, women haul manure on wooden litters, and children or old people carefully guard their one or two precious cows.

I visited an antiquated dairy plant that was not only inoperative but good only for scrap metal. The plants were linked to collectives where the cows were milked. Because the farmers hated the collectives, families took cows to their homes and built sheds attached to their small cottages. They were dismantling the collective buildings brick by brick, wire by wire.

Dairy project

The biggest challenge in designing a project was that Albanians, especially women are very conservative, seldom leave their villages, and never without a male escort. I asked to speak to some women, and my interpreter approached a house to ask if I could talk with a young woman and her grandmother. I would have never been let in if a male was present, nor been able to talk to the two women so freely.

I asked the young woman, "How did you get the cow in your shed?" She said, "All of the villagers went to the collective and got one or two cows." I asked, "How did you learn to milk the cow?" She turned to her grandmother, saying "She taught me." Milking cows was a specialty at the collective and only milk parlor workers knew how. It was obvious that any project I developed had to start with the very basics – how to properly milk a cow.

Cows were significant sources of household protein, especially important for children. The women milked their cow in the morning and made white brine cheese as the only way to preserve it until dinner. Dairy provided 40% of the family's protein. Dung from the cow was the major heat source for the houses.

Livestock production was the backbone of Albania's agriculture. It was one of the few products where excess milk could be sold in village markets for income to support families. Most other crops were sustenance only, though the potential to produce tomatoes and other crops for export to Italy was just beginning.

I visited the Ministry of Agriculture and the Agricultural University; the latter was burned down the next year by student protestors. I immediately knew that extension services from the government or the university would be a failure given their dysfunction, though I did find some young well-trained agricultural women who had the knowledge and drive to help the struggling new dairy women.

Conceptually, the approach was a "Dairy Campaign," careful not to use extension agents or any such term linked to the government. It had to be independent, and my inspiration was the Voter Registration Campaign from Chile. Conceptually, it was the same.

I designed *waves of dairy training* which would have a core of woman trainers who would go out into the villages, reach out to women and demonstrate how to milk a cow, prevent mastitis (an inflammation of the udder), make simple cheeses, and provide proper feeds and forage for grazing. Since women could not travel from their villages because they cared for their children, managed the vegetable garden, and milked their cows, the project had to bring expertise to them.

In time, the approach became known as "Tupperware parties" in which "star" women leaders were trained and returned to their villages to teach other women.

I met with Dianne Blane, the recently arrived USAID mission director who had taken a room in the hotel. She had chosen her own money changer since the banks did not work, and money changers surrounded the only bank in town. The bank surveyed these money exchangers each evening and posted the "exchange rate;" marks and dollars held the highest values.

I told Dianne I would put the proposal under her door since I had an early flight the next day. With only 18 months remaining on the grant, I recommended that we hire a local project director. When I arrived in Rome, I called her and ask if she had received the proposal. She had not gotten it since I had put it under the wrong door.

I described my approach to her and said," We would hire a local project director." She said, "That was not acceptable." She wanted an American chief of party (COP). I told her to ignore the earlier proposal and that I would send her a revised proposal and new budget using an expatriate shortly. I rewrote the proposal in the Rome airport and faxed it to her while waiting for my flight from London to D.C.

We searched for an American COP and later found the perfect person, Debby Wagner, who was already in Albania working on a less-than-successful project by Virginia Tech University to revamp the economics curriculum at the Albanian agricultural university. She received her undergraduate degree at University of Wisconsin-Eau Claire in 1974 in economics and served in the U.S. Peace Corps in Niger. We hired her and from 1995 to 2005, she managed the Dairy Development Project for Land O'Lakes in Albania. The 18-month project continued another 10 years.

During the initial campaign phase, the project reached 3,800 women organized into groups of fifteen, each with an elected key leader in villages of Tirana, Korge, Lushnja, Kugova and Shkodra districts. Field agents for the dairy campaign provided training through demonstrations directly to the groups every quarter. Additional training was provided monthly to key leaders, who were then responsible for training their group.

The women initially received training in three *waves*: milk quality, herd health, business management and marketing. The demonstrations focused on providing information on topics such as sanitation, prevention of mastitis and other diseases, record keeping, cheese making under household conditions, and milk quality tests. Each training topic was accompanied by booklets developed by Land O'Lakes dairy experts and adapted to the conditions in Albania. These booklets were read by friends and family members, thereby broadening their impact.

During the first project extension, field agents continued to teach the original 3,800 women with new topics such as dairy breeding, forage production, and association development. The program added another 1,200 women in the villages located in Kavaja and Durres districts. It was expanded to foster small rural businesses, such as family-based mini-processing plants and milk collection points, and creation of cooperatives, credit unions and associations to advocate for women's issues and support dairy producers in Albania.

Kristin Penn of Land O'Lakes with Albanian dairy woman

I returned to Albania in November 1992 with a team from Land O'Lakes led by Kristen Penn. She is totally "Minnesota nice, and loved animals – dairy cows and her beloved Australian sheep dogs. Her mother was an art teacher in the Lindbergh High School which Judy and I visited. The high school was built with similar features of an airport control tower, since it was aviator, Charles Lindbergh's hometown in Minnetonka, MN.

A former Peace Corps volunteer in Africa, she began as an intern in the international development division in 1990 and eventually travelled to over 100 countries developing Land O'Lakes projects, especially in dairy fields. Whenever there was a particularly tricky proposal she trusted me to draft it, such as in Albania, Macedonia, Montenegro and Ukraine. In 2017, she is a senior agricultural official at the Millennium Challenge Corporation, currently stationed in Niger.

We saw the country's economic progress immediately. Now there were hundreds of derelict cars driving on the road which must have been collected from all over the former Yugoslavia. Our team had four laptop computers. We thought we had more computing power than the entire country – we did not find a single operating computer in our visit.

We explored how to expand the Land O'Lakes project to include agricultural government policy and respond to another expected RFA. An earlier group from Oregon State suggested that Albania could produce commercial red wine – which we found undrinkable.

We drove by a field of Mercedes, stolen mostly from Italy. We were told that you could order the Mercedes of your choice if they did not already have one you desired. We lost the proposal. Some RFAs are worth losing. The ability to change government agricultural policies and create market information systems is slow and difficult. I try to avoid working with governments as much as possible.

Credit Unions

By October 1993, the political situation in Albania was getting difficult. I was asked by USAID to prepare a base document for an RFA on the formation of trade associations and credit unions.

At the USAID headquarters in Tirana, I was told to vary my walks and take care because of pickpockets. At a debriefing, a US police advisor had just arrived to start professionalizing the Albanian police force. In a roundtable, every NGO leader pointed out to him how their apartments had been broken into or cars stolen.

USAID offices located in Hoxha mausoleum

While I was there, a USAID person on temporary duty (TDY) had accepted a "too cheap" computer from one of the Albanian project staff. When the NGO reported, it stolen, the police came to her hotel room, and she threw the computer out the window. She was later fired.

When I wrote my report on the need to form credit unions, I assumed it would be carried out by the World Council of Credit Unions, one of my association members. The USAID mission decided to award Land O'Lakes a subcontract with the Irish Credit Union League. They formed village credit unions using the network of women dairy farmers: nine were created from 1997 to 1999.

The credit unions mobilized the farmer savings and encouraged them to work together in meeting their needs and improving living conditions. Most loans were for home reconstruction, medical expenses, furniture, and simple agriculture equipment.

I recommended the formation of trade associations. I found that the existing associations were informal and created merely to get donor funding. Free lunches were the major draw to attend them. Only Land O'Lakes was able to create an effective association of dairy producers in the emerging small dairy industry because of their strong women's base and leadership.

I visited several village milk collection sites and small family-based dairies which had been formed for cheese and yogurt. Some were primitive in which they used candles to pasteurize the milk. Small cheese facilities were growing rapidly. The dairy industry in Albania was built from the ground up, centered on dairy women

In March 1997, civil unrest began to envelop the country due to the collapse of pyramid investment schemes. The majority of Albanians had invested their life savings into these Ponzi schemes on the promise of returns with high interest. Large numbers of Albanians took to the streets. Armories were looted. Gunfire was heard 24 hours a day. US marines were sent in.   Later, Albania became dangerous because of the conflict in Kosovo and incoming Jihad fighters – the USAID mission and project staffs were evacuated twice.

After the collapse of the pyramid schemes, rural areas emptied with migration to cities. When rural woman left rural areas, the dairy industry became more commercial and farms consolidated.

By 2004, Land O'Lakes shifted the project to an Albanian "Seal of Quality" similar to my design in Macedonia. The project focused on quality standards for dairy and meat products in which a product label signified rigorous testing, consistency, and quality.

Albanian rural life changed beyond recognition in those 10 years. Many of the Muslim women moved to Italy, U.K., and U.S. and they became less conservative and few wore head scarfs.

After the U.S. Embassy evacuated Debby Wagner, she ran the project from the Land O'Lakes Warsaw office for several months. She described her ordeal when I caught up with her in Poland. She said it was dangerous because there was a covert effort to blow up the U.S. Embassy as the conflict in Kosovo heated up.

Debby Wagner told me how much she loved the people of Albania who had gone through such hardship as she proudly introduced me to her adopted orphan daughter.

Unfortunately, Debby became seriously ill and on departing Albania, she received the President's Medal of Gratitude in March 2004 for her leadership in helping small livestock Albanian producers. After a long illness, she died at age 59 in May 2012. I owe Debby Wager so much. She gave life to a concept that I thought up and ran one of the most successful assistance programs in the poorest country of Europe.

Albanian Woman with her heifer

Chapter 19: Coops in Montenegro & Bosnia

Jeton Starova and I decided to try to establish a dairy coop in
Montenegro. In May 2007, I travelled from Montevideo, Uruguay
where I was attending a cooperative insurance conference to
Argentina where I had a ticket from Buenos Aires to Podgorica,
Montenegro. No one at the airline counter knew where it was
located, much less the country. They did get my ticket right for the
flight.

I met up with Jeton Starova in Dubrovnik, an historic Baroque city-
state that had recently been bombed by Serbians. There was a sign
at the main entrance marking every bomb site and damaged
structure that had been repaired. There were still mine fields in the
nearby hills from where they had been shelled by the Serbian army
-- another vivid memory of the ethnic and Balkan conflicts.

Dubrovnik under artillery attack

In college, I had wanted to go to Montenegro where most of the
partisan battles took place during World War II. I read all Milovan

Djilas's books. Fighting with Tito's partisans during World War II, he led Tito's Yugoslavian break with the USSR. A Montenegrin, Djilas was vice president and heir apparent in 1953.

Djilas's criticism of communist rule led to his expulsion from the party and imprisonment for eight years. He wrote *The New Class* (1957) and *Conversations with Stalin* (1962). Finally expelled from the country, he continued to write about the pitfalls of communism from his home in Vermont. He wrote a large tome on the history of Macedonia and another on his war diaries.

I met Djilas at a Democracy Conference years later. I learned unlike Russia's Aleksandr Solzhenitsyn and Andrei Sakharov, to my disappointment and total surprise, he was known in Montenegro not as a dissident, but as a traitor.

This small mountainous country has diverse nationalities and ethnic groups: 41 per cent consider themselves Montenegrin, 31 per cent Serbian; seven per cent Albanian; and 73 per cent are Orthodox, 22 per cent Muslim and five per cent Catholic.

Montenegrins are viewed as militant or "super" Serbs, often serving in the military. Slobodan Milosevic was born and grew up there. It was the epicenter of the Tito partisans' guerrilla fighting with many Serbs aligned with the pro-Nazi Chetniks, well depicted in Djilas war diaries.

Like Albania, most of the dairy cows were in collectives that had collapsed. The biggest herd we found had 12 cows. The focus of the project was to build on these small herds and produce yogurt and cheeses which can be done with small herds. In fact, we met a family who made yogurt from about 25 neighbor's cows.

I thought that Jeton could be a chief of party until we heard the frequent racist slurs against Albanians as he translated into perfect

Serbo-Croatian. It reminded me of the racist comments against blacks as I grew up in Virginia.

We were working on the proposal when we went to the hotel desk to check on our bill. Despite a sign, "We accept Visa and Master Cards," the hotel only accepted Diner's Club. Jeton and I pooled our money to pay the bill, flew to Belgrade where we could get money wired to us, and stayed in a deserted and a shabby Hilton with worn red carpets because of the U.S. and U.N. boycotts. Those were unnerving and dangerous times.

As an Albanian, Jeton was uneasy in Belgrade and did not leave the hotel. He said, "Emotions were high since the war had just ended in Bosnia and was still active in Kosovo. Belgrade was run down and full of war criminals." Since Jeton spoke without an Albanian accent, he was okay unless someone asked for his documents or he told them his last name. We travelled together to the airport where he waited eight hours for his flight so as not to travel by himself in a cab.

I submitted the proposal to USAID in Washington. It was going nowhere until the Montenegrin government allowed US overflights in its bombing campaign in Serbia and Kosovo from March 24 to June 11, 1999.

The State Department immediately searched for a project to reward Montenegro, still technically a part of Serbia. My proposal was the only one available, and it got approved immediately without any review.

Project begins

The project started belatedly in August 1999 because of the Kosovo conflict. At the time, only a handful of Americans were in Montenegro with no presence of USAID or the State Department.

US government officials were not allowed into the country so our project manager, Roger Steinkamp, was on his own.

Americans at the time were subject to arrest by Serbian authorities, but they were protected by the Montenegrin government. The opposition parties were avid supporters of Slobodan Milosevic. Threats against Americans were common. Land O'Lakes project staff let it be known, "We are allied with neither the government nor the opposition."

Although Montenegro was not a primary target in the conflict during the bombing, some US bombs did destroy houses in Danilovgrad and a primary school in Murino which killed four children.

In December 1999, the political climate was tense with the police force of Montenegro and the Serbian federal army in a standoff at the airport. The State Department called Land O'Lakes and suggested evacuation. The project staff stayed. The tense political situation continued until elections and the fall of Milosevic in October 2000.

State collectives (zadrugas) collapsed, and dairy cows were distributed to members. There were 55,000 dairy farmers who had only two or three poorly producing cows. Three large dairy plants and several emerging private plants lacked quality milk and were below capacity. Milk subsidies resulted in high prices and a lack of incentive to produce quality raw milk. There was not a single private farmer association.

The Land O'Lakes training programs began by sharing its cooperative values, mission and business practices with dairy farmers who requested help in forming coops, including drafting bylaws and developing member services.

Training focused on democratic governance and transparent structures. As coops were formed, a rating system was established to compare and create peer pressure among cooperatives to adhere to democratic principles and practices (e.g., open board and annual meetings with agendas and minutes; accurate and transparent financial books).

Training emphasized "doing" rather than merely "talking" about coops. As a result, elected boards of directors reflected member diversity with different political views, religions, and ethnic backgrounds. To my absolute surprise, within a year, thirty-five farmer cooperatives were formed with 12,000 paying members, and a Farmer Trade Company united them in purchasing inputs and marketing. These cooperatives were set up and initially financed through animal feed donations from Italy and the U.S.

The project assisted refugees from Kosovo who received donated cows but lacked know-how in proper feeding and milking practices. The refugees could not maintain most of the cows which were sold to local farmers who built their herds.

The cooperatives experienced few inter-ethnic, inter-religious, and political conflicts. Cooperative members rose up against several old-style leaders who tried to dictate policies.

Radosav Rasovic

By May 2004, there were 48 well-functioning cooperatives in which 244 farmers owned more than 15 milking cows. According to Radosav Rasovic, the Land O'Lakes deputy, they had diverse leadership that was Orthodox, Catholic, Albanian, Muslim, Bosnian, Serbian, and Montenegrin. From 1999 to 2002, he founded 33 of the farmer coops, the National Farmers' Association, and the trading company.

I returned to Montenegro twice--once to write a regional trade proposal to try to reconnect companies in the former Yugoslavia that were not funded, and a community development proposal. Several Montenegrin companies I visited were reestablishing old trade patterns, like a greenhouse for roses that shipped them throughout the region for International Women's' Day.

USAID was moving away from agriculture to focus more on community building, so the proposal died. This time I got to spend a full day in Dubrovnik, in particular, touring its nautical museum with a 2,000-year history of sailing and international trade. As a city-state, the Popes allowed only Dubrovnik to trade with the Arab world. The town had repaired most of the damage from the bombing, yet it was still pretty deserted. That was before the cruise ships began to flood the narrow streets and small plazas with tourists.

Roger Steinkamp

In May 2007, my final trip was to respond to an RFA for community building. Again, it was a challenge to position Land O'Lakes for this type of project.

A former ag vocational teacher from Minnesota, Roger Steinkamp, the current project manager, had strong views, was quite stubborn and outspoken. He kept pressuring the USAID mission in Serbia for more funding, so to me, he was not acceptable as the chief of party. I warned Land O'Lakes about keeping Steinkamp but they insisted. The proposal did not win. A good friend and colleague, Bob Flick wrote the winning proposal and spent a year as chief of party building on the Land O'Lakes success in strengthening the farmer cooperatives.

From these trips, it was evident that Montenegro was moving towards independence. I got to know the staff at the Montenegro consulate in D.C. and helped them lobby for separate USAID mission and funding. I arranged for the Land O'Lakes Board of

Directors to attend a formal dinner hosted by the consulate as thanks for our assistance.

Serbia

Again, I tried to position Land O'Lakes for community building in Serbia. I wrote a proposal to respond to an RFA. I travelled to Belgrade and, of course, went to see and photograph the Chinese Embassy that the U.S. bombed accidentally.

Bombed Chinese Embassy

I visited Novi Sad with its downed bridges due to US bombing which had temporally closed the Danube to commercial traffic. I drove the length of Serbia to Montenegro where you could see thousands of refugees, Serbs who had been displaced by war in Kosovo and Bosnia and were crammed into schools and public buildings. Again, I lost this proposal because Land O'Lakes was not credible as an implementer for community development projects. It was too much of a stretch.

Croatia

I learned more about the ethnic conflicts with a trip to Croatia to see how Land O'Lakes could help there. The American Refugee

Organization, located in Minneapolis near Land O'Lakes headquarters, was interested in economic and dairy development to entice refugees in Bosnia to return to Croatia. I was driven up to the border between Croatia and Bosnia. In this region, most Croatians fled or were ethnically cleansed during the Bosnian wars.

As we drove along the mountain road, we passed railroad stations cordoned off due to land mines. Bullet holes were evident in nearly every house along the road. We could see only a few old people peering at us out of their shaded windows. There were few cars and no obvious activities.

The American Refugee Organization that guided me was bussing refugees from Bosnia to Croatia to show them it was safe to return to their homes. Only the old were willing to return having pensions to support themselves. At the border town of Dvor with a long history of ethnic intermarriages, I asked a young woman, "How you decided which ethnic group you are in? Her response was, "You choose who you are."

Bosnia

My final trip to the Balkans was to Bosnia where the Land O'Lakes project encouraged displaced people to return to their pre-war homes. Jobs, family income, and safety were the major obstacles for minorities who had been subjected to ethnic cleansing.

Land O'Lakes used the words "association" and "cooperative" sparingly in the proposal. The USAID project review committee felt strongly that, in the early stages of the return process and the negative Yugoslav experience with cooperatives and associations, they had little chance of success. They approved the project and were wrong about cooperatives.

John MacKillop relocated from Macedonia to lead this effort in Bosnia. Within the first two months, Land O'Lakes assisted local producers with market research that indicated a large market for traditional cheeses they produced in Srebrenica, Kotar Varos, Knezevo, and Kupres, where some of the worst ethnic cleansing had taken place.

The market information was presented at an open meeting for producers, and MacKillop left them with the open question, "Who is going to take advantage of this opportunity?" The meeting was the first-time local Muslims and Serbs had been in contact since the war.

Several key people came forward and agreed to participate in an ethnically mixed working group. They met every two weeks. Land O'Lakes assisted them with a feasibility study for a centrally located and community-based cheese plant and carried out additional market research at their request.

After six months, the working group requested information regarding cooperatives. Land O'Lakes helped them develop bylaws through a gradual process over three months so they fully understood its basic principles. Initially, they had to register as an association, and later, with favorable changes in national cooperative law, re-registered as a cooperative in September 2003.

The board of directors consisted of seven members of whom two were minority Serbs; and the supervisory board had three members of which one was Serbian. The office was located in an ethnically mixed village primarily because the community donated the space.

The cooperative was formed to pack and market its members' sheep and cow cheeses. The packing facility was located in a

Muslim village with two staff, one Muslim and one Serb. The cooperative paid producer's prices for their cheese, 40 per cent higher than they had received historically.

Initially as a business, the cooperative had problems: accounts payable and receivable that remained too high as well as a cash flow problem. Fortunately, when the cash flow problem flattened out, the cooperative did fairly well. The price of cheese to retailers provided them with a 15 percent margin.

Logo of Bosnia Cheese Cooperative

The cooperative's success played a role in mitigating conflict. The actual number of people who have returned due to economic opportunity is difficult to determine, but there was a dramatic increase in agricultural investment by those who had returned to their pre-war homes and farms.

Because the land is near the former front lines, land mines remained a problem for children, dairy cows, and agricultural development. In spite of these dangers, minority returnees began to feel safe and wanted to return to farming. They invested in physical assets, as they perceived a more secure future.

They saw the benefits of the cheese cooperative which improved their products and were able to sell cheese at increased prices across ethnic lines. The cooperative served as a venue for dialogue where conflict mitigation begins.

In Srebrenica, a livestock association that Land O'Lakes helped with donations resulted in many minorities returning. While reconciliation talks may be useful, I saw that economic opportunities were the major motivations for those willing to return to their former homes and farms.

Yugoslavia broke up into seven sovereign countries: Bosnia and Herzegovina, Croatia, Macedonia, Slovenia, Serbia, Montenegro, and Kosovo. As a student of War World I, now 100 years ago, it began in the Balkans – ignited by the assassination on June 28, 1914 of Archduke Franz Ferdinand and his wife, Sophie in Sarajevo. I knew that the Archduke was killed at a bridge, and I was determined to find it. There was only a small plaque to identity the location.

In Sarajevo, I saw the damage from the 1,000-day siege in bullet-ridden buildings and signs "Warning Land Mines" around the train station and I picked up a pamphlet about the underground shelters used during the siege.

Then and now, the ethnic divisions have not healed. Myths such as Slavic unity were dispelled with the collapse of Yugoslavia. Politicians and parties in the Balkans remain based on ethnicity and exacerbate the divisions. Citizens think of themselves by their ethnic background, not national allegiance.

Underground shelter in Sarajevo

I participated in several USAID-supported reconciliation projects. My impressions were that the "good guys" got together, but the bad actors were not present.

The most glaring omission was a lack of mediating organizations – churches, human rights groups, NGOs like the League of Women Voters, and ethnically diverse cooperatives. In the Balkans, I found that cooperatives can function as mediators because they are driven by economic imperatives – markets, access to raw materials, and economies of scale by working together. To some extent, I believe that cooperatives have bridged ethnic gaps based on common values of trust, self-help, and collaboration.

I wrote a paper entitled *Cooperatives in Conflict and Failed States* which I presented at an international agricultural development forum on June 2, 2004. I said,

"Cooperatives are special purpose organizations that have unique attributes compared to other forms of enterprise. They are independent, member-owned and democratically governed businesses, created with equity financed by members who invest in order to benefit through their patronage."

Cooperatives are built on a collective identity and shared destiny. This characteristic is the underlying factor in the rise of cooperative networks in the face of national and/or regional conflict and hostile, monopolistic enterprises and or middlemen/usurers. The paper detailed the distinct contributions, attributes and examples of how cooperatives achieve economic and social development during conflict and in failing, failed and recovering states including Bosnia, East Timor, Lebanon, Mozambique, Rwanda, Macedonia and Nepal.

I concluded, *that cooperatives are often imbedded in cultures where violence is prevalent and can result in rapid economic development as ethnic bridging institutions. They have successfully helped create jobs for returning minorities and ex-combatants to conflict regions and have been particularly effective when markets are distant and high-value.*

To become transformational, cooperative networks need to be created beyond initial ethnic or group minorities. While anecdotal and historical information confirms these cooperative impacts, more empirical data is needed to better identify traits that mitigate against violence and make the case that cooperatives in such circumstances may be a preferred development option.

Chapter 20: Agricultural Reforms in Russia

With the break-up of the Soviet Union, the rise of Boris Yeltsin, and the march towards democracy and a market economy, I was optimistic.

In a joint session of Congress on September 11, 1990, President George H.W. Bush declared a "New World Order" with the end of the Cold War and a new millennium of democratic expansion and free market growth. It was in this spirit that the administration and USAID began projects in Russia, Ukraine and Georgia.

None of us foresaw the rise of Putin and the return to authoritarian rule.

When travelling throughout Russia, I saw the old women pensioners selling pencils or other items on street corners, the breakup of collective farms, and the rise of a mafia who were easy to spot. The new oligarchs came with body guards wearing Adidas clothing and shoes. When you met with them, they would say, "Don't worry, we can arrange everything for you."

The government and reformers wanted technical assistance to "decollectivize" and reorganize their farms and privatize agribusinesses. The challenge was great since Russian agriculture had little experience with private farm ownership.

Prior to the turn of the 20th century, farming had always existed as a landlord/peasant system, with landed elites owning vast tracts of land and peasants existing as serfs. From 1906 to 1911, small tracts were given to peasant farmers. When Joseph Stalin assumed power in 1924, he began forced collectivization of farmland. In 1929, Ukraine had private farmers, but virtually all landowners were killed or sent into internal exile, many to Siberia and Kazakhstan.

Many of the collectivized farms that I visited were "little villages" with multiple services like grocery stores, bakeries, and doctor's offices. These auxiliary systems collapsed, businesses left the collectives, and the large farms were privatized with shares that were supposed to go to the farmer-workers, but really were controlled by former managers. When managers took over the farms, they never paid dividends, and kept farmers as workers.

In many cases, small plots of land were provided to collective members where they grew food for their families, but it never amounted to private farming systems like in the U.S.

In 1992, I decided to take Nelle Temple Brown on a tour of the Farmer-to-Farmer programs just starting up in Russia. Nelle was Congressman Doug Bereuter's staffer on the House Banking Committee. She is the most quietly religious person I have ever known. She mentored others in religious faith, saw the Bible as allegorical, and led a prayer group that tried to redeem Kaddafi and other brutal dictators. Since Bereuter was skeptical of expanding the Farmer-to-Farmer program to Russia, I wanted her see cooperative-based efforts first hand and report them back to her boss.

We stayed at the Intourist Hotel, a hulking glass, stone and concrete building across from the Kremlin. Like Soviet-style hotels in Eastern Europe and Far East Russia where I went, it was dark, dank, with large empty first-floor atriums, worn out stuffed chairs, and terrible service. Built for foreign visitors, who by Soviet rules were required to stay in special locations under supervision, the hotel was a strange combination of East meets West as guests rubbed up against traders looking to make an illegal buck.

When we arrived, the new manager had fired the translators and, not speaking any English himself, hired new staff who claimed to speak English, but didn't. It was a challenge to register, but we did find the last remaining English translator to help us. We had to pay in advance for our rooms with exact change, so we scrambled with other guests to work out the right amounts. When we left, we had to go to two other places in the hotel to pay our bills for telephones and the restaurant.

Hailing a cab was a challenge. The local mafia controlled the unmarked taxis that were allowed to line up at the hotel entrance. To avoid the mafia cabs, we walked two blocks to get a roaming, also unmarked cab and hoped we weren't going to be mugged.

Most surprising was how Hiltons and Sheridans sprung up so quickly and as a rule would not hire anyone who had been in hotel management in Russia because of their inattentive attitudes. On my last trip to Moscow to carry out a Land O'Lakes evaluation, I stayed at an upscale, clean Swedish hotel that would rival any in the West.

Based on our trip, we wrote an article for the Christian Science Monitor, *Grass-Roots Leaders in Russia Embrace Change* (December 18, 1992). A snapshot of early changes underway, it read,

"SHELL shocked by rapid changes, Russia is a country in psychological depression. Many Russians are passive and barely coping with day-to-day life. While Boris Yeltsin is important to the success of overall reform, so are the grass-roots leaders who are embracing private initiative. These nuts-and-bolts leaders are trying to cast off 75 years of mismanagement. Undaunted by continuing

bad economic news, they are squarely facing change, and they need our help.

After driving past the small grimy towns of Lenin and Marx along the Volga River, we met one of these people, an energetic former senior communist who was recently hired as manager of the Sokol Farm. With advice from a successful Minnesota farm couple, he reorganized the farm into 13 small agribusinesses and 12 individual holdings. He linked up the former collective with a defense electronics firm to gain investment capital in exchange for supplying the plant's employees with quality produce. He reflected ruefully that he had wasted his most fertile years in communism and wants to produce concrete improvements in farm life and enterprise. He expects to work himself out of a job in two years, when the transition to profitable private ownership is complete.

Another leader of 8,000 private farmers in the Saratov region left a senior management position in a military firm in 1990. A United States volunteer is helping him assess antiquated crushing equipment for sunflower seeds to produce higher quality oil for a U.S. joint venture in popcorn. He told of painstakingly training himself to take the initiative by looking into the mirror and asking his "boss" what he should do today. Neither of these private farm leaders have an agricultural background.

A few Moscow professors and students have formed Russia's first national consumer advocacy group. Wizards of media, they are publishing a magazine like Consumer Reports, advocating consumer protection laws and promoting consumer cooperatives and credit unions. Meanwhile, U.S. credit-union staff is helping strengthen newly formed credit unions in Suzdal and St. Petersburg. The group's strategy is to work with regional and local governments to pass model credit-union laws, creating pressure for national legislation. In a country where consumers are daily abused or ignored, have no recourse for faulty products, and have few places to save, these leaders are helping to start a grassroots movement based on existing informal mutual-aid groups.

A banker in Podolsk near Moscow is receiving advice from seven top U.S. farm credit specialists on how to transform his bank into a central institution with branch offices to provide credit to Russia's 120,000 struggling private farmers. His is the only bank owned by private farmer's groups. He told us no one tells him "no" or "yes," so he just figures out how to move ahead on his own.

The elected head of a national research institute in Pushchino is a leading world scientist in the use of bacteria to detoxify polluted soils. He is creating high-tech commercial ventures and reorganizing his staff into a university to qualify for additional grants. He is helped by two U.S. land-grant universities and a major California fruit and vegetable co-operative. He said the scientists under him support the idea of change, but not for themselves. One said that all he wants from a joint venture is enough money to feed his family and to go on doing research.

Like plants sprouting in the cracks of a sidewalk, these leaders have made the complex mental shift toward initiative and self-reliance. They are under extraordinary pressure, working against the inertia, passivity, and fear in the old system. Given the Russian saying that 'the nail that sticks up gets hammered down,' their courage in exercising initiative in these uncertain times is awesome.

Organizations in Russia may at first look like those in the West, but they are built on different rationales and motivations. Banks are designed to disburse soft government credits and to collect private savings for government use while providing little interest, despite 2,000 percent annual inflation. So-called employee cooperatives are built on taking free goods from state supplies for private gain. U.S. advisors need to delve deeply into underlying assumptions before *making recommendations. Our most useful people-to-people help is encouragement, moral support, dialogue, and information on alternative ways to establish private operations.*

Our task is to help these new grassroots leaders reorder their country's rich human and natural resources. Our aid should help them imagine, create, and organize transitional and nascent organizations that promote private initiative and nurture trust. Countering the legacies of passivity and a dysfunctional economic system will take all the courage, patience, and energy these leaders can muster."

What I did not write about the Sokol farm is that in addition to advice from US advisors, the German assistance agency (GTZ) decided to build a small dairy. The German advisors did not trust the local cement, or workers, so they brought in everything: concrete, machinery, German technicians, and workers.

The project was designed to resettle Volga Germans whom Catherine the Great had invited to immigrate and farm Russian lands including Mennonites, near what today is called Volgograd though Putin is thinking of renaming it back to Stalingrad, bowing to renewed patriotism and his revisions of history.

With the Nazi invasion, Stalin worried that the Volga Germans would collaborate with the invaders and relocated them to Kazakhstan. Since Germany had the "right of return," the goal was to resettle them where they had been deported many decades ago. Few Kazakhstani of German origins stopped and most went all the way back to Germany in the 1990s.

On my next trip to Russia with a team of cooperative leaders, we were looking for agricultural projects. There is a ring of 17 airports around Moscow. Without a Russian guide, it was impossible to get through the checkout lines, get to the right holding area, wait for the flight, and then walk out to the airplane.

On the TU 144 plane, you sat on what felt and looked like lawn chairs. As foreigners, we paid $250 each, the mostly Russian military on the flight paid $14. They were going to Saratov which is a major fighter manufacturing center.

We had arranged a tour of this agriculturally-rich area along the Don which flows into the Black Sea. When we arrived at the dingy dark hotel, the woman at the desk asked for our passports which she took to the police station, and for our internal passports. We informed her that Yeltsin had eliminated these restrictions on traveling among regions.

There was no food at the hotel so in the morning we walked to a cafeteria with some of the saddest waitresses that I have ever met. They were mostly milling around with little to do and few customers. They had dead-end jobs. All we could see that looked edible was some watered-down soup. I paid with the littlest bill that I had, and among the change was given an old two-kelpie coin that I calculated was worth one hundredth of a penny.

We asked our Russian hosts to see a map to discuss the farm areas, and there was a huge hole in the middle with roads going towards the void. I asked what is there and they responded, it is where Russian mobile ICBMs are located.

We visited an agricultural college that evening as it began to snow. An Italian joint venture ice cream shop had just opened. There was a line of at least 100 people waiting in the middle of the street in the snow waiting for a tiny scoop of ice cream.

Later, we sent a group of U.S. farm credit experts to the college. They were to teach how capitalist agribusinesses and cooperative banks work. They prepared lessons on the A B Cs of credit but found the students asked highly technical questions, some of which stumped them. Russian students are well educated, especially in math and sciences. Usually, they avoid management or other fields where they were forced to become part of the communist system. They quickly grasped the intricacies of modern Western finance and banking.

Tri-Valley Growers

Over the years, I recruited six cooperative organizations to the US Overseas Cooperative Development Council. I wrote their proposals, and they joined the association. Tri-Valley Growers (TVG), a large California fruit and vegetable cooperative, was one of them. I helped them get a Farmer-to-Farmer program with a West Coast twist since few volunteers had been recruited from the Western states and few assignments had targeted Far East Russia.

Many of their cooperative members and canning facilities were in Modesto, California which had a heavy concentration of immigrants from Russia, especially the Far East which was not subdued by the communists until about 1923.

Tri-Valley was struggling to survive as the largest tomato cannery in the world. Consumers were shifting to fresh tomatoes and fruits. The cooperative was losing gobs of money. A Harley Davidson-riding new CEO drove it into the ground.

The board of directors decided to end their Russian and Georgian programs and withdraw from USAID which they saw as a distraction from their efforts to rescue the cooperative as it was going bankrupt. It gave me the opportunity to evaluate their programs objectively without regard to continued USAID support. I had carried out a mid-project evaluation as they started up the program and wrote the final report as they phased it out.

From 1992 to 1995, Tri-Valley Growers sent 75 technical advisors to Voronezh and Moscow Oblast (county) who assisted 43 agribusinesses and related institutions. I visited project sites, interviewed the beneficiaries and returned to the US, where I interviewed the American volunteers who had provided technical assistance to the same projects I had visited. It was a unique evaluation since I was able to interview both recipients and givers of advice. Rather than a traditional evaluation, I wrote these vignettes.

Organic agriculture

Russia's dominant agriculture traditionally relied on chemicals, but this was beginning to change as private farming emerged. Most of the 300 private farmers in the Sergiev Posad region of the Moscow Oblast farmed organically because they could not afford expensive chemical fertilizers or pesticides. New certification programs by the Farming Development Service (FDS), a non-profit extension service, in conjunction with EcoBios (a German/Russian initiative), were teaching these farmers sustainable agricultural techniques. Once certified, the farmers received 10% more for their potatoes, carrots, and cabbage from specialty markets in Moscow where customers paid a premium for organically grown foods.

This move to organic agriculture was not limited to this single region. The Farming Development Service was attached to the All-Russian Agricultural College, a correspondence and distance learning center with over 1,000 students and prepared curriculum for technical colleges throughout Russia.

Organic farming is not new to Russia. Trager Groh, a Tri Valley Growers advisor from New Hampshire, reintroduced the techniques based upon his own work with Russian emigres. He told the local growers that in New Hampshire, he had watched three waves of

Russian emigrants cultivate organically and said "I am just bringing these techniques back to their homeland."

"The private farmers have been slow to cooperate," said Natalya Andreeva, director of the FDS. "It will take time for the farmers to work together since they were forced to cooperate when they were part of the recently-dissolved collective and state farms." After four years of struggling as individuals, she said, "The time was now right, and FDS is creating voluntary marketing cooperatives."

Overcoming the communist legacy of "we pretend to work, and they pretend to pay us" was not easy.

Vegetable storage

A former state-owned Kominternovskoe Vegetable Storage company shifted from bulk commodities to purchasing and storage of higher value apples, potatoes, and cabbage from private farmers. The dynamic woman manager, Alexandra Nikolaevna Mogilevskaya, said, "I like the new stock company since we are free to make our own decisions, not dictated by the state." Of course, she was the major stockholder and manager.

She said the biggest problem was the quality of her employees who showed up but were not inclined to work hard. In June 1993, Greg Billikopf provided her with advice on how to change her employment practices combining a regular salary with incentive pay. Through shifting to "piece work," 100 of the 170 employees remained with the company that is now five times more profitable. Employees understood that their salaries were tied to the profitability of the company.

Meat Processing

We flew to Novovoronezhsky near the Kazakhstan border and met a budding capitalist. "I was always a capitalist inside," said Ivan Verba, the plant manager of Novovoronezhsky, a meat processing company. The first American he met was Tri Valley Growers adviser Stephen Kurylas who helped reequip and modernize his plant. "I learned not to think of Americans as my enemies. While today Russia is depressed, someday our companies will be good business partners," he said. I am disappointed that the rapprochement did not last.

Ivan Verba credits most of his meat plant's success to Stephen Kurylas, a former veterinarian and meat inspector for USDA. With his advice, the plant expanded its sausage lines from 8 to 40 and replaced 70% of the plant's equipment through plowing profits back into operations. The plant acquired a local farm to access meat supplies and diversified into blue and grey fox fur production.

The Novovoronezhsky meat processing company profits increased by 300 percent. Ivan Verba was the elected mayor of a small town outside of Voronezh where the plant is located. He was one of the few elected officials from Yegor Guaidar's reform party in a region still dominated by former communists.

He said the workers called him back to manage the plant when it was privatized and commented, "I prefer to make profits than being a public official." He is a true democrat as a politician and business manager in a region of Russia that is resistant and slow to change.

The Novovoronezhsky meat processing company remains today as one of the most successful in Russia.

Bread plant in Voronezh

For the next interviews, I went to Voronezh which resonated with me for two reasons: Here was the site of the famous Kursk tank battle that was the turning point of the Eastern Front during World War II and I was born that very week in July 1943. It was also where Peter the Great, who had travelled incommunicado in Europe, brought Dutch craftsman to build a 250-armada fleet in 1700. In the middle of Russia and on the Don River, we visited a museum with model ships. The shipyard is still active.

The local Tri Valley project manager was Asya Tarakanva who spoke excellent English and loved modern American authors like Hemingway and Fitzgerald. She challenged me to remember these books that I had read so long ago. She was married to an "intellectual" who did not believe in work. She supported him and her parents. She gave me an insight into the role of women in Russia who were bread earners, scavengers in long food lines, true heads of household, and cared for both sides of in-laws. No wonder she was basically pessimistic about her future.

It was here that the Tri-Valley Growers country manager almost died. She was traveling from Moscow to Voronezh on an overnight train. She was drugged, robbed, and carried off the train by medical staff. The drug used was a blood pressure medication. According to US doctors, it was potentially fatal. She was hospitalized for five days in Voronezh. She lost a significant amount of cash that she was carrying to open a bank account since bank transfers were impossible at the time.

I interviewed the owners of the Bread Plant #5 in Voronezh, which was nearly bankrupt in early 1994. Its roof was leaking, everything was rusty, and the equipment obsolete from its founding in 1946. The bakery needed money to fix and buy new equipment with 75% of operations still done by hand. Desperate for help, Nina Dubliakova came to the Tri Valley Growers office. A business miracle transpired with that knock on the door.

Nina Dubliakova (right) and me

The plant had been privatized in 1993. The workers kicked out the old manager in an election. Nina Dubliakova, an engineer and former employee of the local bakery association, was hired to turn the plant around. She said, "Before we were dictated to and now we can dictate in response to the marketplace, not the government. Before the state determined our recipes, now we make up our own." Bakery #5 was under increasing market pressure from the four larger bakeries, freed to compete against each other.

The first task of the new management was to prepare a business plan to become profitable and potentially to access Western funding. With accurate financial data and newly motivated workers who were fearful of losing their jobs, the plant began to turn a profit within several months. With initial profits, the management bought two delivery trucks, computers and a mixing machine.

Obviously, I much prefer visits to bakeries than animal slaughter houses. Their giant leap to profitability came about through the advice of Farmer-to-Farmer volunteer, Joe Tuck, a ponytailed general director of the Alvarado Street Bakery, who came to help them out and hosted two senior managers on a visit to his workers' cooperative in San Francisco.

Joe Tuck advised the new management team to diversify its recipes and assortments from two types of bread to about a dozen higher-priced pastries. With the same ingredients and shelf availability, the new assortments resulted in 50% increased sales in the first year, and 200% by the second year. Another recommendation was to market their products directly through kiosks.

A third suggestion sent sales skyrocketing. On his advice, the managers decided to change the return policy on day-old bread from shops selling their breads and pastries. Usually, they paid back to shop owners 75% of the price for returned bread which is used as part of the ingredients in preparing new bread.

Plant #5 pays the shop owner 100% of the selling price. The returned bread is put into plastic bags, extending its life by 1 1/2 to six days and they sell the bread directly from their own outlets at a discount. The result is phenomenal. Their exclusive outlets increased from 43 to 72 and volume of returns from two tons to eight tons a day within 20 months. The employees work on weekends to keep up with business.

Joe Tuck advised management on how to assure quality control and incentive programs. The newly-motivated workers make sure that all recipes are exact with regular testing of the dough mixes or they will lose their bonuses.

The bakery restructured its marketing department that develops new products, undertakes advertising, and carries out market research, the latter unheard of in the region. "We test new products at our own store," Nina Dubliakova said. "That way; we can observe and evaluate our customer's response before moving new products into the marketplace."

On my final trip to Voronezh, a year later, conditions had improved for private farmers and the food industry. Most individuals were more optimistic and expressed concerns about the upcoming elections. Few farmers and citizens wanted to go back to the old system. Less than 20 people demonstrated to return to the old communist system during the attempted coup in Moscow. Several hundred demonstrated in support of Yeltsin.

There were two Western-style cafes on the main street. Both were crowded and patrons waited in long lines to get in. Prices are high by Russian standards, but clearly a cafe of choice for the town's people. When McDonalds opened in Moscow, a similar phenomenon occurred with customers winding around for two blocks.

Business competition was carefully controlled. Monopolies were still the major way of doing business. The kiosks had Western products including cigarettes, MARS candy, and liquors. Private business licenses took over two years to obtain or were never granted. Much of the imported products were sold through street vendors and kiosks where they are often controlled by individuals beholden to the mafia. You could see the oligarchs taking control – the communists just became robber barons, not capitalists. I will never forget the sight of a brand-new Cadillac outside a restaurant as one of the Mafioso walked in with his body guards.

Honey and Far East Russia

My final Tri Valley evaluation was in Far East Russia where Derek Brown and I took an Alaskan Air flight from San Francisco to Anchorage and on to the Sakhalin Island where Shell was developing oil wells and on to Vladivostok. Alaskan Air took its own mechanic, and we saw abandoned Russian airplanes littering the airfields as Aeroflot was dismembered with the breakup of the Soviet Union.

Vladivostok is at the end of the trans-Siberian railway and we took the train to the micro-climate, agricultural area of Spassk. The local Russians took us on a seaside picnic that featured more vodka than food; that evening, they took us to a concrete plant where we swam nude between hot and cold water, lubricated with vodka.

I got an idea of how the mafia worked in this small town when I asked a street vendor who was selling Western clothing how he gets his supplies. He told me that he had to pay for protection, and when he ordered clothing, the mafia took about a quarter of the clothes.

Driving along a Russian highway, a policeman raised his baton to stop cars, and did a shakedown for rupees. In another case, my driver had flashing lights and drove at excessive speeds. He was pulled over by a policeman, gave him a bribe, and immediately took off again with lights flashing as he sped along.

We met with the Beekeepers Association in Spassk, talked about the volunteer assignment and later I was able to meet the volunteer, Alan Buckley in San Francisco. Alan Buckley grew up in Modesto, California and had many classmates in the 1920s who were White Russians who fled Far East Russia. With a passion for bees, he had long known that the *best honey* in the world came from the small agricultural town of Spassk. Now, he was having an adventure of a lifetime providing these Russian entrepreneurs with honey marketing assistance.

After walking several miles into the lime tree forest (it's nectar gives a distinctive taste to the honey), Alan Buckley begin putting on his beekeeping paraphernalia. His host, Victor Katchan, in contrast, stripped to his bikini shorts. Seeing each other, the difference in bee handling attire caused both to laugh.

Buckley spent most of his two weeks listening to his hosts. Bee pollination is his second career which began when his daughter asked him to help with her 4-H project. He produces hundreds of beehives, since bees are the only way to pollinate almond trees in Sacramento valley. His first career was as a stockbroker, and he knows sales. He carefully waited during his assignment until the right moment to make his recommendations on how to market honey. He felt the need to bond with his Russian hosts first. He told them that they needed to change their marketing from large glass jars to distinctive plastic containers, capture the local market and, then, seek out new markets.

On returning home, Alan located and shipped $15,000 worth of 12 oz. plastic bear jars, tanks, strainers and other equipment on his own -- an investment he did not expect to recover anytime soon. Each bear jar had a label that said in Russian, "Packed under American Standards." This demonstrates the values Russians place on US quality, though there are no such "standards."

Far East Russia has a particular memory for me. I had just come from traveling to Guayaquil, Ecuador to look at a cooperative housing project for low income residents with the Dutch-based Foster Parents Plan. I got violently ill from bouillabaisse. I nearly went to the hospital from the hotel because my stomach was so upset. For the first time in all my travels, I asked to see a hotel doctor.

The trip to the Far East followed, and when I returned to San Francisco to meet my wife and niece, I felt lousy and was peeing yellow and had a yellow complexion. It takes exactly 40 days for hepatitis B to appear after being infected. The doctor at an urgent care clinic told me to "get on the very next red-eye and get home as soon as possible." I was going to get very sick. I did and I was.

My next assignment was to strengthen the Land O'Lakes Farmer-to-Farmer Program in Russia and Ukraine. I travelled to Moscow where the project director, Will Bullock, took me to a hotel for the afternoon, and said, "Get some rest because we are taking an all-night train to Vologda." Vologda is the home of Ivan the Terrible, the Russian ruler who wanted to move the capital there from Moscow.

As a non-aggie, my colleagues always assigned me to go to slaughterhouses of cattle, sheep and chickens, a good reason why I became a vegetarian. I prefer sweet smelling bakeries, green houses, and florists.

The House of Flowers was originally part of the greenhouse operation of a state farm. Oleg Yevgemevich Nikitin, together with other greenhouse personnel, privatized the greenhouse. He began a family company to sell fresh cut flowers. His wife, daughter, son and son-in-law were the backbone of the company; each had an artistic background, important in flower arrangements. Oleg turned the greenhouse from a losing vegetable operation into a profitable flower operation as other greenhouses in the region went bankrupt.

Oleg Nikitin knew little about nursery operations and turned to Land O'Lakes for assistance. John Gerten, owner and operator of a successful family-owned greenhouse and garden center in Ohio, provided technical assistance in December 1997.

Oleg gave us a tour of the nursery and later invited Will and me to his apartment. It was small with bunk beds but tastefully done. It showed what a typical family apartment is like, but in his case, he had invited his daughter and her husband to live with him as they built the business. This made a tight living space, but they were very gracious hosts.

The first and most important recommendation they adopted was to hire a young manager, right out of the military, who is a "new Russian not spoiled by the old system." John Gerten left a detailed list of management, marketing and technical recommendations that the former soldier was implementing one by one. Oleg Niktin said that Gerten "revolutionized our way of thinking."

Manager of House of Flowers

For example, by shifting work schedules (cutting flowers every day, not just on weekdays), there was an immediate increase in production with daily deliveries.

New flower varieties, double plastic insulation (more effective and less costly than traditional glass), the addition of advertising, two new shops, and other changes increased sales to about $500,000 rubles. The young manager said, "The most important recommendation was a new attitude towards your job and work."

In Vologda, there was only one private restaurant called Hanoi and run by North Vietnamese. In Arlington, I often went to Vietnamese restaurants owned by refugees from south Vietnam. Another indication of the Cold War. The Vologda administration opened the former US Embassy as a museum and invited the U.S. Ambassador James Collins to attend the opening in June 1998. He visited The House of Flowers.

We travelled way north to a small logging community. I felt right at home with a village full of blue eyed, tall thin men who looked exactly like me. It was surreal. I know now from where my German heritage comes.

Seven farmers had been struggling to make their farms profitable. The farms, owned by three brothers and four friends, produced rye and feed grains. They found that it was not possible to receive cash for their grain, so they received eggs in barter for their feed grains from a state poultry plant, opened two stores and started to sell the eggs there. Due to lack of trust, barter was the common way of doing business at the time.

In their search for a market for their rye, the farmers worked out a barter system in which they traded 30% of their rye and received 70% back in flour from a local mill. They sold this flour from their store. Without packaging for the bulk flour, sales were slow and this led them to add two bakeries to their operation to bake the flour into bread and sell this bread at their stores.

The next step they took was to prepare a proposal to build their own flour mill and they turned to Land O'Lakes for technical assistance. Glenn Babcock taught them the principles of cooperative management and operations, new plant technologies, and helped them prepare a business plan.

With the business plan, they got a loan of $50,000 rubles from the Russian Farmers' Foundation to acquire a flour mill. The cooperative bought a building and renovated it. The mill had a capacity of 500 kilograms of wheat flour per hour and 360 kg of rye per hour.

In this lumber town in the north of the Vologda region, the new mill is especially significant. Not only is the flour mill providing jobs, but because of their vertical integration, the cooperative can provide a lower-priced food staple for the community.

Kaliningrad Institute

The final project assessment was the Kaliningrad Institute for Retraining and Agribusiness. We few to Kaliningrad which is located as a Baltic port city wedged between Poland and Lithuania. It is the former Prussian city of Konigsberg which was overrun by the Red Army in 1944. Germans either fled or were deported. Today the town is a major military base with excellent climate and soil for agriculture. While there is German architecture, there are no Germans, and the few who visit to see their former homes are unwelcome.

In March 1998, Dale Dunivan worked with the Institute's staff to help them transition from the centralized management and resulting education system, to focus on private farmers then emerging from the collectives. The Institute wanted to become an extension service similar to USDA. Dale brought educational materials which were translated into Russian and discussed appropriate agricultural policies to encourage private farming.

A second advisor, Tom Belich, carried out marketing training and put together a program of technical assistance programs and practical courses. His most critical help was to transform the Institute from 100% government funding to a fee basis. Because of these efforts, the Institute was able to attract grants from the Eurasian Foundation to cover 50% of its budget in 1997; and 80% in 1998.

The Institute is still offering courses today and is mostly funded through student fees. It outreaches to 5,600 independent and 400 remaining large collective farms. While Kaliningrad can be self-sufficient in food production as a tax-free zone, food imports from

Poland and Lithuania are cheaper so the focus is on dairy and livestock including mink for export.

Kaliningrad in the heart of Europe

Reflecting on Kaliningrad, I remember how the military base was decrepit and most naval ships so rundown that they could not leave the port. I met a former Soviet missile launch officer like me. We traded comments that we were both in the Cold War together with "our missiles aimed at each other."

Kaliningrad is a thorn for NATO as a European outpost where in June 2015 the Russians conducted exercises for 9,000 troops and 55 naval ships. There is fear that Putin may put short range nuclear missiles there.

As a military base squeezed in between two NATO countries, Kaliningrad is a metaphor for the rise of military aggression, xenophobic patriotism, Russian oligarchic billionaires stealing public goods for private gain, and the rule of Putin. Under it all, there are democrats, advocates for free enterprise, and pro-Western reformers – but they cannot overcome the momentum of Russian authoritarianism.

We were so hopeful about democratic change, free enterprise and a non-polar world. Kaliningrad reminds us that change and reform is not a straight line. Maybe in time, the individuals and organizations we helped will emerge as a grassroots movement that embraces Western values, ends corruption, and engages in democratic reforms.

Workshop in Moscow

As Will Bullock and I flew back to Moscow, he noted an e-mail from the Minnesota staff who wanted information on tourism. At this point, we had been traveling and working for three straight weeks without rest.

We schemed on the flight and decided after the three-day workshop, that I was to lead, we would send the three Land O'Lakes headquarter staffers outside Moscow to develop "volunteer assignments." We laughed and chose to send them to the most difficult former communist leaders and old-style Soviet institutions that we could think of. They loved it and returned excited and motivated about the challenge. As a reward, and at my expense as "not allowable" under USAID rules. I treated everyone to a night at the Bolshoi ballet.

The free enterprise leaders we met – many of whom had been communist officials -- had an uphill battle with corruption. Most privatization efforts resulted in giving "public property" to communist functionaries or to the mafia and giving worthless share capital to farmers. It was impossible to do business without "corruption and bribes."

Privatization in Russia

Similar to people-to-people programs, I designed a proposal for privatization programs in Russia that would rely on company-to-company assistance between similar types of firms.   Shock economic plans in which state companies were immediately privatized may have worked in the Czech Republic and Poland, but generally they resulted in massive economic suffering in Russia. Reform governments fell as a result of the displacements and hardships.

The concept behind the Western approach to privatization was to sell shares of public companies to their citizens since they were basically owned by them in the socialist economy. It seemed to have worked in Eastern Europe but was a failure in Russia.

There the communists, nomenclature, KGB, and mafia controlled the process and repressed the emerging democrat parties and business leaders. Economics is tied to politics. Russia did not have honest and competent leadership to lead the transition to a market economy. Jeffery Sachs, the well-known Harvard economist and Russian advisor, advocated shock therapy and immediate privatization. He resigned because he found corruption was growing.

There was an alternative approach to privatization that Margaret Thatcher carried out in Great Britain. Like most privatization schemes, it favored those who are strongest in control of the market and hurts public employees and their unions. She famously privatized the railroads and auctioned off restaurants at the stations to private entrepreneurs.

I wrote a USAID proposal for privatization which relied on the US consulting group, Tower Watson that had acquired the company which designed the Thatcher program. The proposal had a consortium of major US international companies (Texas Instruments, 3M, and Land O'Lakes) to provide advice in the transition to private ownership. The underlying assumption was that Russia had to have in place an independent regulatory system prior to beginning to privatize and selling state companies by sectors. Otherwise, the sale of shares is rigged, often on the cheap, steered to insiders and to the political, often corrupt, and powerful.

My proposal made the finals, against several large U.S. accounting firms (Deloitte, Ernest & Young, and PricewaterhouseCoopers) that wanted to use the USAID funds as "lost leaders" to enter Russian accounting markets. Unfortunately, Tower Watson was unwilling to provide consulting services at USAID rates so I lost the proposal.

Agricultural privatization was slow. Starting in 1993, the privatized kolkhoz and sovkhoz collectives became corporate farms. Household plots continued as before from the Soviet period. Not until the 1990s, did "peasant farms" begin to emerge and now these farms and private plots control about 20% of agricultural land and increased agricultural outputs from 26% in 1990 to 59% in 2005. Most of these changes could only occur with land reforms in 2002 and real ownership including the right to buy and sell land and own buildings. It is fair to say that volunteer U.S. people-to-people assistance helped in this transition.

However, the grassroots democrats and free market entrepreneurs were not able to overcome the stacked, entrenched, and corrupt political system. I was so hopeful and equally depressed when nearly all of the former Soviet bloc countries became more authoritarian often led by former so-called reformed communists.

Chapter 21: Farming Reforms in Georgia

In the 1995 final evaluation for Tri-Valley as they terminated their relationship with USAID, Derek Brown and I flew to Georgia to review their projects there. We drove to a valley beneath the Caucasian mountains where fighting was destroying nearby Grozny and the Russians had cut off hydro-electric power to Georgia.

Relief organizations imported kerosene heaters to get families through the winter, including our staff who huddled around their heater in the kitchen most nights.

Turkish bath in Tbilisi

Georgia produces brandy. At an ancient Turkish bath, I met a California brandy expert who just got fired from the project which was financed by former Secretary of State George Shultz. He said he tried to teach the workers about quality but failed. He brought in Remy Martin, Hennessy, and Courvoisier brandies, took the labels off, and had a taste test. The workers preferred their own foul-tasting brandy. With that, he said," I gave up."

Forth century Svetitskhovel Cathedral

We visited the most famous cathedral outside of Tbilisi. We were told the legend that the priest who was architect's patron had his right arm cutoff so that he could never design a better one. The arm was symbolized in a relief on the north wall. At the service, I listened to Gregorian chants from one end to the other in the sanctuary.

We drove to the Alazani project site along roads without signs, asking people at each turn for directions. With no open gas stations, it was not easy to get gas which was sold by individuals in jerry cans along the way. Our driver was a recently graduated doctor who could not find work.

When the collectives collapsed, farmers just took the cattle, and often even the bricks and telephone wires to their own houses. They feared that the "authorities" would take back the cattle that they acquired.

"When I considered joining the association, is it like the communists? Are you going to take my cattle?" a woman farmer told me about the newly formed Alazani Valley Growers Association. It's a serious question since many farmers assembled small herds when the state farms and collectives disintegrated as Georgia broke away from the former Soviet Union in 1992.

The 100 farmer-strong Alazani Valley Growers Association was the first bottom-up farmers' group that Tri Valley Growers adviser Sarb Basrai helped get started. "They needed confidence and some legal advice so I got them together with the Tbilisi young lawyers association in preparing by-laws," he said.

Local farmers in this fertile valley under the shadow of snowcapped Caucasian mountains joined the association to advocate for private land. Most farmers leased plots from the former state farms and many of these leases were up that year.

"If you don't sell us land, people will starve. Farmers will not plow anything without ownership," said Jemal Khiatashvili, chairman of the association. I was impressed when I visited his home which was lined with books.

Alazani Valley Growers Association

417

These farmers participated in the Tri Valley project to distribute wheat and corn seeds. However, much of the land in this rich agricultural valley remained fallow because of lack of inputs and credit. At the time, some 26,000 of the 400,000 private farmers in Georgia were members of the Private Farmers Union (PFU) that received repeated technical assistance from Tri Valley advisors.

In 1994, the director and deputy director Raoul Babounashvili and Koba Kobaladze came to the U.S. for one-month training where they spent time on an Iowa corn farm. "We didn't know how important it was until TVG began bringing in hybrid corn seeds and we helped distribute them and tell farmers how best to plant them," said Koba Kobaladze. "We transferred our personal knowledge from Iowa about plant chemicals, soil preparation, storage, and types of hybrids directly here," he said.

Six-foot tall and blond, volunteer Sue Wilkinson made a lasting impression on the PFU staff. "She was particularly helpful," Raoul Babounashvili said, "since she taught us modern desktop publishing and computerized our accounting system." She designed a data bank on PFU members with crop and other information. Tri Valley Growers contributed a computer, printer, scanner, copier, and software for the only private farmers' publication in Georgia.

When Ed Plissey held a seminar at the PFU on growing potatoes with the minimum use of herbicides, it was the first time that Georgian farmers learned about the US experience with potatoes. "We wrote a series of articles based on his lectures for the newsletter," said Raoul Babounashvili "that points out the importance in rotating potato varieties to avoid viruses and the need for quality potato seeds. We are trying to get potato seed production started here in Georgia as a result."

Restarting corn and wheat production

The Asgrow Seed company was about to burn its excess maize seed before they received a call from Luke Hingson of the Brother's Brother Foundation, which links donors of commodities and medical supplies with development and relief organizations around the world.

Hearing about the availability of seeds through Save the Children, Derek Brown, the Tri Valley project manager, saw the opportunity to combine donated seeds and US experts to jump start Georgia's agricultural economy and strengthen some 25,000 private farmers. "The window of opportunity was brief because American seed producers do not want to hold excess seeds after they've cleared all their orders. So, we took the risk and got the seed, then, figured out how to get it to Georgia," said Derek Brown.

Fortunately, Save the Children in Georgia financed the transportation costs, and Tri Valley local staff handled the logistics. The four containers of American seed, along with additional seed purchased in the region, resulted in the delivery of 122 tons of hybrid corn seed just prior to spring planting. "The timing had to all work out," Derek said. "Other donors had promised seeds and other inputs, but we delivered."

In addition, Tri Valley brought in 150 tons of parent wheat seed for multiplication provided to 10,000 private small farmers in 26 districts in time for the fall planting. Tri Valley imported fertilizer and herbicide for winter wheat planting. "Key to the project's success," Derek Brown said, "was the use of US volunteers to help select the right seeds and make sure they were properly planted."

The American hybrid corn acclimated very well to local conditions. It was found to be drought and wind-resistant," according to Raul Babjuashvili of the Private Farmers Union. "In some districts, we had record crops of 12-14 tons per hector," he said. The increases in yields were 2 or 3 times higher than local varieties. The farmers became believers in high quality US hybrid seeds that outperformed expectations with five or six ears per stock rather than one or two.

Research station

Dramatic changes occurred as the result of two visits by Mathias Kolding, a retired plant breeder from Oregon State. On his first trip, he helped develop the wheat seed program and selected the American cultivars which made up the 40-metric ton of wheat seed sent to Georgia. On the second visit, he brought 1,157 wheat and 150 corn varieties to facilitate local breeding and research. These publicly-held as well as many private and patented varieties bred by him were worth about $100,000 and would cost a research institution millions of dollars to replicate.

I observed the experimental seed fields at the Mitskheta research station, located in the ancient capital of Miskheta. The cross-breeding combines the best genetic attributes of American and Georgian wheat that is multiplied and supplied to local farmers. It is believed that wheat originated in the Caucasus so this program truly merges the old and new worlds.

"We were very surprised Matt Kolding did it for us. He brought everything with him. It's the very best seeds of American science," said Jurnber Patiashvili, Director of the station. "Before we could get only poor-quality seeds from the Soviet Union," he added.

Tri Valley provided people-to-people assistance in the transition to private agriculture. Agricultural collectives collapsed and land was dispersed into individual plots. By 1995, the agricultural sectors had mostly recovered. Due to the on-going conflicts with Russia including its support for the breakaway states of Abkhazia and South Ossetia, most Georgian products, especially wines and processed foods, are shipped to Ukraine and other former Soviet Union republics.

Tri-Valley was present during this most critical transition to private agriculture.

Overlooking historic Miskheta in Georgia

Chapter 22: Market Reforms in Ukraine

I thought that the Ukraine was more promising than Russia since we would be working with Western-oriented leaders along the Polish and Hungarian borders. They were more Euro-centered than Ukrainians in the east by the Russian borders.

In 2000, I visited the Horachek farm and retail store near L'viv, across the border from Poland. The store was founded in 1988 when Myroslav Horachek received a government grant that helped privatize his store and expand his farming operations. Most startups involved vertical integrated family enterprises since trust and legal protections did not exist in buying or selling among individuals or businesses.

In early 1997, due to the demand for milk, Horachek decided that he wanted to increase his own milk production and build a bigger herd.   Because Horachek had been involved primarily in trade prior to receiving his land, he had no formal training in agriculture. He asked for an American advisor.

In September 1997, Lee Stadnyk of Land O'Lakes worked closely with him to balance several different feed rations utilizing ingredients readily available on the farm. Horachek noted that prior to the assignment he had known almost nothing about animal nutrition. As a result of this new information and changes in the rations, milk production increased by 15%.

Lee recommended that the farm enlarge a well to increase water for the herd so the farm could expand to twenty head of cattle. Horachek purchased young 3- to 4-month-old calves. At the time, the Horachek farm was the best private family farm I have ever seen either in Ukraine or in Russia. It was well managed and prosperous.

I recall the conversation with Horachek who was probably in his early 30s. His grandfather was present, easily in his 80s. I asked the son, "Could I ask your grandfather about Stalin's forced collectivization?" Reportedly, they killed 20 million so-called Kulaks, who were really the more progressive Ukrainian farmers. His grandfather related to me that his wife and two children died of starvation, and most of his family was sent into exile. He never heard from them again. Then, tears welled up and he broke down and could not continue. I thanked him profusely.

Baptist bakery

I next drove to the Leshko Bakery which is a good example of the great impact that a small group can have when it bans together for the sake of the entire community. The Soviet system deprived its citizens of mutual trust. Trust is essential to private enterprise, and especially in group-based businesses and cooperatives.

The close relationship between the Baptist Church and the Leshko Bakery provides a model for how trust can be restored. In the small Vekyki Luchky community, the bakery and retail operation makes and sells bread, baked goods, and pasta in southwestern Ukraine.

Its close ties with the local Baptist community began six years earlier when US Baptists offered the community two used baking ovens. In 1992, Yuri Leshko stepped forward and built the facility and obtained the rest of the equipment to open the bakery. This new business employs 23 members from the local Baptist community. It demonstrated a new way of doing business.

Leshko contributes 30% of the bakery's income to the church. The bakery was making possible construction of a new church for the local congregation next to the bakery. The church, in turn, had a daycare facility that provided working parents, including several bakery employees, with a safe, reliable childcare option. In accordance with their religious beliefs, the bakery does not have any locks on its doors. Not only has this not led to any thefts, but Leshko believes that the business has not been approached by the ever-present protection racket because of the bakery's religious connections.

Over the course of the week he spent at Leshko Bakery in June 1997, Trevis Gleason discovered several problems with the bread-making process and provided useful advice to correct them. For example, the yeast is now mixed in water which eliminates the unpleasant yeast smell that otherwise results, and helps the dough rise more quickly. In addition, salt is added only at the end of the dough-preparation process, which allows the gluten to form more quickly and the dough to rise fully. The bakery profits have grown by 15% as a result.

The bakery was operating around the clock, two shifts to maximize production. During peak times, they are not able to meet demand. The Land O'Lakes advisor introduced the bakery's employees to a more efficient technique of bread placement in the ovens. This method increased total oven capacity from 90 to 150 loaves and saves energy.

Agricultural university

We drove over the mountains to Transcarpathia on the Hungarian border. After Ukraine gained its independence in 1991, this region became the first to grant parcels of land to residents. Many individuals in Transcarpathia became landowners and private farmers. Most had little or no experience in farming, and even fewer had entrepreneurial skills to run a business.

Ukraine's agricultural schools were ill-suited for the transition to private agriculture. Since schools were developed to support the Soviet agricultural system of subsidized state and collective farms, their curricula were not relevant to small independent farmers. The knowledge and access to information on modern farming techniques and statistics was limited.

Mukachevo Agricultural Technical School is a 4-year institution of higher learning in the southwestern region. Land O'Lakes recruited Dale Donovan, a private farmer and educator with many years of teaching experience; he provided assistance in curriculum development to make the technical school responsive to the needs of the emerging private agricultural sector.

Donovan updated the content of their courses, provided educational materials to be translated, and taught instructors about agribusiness marketing, bookkeeping, and management. He shared how to develop agricultural statistics. The assistant director said, "The statistics for farming in the West are especially important because they allow us to gauge our own performance and compare it to what is truly possible."

I learned about the pervasive corruption in Ukraine during this visit. At a private restaurant, I noticed a group of policemen eating nearby. I ask the owner about the policemen. He said that he had to provide free meals to 17 different police, building, and health inspectors, and other government officials; otherwise, they will close him down. At the restaurant, a young female student at the nearby university told me that she had to bribe the administration to get into the school, and then every professor to get into classes and again to receive her grades.

Fruit and vegetable proposal

My most challenging assignment for the Ukraine was to position Land O'Lakes, a dairy cooperative, to manage a USAID fruit and vegetable project. The competitors for the Ukraine Agricultural Marketing Project (AMP) had spent months preparing for the RFA. With only ten days in Ukraine, I had a leg up because our proposed Chief of Party, Robert E. Lee, was well-known by USAID/Ukraine staff for his work on land privatization. (He is not related to the General Lee of the Civil War.)

The RFA had a requirement to rank and select oblasts to work in. On a visit to a Costco-type grocery store, I found that they had plenty of imported canned goods, but few fresh vegetables. That would be the focus and engine of the proposal.

Andry Yarmak

I knew the proposed deputy, Andry Yarmak, who had helped us in the marketing component of the Macedonia Seal of Quality project. He was the leading Ukrainian agribusiness market expert, frequent commentator on the air and worked with the first agribusiness information services. He works for the U.S. Food and Agriculture Organization (FAO) where in 2015 I visited him in Rome.

426

I asked him "Why don't we have the consulting staff call around, identify the best oblasts where there are leading fruit and vegetable companies and local NGOs we would work with?"

I thought we would fly to Dnipropetrovsk where APK-Inform is headquartered, the only agricultural information company in Ukraine. "No," he said, "We will take the overnight train." We talked on the train about the tension between the Eastern pro-European and the Western pro-Russian regions. It was the first time that I had visited the Russian-oriented city of Dnipropetrovsk. We won the proposal because we assembled the best team and had the best information from our marketing survey.

A primary objective of the project was the formation of farmer groups and associations to join forces and gain benefits by working together. This helped farmers obtain higher prices and, through group buying, pay less for input supplies and equipment. The project, known as Agricultural Marketing Project (AMP), united farmers in creating joint facilities – storage and packing - to help extend the season and increase prices, by selling directly to rapidly growing grocery chains. The project assisted 42 farmer groups with 1,250 members with marketing, planning, and organizational assistance.

For example, Oleksandr Kravchenko was a successful leader and newcomer to agriculture. In 2003, he produced tomatoes on 18 hectares of non-irrigated land. By the 2006 season, his cooperative formed with his friends cultivated 118 hectares and sold their products directly to retail chains and processors. The cooperative managed a cold storage facility, cucumber sorting line, and a washing, sorting and packing line. He said, "Increased incomes and a growing number of jobs have proved the effectiveness of the cooperative's activities."

The project's Market Information System (MIS) improved decision-making. It provided targeted client groups in the supply/value chain with technical and marketing ideas, market news, price information, commodity forecasts, and purchase/sale opportunities on fruit and vegetable markets throughout Ukraine.

The AMP project developed and implemented a unique market information system which included data collection, analysis, and presentation. The information was used to evaluate up-to-date data on fruit and vegetable prices in the different regions of Ukraine and identified new sales opportunities and market channels.

Retail prices for 42 target commodities monitored at farmers 'markets and supermarkets in 16 regional centers were reported weekly to readers. The market information system posted about 1,200 "bids and offers" weekly from producers, buyers, and farm input suppliers.

Yaroslav Mayovets said, "With the help of AMP and thanks to advertising in Agrooglyad, Vegetables and Fruits journal, I sold my products to a canning factory while not one of my colleagues sold anything. I hope for further successful cooperation."

This Land O'Lakes project achieved impressive results: $44 million in sales, 4,745 seasonal and 1,096 permanent jobs, and a robust and leading Market Information System with 30,000 users monthly. It helped create and support 42 fruit, berry and vegetable cooperatives and farmer's groups, increased production by 20%, improved quality, packaging, and linked them to fast growth urban markets.

I returned to Kiev, the capital of Ukraine, several times to develop additional projects. I tried to link the AMP project for agricultural credit with an on-going Canadian credit union project where all of the staff from Toronto spoke Ukrainian.

I wrote a proposal to address human trafficking since Ukrainian women were recruited by friends and relatives and turned over to traffickers at the border to Russia or sent to the Middle East. Most of these women came from rural areas with little hope of jobs. They were lured abroad as cocktail waitresses or dancers but abused and put into brothels. We hoped to help develop rural jobs as a way to prevent this trafficking.

I traveled there in the winter in which Robert Lee said, "It is warmer in Kiev than at my home in Maine" as he showed me a picture of snow up to the rafters of his house.

Some of the most dynamic AMP results occurred in Crimea, Donetsk, and Luhansk – conflict zones - now cut off from their traditional markets in Ukraine. The project proved that farm associations can link different ethnic regions.

A new USAID country team arrived in Ukraine and decided to terminate this successful Land O'Lakes project in favor of a project that promoted government reforms. That project was a total failure due to corruption and a weak government with little real commitment to reforms.

The world witnessed the growing tensions that later unfolded in the Ukrainian and Russian conflicts. I did not anticipate the annexation of Crimea by Russia in March 2014, or the war in Donbass in April 2014. Nor, the thousands of protestors in Independence square next to the hotel that I stayed in who fought for democratic and anti-corruption reforms.

Development assistance is no match against armed revolts and conflicts that divide nations. It was easy to see how corruption, greed, and bad governance held back Ukraine. The country is a long way from becoming Western and integrated into Europe.

The former Soviet Union countries rank at the bottom of transparencies corruption indexes, worse than many African countries. While helping the rising class of private businesses, they faced corruption in contracts, issuance of permits, and law enforcement as well as land distribution, titles and construction. As a new form of imperial nationalism arose fueled by economic depression, there remains pervasive and systematic corruption in Russia, Georgia, and Ukraine.

AMP-supported women selling fruits and vegetables

Chapter 23: Sweet Retirement

"15, 12, 9, 6, 3, 0" was my countdown. I began counting for retirement, not by days but board meetings – three a year - which I managed as executive director of OCDC. At age 62, I could take full retirement from the National Rural Electric Cooperative Association and my 401(k) in a lump sum on my birthday, July 19, 2005.

Retirement did not mean I would end my efforts to create cooperatives. It gave me an opportunity at my own pace to promote Fair Trade cocoa cooperatives another ten years.

I gave my board a two-year notice that I would retire and urged them to take charge of the organization. I was the founder and provided most of the leadership. They undertook a comprehensive review of OCDC – at least one member wanted to disband it, but most saw its value in earmarking Congressional funds and accessing USAID leadership.

For the last 20 years, I had an arrangement with OCDC to work 75% of my time for the coalition and 25% as a consultant to its members. In fact, the ratio was reversed in which I mostly wrote proposals. Without any contract for 23 years, I got positive reviews; many members valued my ability to raise specific USAID funds for their organizations.

After July 2005, I stepped down progressively into retirement. For the first year, I worked for NRECA International and Land O'Lakes International four days a week; the next year, I worked solely for Land O'Lakes two days a week, and then I became a consultant with my own hours and worked from home.

I had read a book, *My Time* by Abigail Trafford who recommended in retirement doing what you loved as a teenager before you had to work for a living. I wrote to her how important the book was in planning my retirement.

In a *Washington Post* column, she wrote, "Some sailors change the way they sail as a way to shift to this new stage of life. Ted Weihe of Arlington has sailed all his life. 'If I'm not doing it, I'm thinking about it, I'm reading books about it,' he says. As a teenager, he raced on the Chesapeake Bay and belonged to the Sea Scouts. As a student at Georgetown University, he sailed a catamaran on the Potomac.

Last year, he decided to retire from OCDC. At the same time, he stopped cruising, downsized to a smaller boat and returned to racing. "It's going back to his youth – going back to being a teenager," says Weihe, 61.

His personality hasn't change, it's his life that is changing, racing sailboats is a way for him to keep his competitive identity– and do what he loves to do."

I assumed that Judy and I would stay in Arlington where my 95-year-old mother at the time lived in Goodwin House, a nearby Life Care Facility. One day we were talking to her about living there and she said, "It is the happiest time of my life." With her comment, I felt that we could move – at least to Annapolis to be near our sailing club.

Judy had other ideas – she wanted to move to Florida. I told her, "I hate Jacksonville, Orlando, Fort Lauderdale, Miami, Tampa, but would consider Sarasota where I had raced my Shearwater

Catamaran in 1964." I knew that there were excellent winds for small boat racing.

Judy found a rental apartment for a month in Sarasota, and we loved the city. The next year, we bought a two-bedroom villa. She totally gutted it and made it a model home. We were now snowbirds with a 17-hour drive from Arlington to Sarasota.

Watching a blizzard over Washington on TV, we decided that we did not want our house vacant during the harsh winters where a neighbor's homes had experienced water flooding from frozen pipes and sewage backups. We decided to follow what I thought was my new dream to sell the house in Arlington and move to Annapolis. We bought a townhouse, but traffic was about as bad as in Arlington, and our sailing club had lost its allure.

That winter, I was writing a proposal in Annapolis while Judy was in Sarasota. I said to myself, I can write proposals just as easily in Sarasota so got on the next airplane to the warmth of the south. At this point, we knew that we did not want to be snowbirds, sold the Annapolis townhouse, and bought a larger house in Sarasota on a small lake with a pool, and high ceilings to display model boats that I had collected from my travels around the world.

There was another reason to leave Arlington. I had chaired or served on nearly every civic organization and neighborhood association. My moto was: Act *locally and globally* – I did. I was finished, I wanted to focus on sailing year around.

My last efforts were to reform residential zones to limit "McMansions." This effort took 11 years to achieve. On the Planning Commission, I championed LEAD certifications (environmental and energy sustainable buildings) for all new high rises. Both efforts were successful, but I was tired of the late-night meetings – I had nothing else that I wanted to achieve civically.

I remained committed to volunteering in Sarasota, and I found new ways by promoting small racing sailboats, teaching courses at an adult education program on Fair Trade and serving as Rear Commodore of my sailing club in Sarasota.

CONACADO cocoa project

I had written proposals for others to manage. Now, I would manage and direct one myself. My involvement with cocoa coops began in 2007 with a proposal I wrote for Land O'Lakes to work with CONACADO, a successful organic and Fair Trade cooperative in the Dominican Republic. The goal was to link small cocoa farmers more closely into U.S. markets given the recently-approved free trade agreement.   While most of CONACADO's cocoa beans were sold to European companies, new opportunities were emerging in the U.S. artisan markets.

I felt Land O'Lakes was a good match since they invented Cocoa Classics, a chocolate drink, and were the major supplier of dairy ingredients to both Mars and Hershey's. Milton Hershey located his chocolate plant in Pennsylvania dairy country since milk products are a more significant ingredient than chocolate. Land O'Lakes' Carlyle Pennsylvania plant owned by Mennonite dairy farmers supplies most of its dairy products to Hershey.

My challenge was to identify opportunities for CONACADO sales to US fine chocolate companies. The first name that came to mind was Timothy Moley, founder of Chocolove. I knew him from his volunteer assignments in the early 1990s to Sumatra, Indonesia for a feasibility study of Indonesian spices.   In 1995, he came across cocoa trees there and decided to form his own chocolate company.

I invited him to visit CONACADO in the Dominican Republic to look at the potential to directly import their cocoa beans. He is committed to what he calls his "labor of love" with Chocolove, located in Boulder, Colorado. He said, ``There's a whole world of chocolate to explore - a world of creativity and experience analogous to music, art and wine. To make chocolate is an art by itself at the premium quality level." Adding that as quality manager, "Some days I'll eat half a pound of chocolate and end up pretty wired."

Moley at solar drying tunnel at CONACADO

With a background in wine, he believes that specialty chocolates will develop along the lines of wine, not specialty coffee. Since the flavor of cocoa beans tastes different in different countries, chocolate is closer to wine.

Timothy Moley said you can't have one without the other: love or chocolate. He brands his product as a premium chocolate delivered directly from the heart. The approach is accentuated by packaging that includes a romantic poem on the inside each bar.

I asked him how often he changes his poems, and he said, 10 to 12 times a year. With 25 plus flavors, he runs through about 250 poems a year and has only about 300 that he likes. Scientific studies demonstrate that chocolate and love have similar psychoactive compounds (theobromine) that improve moods and happiness.

He puts an historic stamp on each chocolate bar to honor his father who was a philatelist. Moley was willing to come to the Dominican Republic on my volunteer assignment because he wanted time for himself since his father had just died.

One of Timothy's recommendations was to copyright the name CONACADO so that buyers who were paying a premium for organic and Fair Trade cocoa beans could assure their customers of its origin. I wrote the copywrite application and was called by the agent at the Trade and Patient Office. When I said that I was not a lawyer, she hung up. I needed a lawyer to complete the application. I knew Jonathan Kenney, a prominent Arlington lawyer since he came often before the Planning Commission. His office provided pro bono service as I explained to him that CONACADO represented some of the poorest farmers in the Dominican Republic. Subsequently, the copyright was granted and later extended.

At a World Cocoa Foundation meeting in D.C., I came across Dr. Ray Schnell of the U.S. Department of Agriculture who is a world expert in cocoa breeding. With a tropical experimental station in Puerto

Rico, less than 45 minutes away by plane, he and his colleagues had not looked at cocoa breeding programs in the Dominican Republic.

Timothy Moley put me in touch with Brian English at the U.S. experiment station in Puerto Rico who led the study. I arranged for these USDA experts to visit the key government officials and the Horticulture Research Station in Mata Largo. Working closely with Jaime Gomez, they carried out the first and only national survey of cocoa genotypes (varieties) in D.R. They closely examined several cocoa trees at the research station that had been.

At the same World Cocoa Foundation meeting, I met John Kehoe, who headed his own brokerage company, EcoTrade in Miami. He had worked for E.F. Mann, a major cocoa buying company in the Dominican Republic so was familiar with CONACADO and its managers whom I had brought to the conference.

I asked him to prepare a report about how the cooperative could take advantage of emerging opportunities for Fair Trade, organic chocolates in U.S. In a twist of fate, John left his own company and began to work for Timothy Childs, the founder of TCHO, an avid supporter of the Burning Man festival (he loves large movable sculptures), and an entrepreneur.

I asked John and Timothy to visit CONACADO as potential sources for their cocoa beans. When they arrived, John had his shoulder in a sling from a cycling accident the week before, and Timothy broke his toe trying out kiteboarding, a few days earlier. My first job was to take Timothy to a women's medical clinic for a cast.

They hobbled around to see CONACADO fermentation centers and a recently acquired processing plant. Jamie Gomez, a founder of CONACADO and my project consultant, was our guide and had earlier collected the cocoa leaves throughout the Dominican Republic for analysis by Dr. Schnell.

TCHO

In 2005, Louis Rossetto and Timothy Childs launched TCHO whose motto is "where technology meets chocolate," applying new technologies to what was previously an old world, artisans' craft of chocolate making.

Prior to starting this new chocolate company, Rossetto and his wife, Jane Metcafte, were founders of *Wired Magazine* which ushered in the "digital culture." They started the magazine with about $30,000 and sold it for many millions.

Timothy Childs was the brain child behind TCHO. Earlier he co-founded Cabaret Dessert Chocolates which relied on a single-origin cocoa from Venezuela, which proved unstable. He left TCHO to start a new venture in importing Pisco Sour (fortified wine) from Peru. John Kehoe said, "TCHO believes that dark, high percentage cocoa, varietal, and origin labels are placeholders for knowing what chocolate actually tastes like. As with wine, what you taste is precisely, and only, what's in the fruit itself."

"We're committed not only to making the best chocolate possible, but, also to making a better world," said Chief Chocolate Maker Brad Kintzer, noting that their deep connection with cocoa farmers is probably the key ingredient for TCHO's success.

Brad Kintzer (right) inspecting cocoa beans at Acopagro

Kintzer has a serious background in chocolate, having worked at Scharffen Berger where I first met him when I brought CONACADO's Operation Manager, Abel Fernandez, on a marketing trip to San Francisco. When Hershey's bought, and closed down Scharffen Berger, Kintzer moved to TCHO which has recently relocated from Pier 17 in San Francisco to a larger facility in Berkeley. The early investors are now minority partners to a German holding company that is substantially investing in promoting the TCHO brand nationally. In 2018, a Japanese company bought the company that is expected to make major investments to expand its marketing nationwide.

I sponsored a CONACADO marketing trip to a natural foods expo in Boston where I met Rob Everts, co-president and Dary Goodrich, the chocolate manager at Equal Exchange.

When Land O'Lakes decided not to continue the CONACADO project, I searched around for an alternative sponsor. John Kehoe at TCHO followed up my earlier contacts with Rob Everts and Dary Goodrich. We began discussions on teaming up.

Equal Exchange

When Rob Everts joined Equal Exchange in 1997, he had 20 years of experience in organizing workers, consumers, and voters. He had worked for Cesar Chavez and Neighbor-to-Neighbor where he helped lead a successful nationwide boycott of Folger's coffee that did not support a peace accord in El Salvador's bloody civil war. He later moved to Costa Rica and worked as a consultant to UNICEF and another NGO.

Evert's experience with UNICEF had not been positive, and he was a skeptical of foreign assistance programs. My first challenge was to convince him that Equal Exchange could lead a different type of assistance program.

Dary Goodrich sampling chocolate

Dary Goodrich presented a different challenge. He is Equal Exchange's Chocolate Products Manager, which covers everything from producer relations and purchasing to new product development – which is growing at Equal Exchange.

Previously, he led Equal Exchange's interfaith programs where he met his wife. A new USAID project would add to his administrative burdens and already busy schedule and work load. He brings his family's Maine-frugality to his efforts by assuring that no funds are wasted or misdirected. I needed to assure Rob and Dary that I would do my best to reduce their workload as much as possible and monitor spending closely to benefit small cocoa farmers.

Initially, both were reluctant to take any government funds, so I explained that the USAID's Cooperative Development Program is flexible and consistent with their mission to help small farmer cooperatives. I had known the manager of this USAID program, Tom Carter, for two decades when he worked for dairy cooperatives in India. I told Rob Evert that, Tom Carter would love to have Equal Exchange in the program since his work in India focused on commercially linking Indian and US cooperatives which is what Equal Exchange does between small farmer coops and US natural food coops.

It was touch and go. The decision to apply for the USAID grant had to be agreed to by Equal Exchange's worker-owners. Just before the deadline for proposals, Dary Goodrich called me and asked, "Can we turn down the grant if we decide not to go forward?" I said, "Yes, but it is more difficult after you have a signed agreement with USAID." They were on the fence until just before the deadline.

Equal Exchange buys its products exclusively from some 50 producer coops and sells them through 175 U.S. natural food coops as well as 10,000 religious congregations, 100 specialty grocery stores, and others. As a profit-oriented worker cooperative, it is dedicated to linking small farmers' coops with American consumers. Equal Exchange is not interested in becoming a technical assistance agency but working with its supply cocoa cooperatives advances its own mission.

This was my opportunity to prove the points that I had been making that Fair Trade was a viable commercial way to strengthen small farmer cooperatives. I understood the unique cooperative aspects of Fair Trade. I gave a 2005 speech to a conference in Berlin on how U.S. cooperative development organizations supported Fair Trade specialty coffee coops in Ethiopia, Colombia, Rwanda, and East Timor.

My assistant Kate Surber and I wrote, *An Introduction to Fair Trade and Cooperatives: A Methodology.* In 2010, during the last year of the Land O'Lakes project with CONACADO in the Dominican Republic, I wrote two monographs: *How Certifications Affect Cocoa Cooperatives* and *The Importance of Quality in Cocoa Cooperatives*; both discuss Fair Trade, organic certification, and the importance of quality.

Equal Exchange's mission and passion to help small farmer cooperatives aligns with my beliefs. "Small Farmers, Big Change" is its slogan in which Equal Exchange builds long-term trade partnerships that are "economically just and environmentally sound; fosters mutually beneficial relationships between farmers and consumers and demonstrates the contribution of worker cooperatives and Fair Trade to a more equitable, democratic and sustainable world".

Equal Exchange's Big Change campaign starts with an idea: what if food could be traded in a way that is honest and fair, a way that empowers both farmers and consumers. The founders - Rink Dickinson, Jonathan Rosenthal and Michael Rozyne - envisioned a trade model that valued farmers and consumers. In 1986, with support from natural food stores and religious organizations, they started with Fairly Traded coffee from Nicaragua as a means to oppose U.S. policies supporting the Contras.

Equal Exchange is a democratic worker cooperative, an alternative to for-profit businesses and operates on democratic principles. It is not designed to maximize profits, nor returns to investors, but to bring to the workplace the rights and responsibilities that Americans hold as citizens in their communities.

Unfortunately, the U.S. Fair Trade which certifies fair trade standards and U.S. companies that follow them, pulled out of the international Fairtrade network, abandoned small farmer cooperatives and now works with large plantations and multinational companies. That is not Fair Trade as envisioned by Equal Exchange, alternative trading companies, and believers in promoting democratic cooperatives.

Fair Trade challenges the existing trade model, which favors large plantations, agri-businesses, and multi-national corporations. Instead, it supports small farmers and connects consumers and producers through information, education, and the exchange of products in the marketplace.

Underlying the Equal Exchange model is the belief that only through organizing can small farmers survive and thrive. The cooperative model is essential for building this change. Fair Trade is not a charity or a handout; it is simply a process of fair markets. Equal Exchange provides high-quality foods at a fair price to consumers. By cutting out the middleman, Equal Exchange pays the farmers more and gives customers a better value.

My pitch to Equal Exchange was that I would design a cooperative development project that fits their mission but expands it by strengthening their supply cooperatives with resources and technical assistance.

I told them that I knew all of the wrong ways to operate assistance programs and guaranteed them that I had an entirely different style consistent with their mission. It would put decision making in the hands of the partner coops; provide most of the resources to them; not rely on high cost expatriates; donate all overhead costs to project activities; and insist on solid indicators and quantifiable results for the small cocoa farmers as beneficiaries.

Despite initial concerns, John Kehoe, Rob Everts and Dary Goodrich agreed that TCHO and Equal Exchange would team up on a proposal to continue the Land O'Lakes efforts with CONACADO in the Dominican Republic and add Peru and Ecuador where both companies buy cocoa beans from cooperatives.

Equal Exchange was already buying CONACADO beans for processing in Holland where most cocoa is processed into its chocolate powder. They were interested in shortening their supply chain. They wanted to buy cocoa powder directly from the CONACADO processing plant, thus providing value-added cocoa to benefit small farmers.

John Kehoe linked me up with Pat Burke to help CONACADO bring the plant up to international standards. Burke grew up in his family's chocolate company, operated several processing lines, and is a major cocoa broker. With Pat's assistance, Equal Exchange is now directly shipping quality cocoa powder to the U.S., bypassing Holland.

Initially, the project focused on quality and productivity. As we launched the project, I could see that the partner cooperatives did not understand the underlying financial structure of self-reliant cooperatives: member equity.

I contacted two long-time colleagues, Bob Flick with years of overseas cooperative experience and Barry Silver who was vice president of the National Cooperative Bank – both Peace Corps volunteers who had worked in Ecuador and Peru respectively-- to help with cooperative finance, board and member education, and baseline studies. The three of us held in common the belief that the greatest failure of cooperative development is that they are not properly structured to operate as group businesses in which members must invest and build equity ownership.

John Kehoe hired Cristina Liberati at TCHO who helped coordinate the project for TCHO. She decided to move closer to her large Italian-American family in Rhode Island and in 2015 became the project coordinator at Equal Exchange.

She manages the day-to-day operations of the project with a close eye to detail. John Kehoe is now the director of sustainability for Guittard Chocolate. He remains committed to small cocoa farmers and defining cocoa on the basis of flavor.

From 2010 to 2015, the project succeeded beyond my expectations as I drafted a two-year extension through 2017. The underpinning rationale I wrote states:

"We believe that for small farmers to succeed in international markets, their cooperatives must not only collect and process their

*raw products but must also provide them with the technical
assistance that helps them to raise productivity levels, add quality
and thus value to that product through improved post-harvest
procedures, quality controls, and gain their loyalty and patronage
with member education and equity programs."*

The program's logic and hypotheses are: increased productivity and
quality results in higher sales and premiums from buyers and more
money to farmers; member equity plans generate allocated capital
and increased loyalty to the coop, and financially stable coops that
have invested in human capital are better able to supply the fine
chocolate markets. At the internal USAID review, the project
extension came in first out of ten proposals, and in the oral
presentation, a reviewer said, "It is the only one that focused on
member equity and coop sustainability."

Member equity

In numerous cooperative publications, I have emphasized the
importance of member equity: members provide products to the
cooperative for processing, and a portion of it is monetized and
placed in a long-term revolving fund.

Member equity is "quiet capital" that backs up bank loans or
finances infrastructure and other ways that the coop can grow.
While I have evaluated many coop projects, I can recall few that
successfully promoted member equity. I determined to change this
in the design and management of "my" project.

Bob Flick member training at Acopagro in Peru

In the first cooperative meetings that I had in Peru to begin implementation, I raised the member equity issue with managers who seemed eager to understand and implement it.

I asked Bob Flick to discuss member equity with managers and boards of cooperative partners. He attended the annual meetings of three cocoa coops in Peru, and two farmer associations in Ecuador to discuss its importance. I enlisted Barry Silver for his financial analysis especially on cooperative financial ratios. We designed training programs at the membership level and for delegates prior to annual meetings so they understood and supported the member equity plans.

At Acopagro, the manager and board instantly understood its importance. There had been a revolt by members who wanted to defund the cooperative and send "unallocated" capital back to themselves. On the other hand, "allocated" capital in the members' name would help increase loyalty and trust.

With help from Bob and Barry, we were able to shift resources from unallocated to allocated capital from the previous three years, thus immediately creating an equity revolving fund. Now members have a personal financial stake in their coop. Similar to an IRA, they can receive their money back on a revolving basis or when they retire, move, or sell their farms.

Our greatest success was Acopagro, the largest and most successful Fair Trade cooperative in Peru. In 2012, the general assembly meetings adopted and, in 2013, expanded their member equity plan based on the recommendations of their managers and boards of directors as well as the extensive field training we supported to their local committees and delegates.

Training workshop in cooperative capitalization

Acopagro increased member investment which stood at U.S. $192,000 in 2010 (baseline) to U.S $834,000 in 2014, a 334% increase. Since 2013, its capital position has become extremely sound (total capital to assets ratio of 28.8% with an optimum but rarely achievable 30%).

In October, 2016, the coop adopted a new check-off system that deducts 1% of the sales of each member with a 4% annual interest rate, rather 120 soles ($31.00) per year, per member that was insufficient to meet the cooperative's financial needs. Over five years, members will receive accumulated equity based on patronage. In 2016, all members were up-to-date with their equity payments and defaults on loans had decreased to a mere 2.53%.

In 2013, I made a presentation to the World Cocoa Foundation Partnership meeting in the Dominican Republic on *Cocoa Cooperatives: The Importance of Member Equity*. I said,

"Producer cooperatives are group-based businesses formed by like-minded farmers who, by joining together, realize economies of scale by lowering production costs, purchasing inputs such as seedlings and organic fertilizers, providing technical expertise and adding value to their products to domestic and international buyers. The farmers expect to increase the profitability of their farms through joining the cooperative. But, in most cases, the farmers do not appreciate or understand the business and financial obligations as a member of a co-operative.

Member equity is the defining characteristic of the cooperative model. Coop members provide the crucial flexible and patient equity capital to help achieve financial stability. "

My presentation was the first presentation to the chocolate industry that relies on cooperatives for chocolate beans and how they should be financially structured. Several audience members sought me out to say, "It is the first time anyone presented to us the importance of member equity in coops."

I tell cooperative leaders that member equity is not new. The history of Western cooperatives provides a roadmap where even poor farmers are capable of supporting their farm organizations such as the Raiffeisen system from the Black Forest's poorest regions in the 1890s, US agricultural cooperatives in the depth of the farm depression in the 1920s, and the Anal dairy co-operatives in India in the 1960s with over 12 million mostly lower caste women farmers with one or two cows.

In all of these coops, members invest through equity based on their usage. The three cocoa coops in Peru and similar savings approaches for a farmers' associations in Ecuador are following the same path.

Bob Flick, Barry Silver, and I drafted a guide: *Too Poor to Invest? The Case for Member Equity in Small Holder Farmer Cooperatives and Associations* offering a methodology to develop member equity plans. We hope to train cooperative and development experts in this critical importance for sustaining cooperatives. We presented the paper and discussed how to begin member equity programs at a Forum on Cooperatives in Development at the National Cooperative Business Association in October 2016 and continued the equity discussions at a workshop for cocoa and coffee cooperatives in Lima, Peru in April 2017.

Our document was revised and improved with expert cooperative writers and graphics staff and retitled: Not Too Poor to Invest: The Case for Smallholder Farmer Ownership. Accompanying the document, Dary Goodrich wrote:

In 2010, Equal Exchange embarked on a journey to partner in new and innovative ways with cacao and coffee co-operatives in Peru, Ecuador and Dominican Republic. With support from the USAID Co-

450

operative Development Program, we set out to develop a project focused on three key factors for cooperative success: quality, productivity, and capitalization. Through conversations with our farmer partners and several cooperative and financial experts, we realized that many farmer cooperatives and associations in Latin America are missing a key component of the cooperative principles - financial investment in the cooperative by members through Member Equity Programs. Over the last seven years, we supported six farmer organizations in building strong member equity programs, allowing farmers to have an ownership stake in their cooperative and build a stronger capital base for the business.

Through this project, we have learned much about member equity. Thanks to the work and original authorship of Theodore Weihe, Robert Flick and Barry Silver, as well as the support of a strong technical writing team of Catherine Ford, Ann Hoyt and Jenny Bernhardt, we are excited to share this document, which summarizes our key learnings (it will be translated to Spanish at a later date). By sharing this, we hope to generate better understanding of the need for member ownership in farmer organized cooperatives and associations, as well as to lay out the building blocks for organizations to implement a Member Equity Program of their own.

This document is the culmination of my many years working on behalf of cooperatives. It has been disseminated widely and taken seriously by cooperative development organizations.

In 2017, we invited Emily Varga to a member equity workshop in Lima, Peru. In 2018, she replaced Tom Carter as the USAID position as coordinator of cooperative development programs. Working closely with her and as she said "getting back to cooperative basics", member equity became a critical component of the cooperative 2018 RFA. In their proposals nearly, all of the cooperative development organizations indicate that they will incorporate member equity into their next five-year programs. The Overseas Cooperative Development Organization has adopted member equity as part of their research agenda.

While it took eight years, my work with member equity in the Equal Exchange project has now ignited a broader effort to properly structure cooperatives so that they can become sustainable.

In 2015 after five years as its manager, I confidently turned over management of the project to Equal Exchange so that "they own the project," my goal all along. I have remained engaged as a consultant on member equity.

I published a book about the project: *Saving Fine Chocolate: Equity, Productivity and Quality in Cocoa Co-ops.* I feel there is now momentum within cooperative organizations on member equity so I can bow out.

Craig Lasher, Jim Cawley, Jason Gross, Beth Lehman, Ted Weihe, Beth Sheehy Jocelyn Rowe and Judith Hermanson at my retirement party from OCDC (left to right)

My retirement

At my OCDC retirement party in 2005, there were kind words about my cooperative career.

Tom Verdoorn and Kristin Penn of Land O'Lakes International Development wrote:

"Ted's help has been uniquely valuable in many ways--through his ideas and concepts, his commitment to development and cooperatives, his support of the poor and powerless, and many others. Ted was always willing to climb aboard one more airplane to visit one more village and provide one more idea on top of the hundreds of successful approaches he had already built into development programs--and, even into policies. He saw the system in its infancy and its youth and helped it grow and mature. He has left positive impacts everywhere, as few others have done.

For Land O'Lakes, Ted served as a guide through the start-up of our international development programs and has helped make our efforts more successful at every step. His vast knowledge of cooperatives and the developing world has helped us and the communities anticipate and build upon foreign assistance priorities as they have evolved across the global community.

I especially want to mention a side to Ted that many may not have seen-his uncanny ability to spot bright, capable and passionate individuals and strengthen their opportunities to succeed on their own- with his help and encouragement. He provides the challenges, helps with some of the guidance and is generous--always--with the credit. There is a roster of such people in our hearts, and Land O'Lakes is privileged to have seen and benefited often from that ability and wisdom.

Ted exemplifies and embodies the cooperative spirit that guides us all, and he helped us build and leverage our competencies and to achieve and contribute so much more together than we could individually.

Thus, we take this opportunity to acknowledge that Ted has gained our respect over the years and to add our acclaim to the new level of honor he holds within the development, cooperative, legislative and donor communities. For these successes, we remain in his debt."

Tom Carter, Coordinator for Cooperatives and my colleague at USAID said,

"Your contributions were not only on the grand playing fields of Congress and the Executive but found practical application in the large number of successful cooperative development proposals that you prepared. More than proposals, you were the architect of cooperative development designs that produced successful activities but, more importantly, left behind institutions that have not only survived, but have thrived. Whether in Chile, Poland, Bosnia or Ethiopia there are cooperatives today that have not only received resources but have benefited from your knowledge of cooperation and your wisdom in applying it.

Although you are often seen as the public voice of cooperative development, the private voice you have played in mentoring, hectoring, teaching and occasionally reprimanding cooperative development organizations have contributed to the growth and quality of all of them. Each reflects in its own way the touch of Ted Weihe."

It is humbling to be praised by my colleagues who supported me, listened to some of my crazy ideas and stood by my side as we advanced cooperative development.

Conclusions

When I grew up, I remember the duck and cover exercises at my elementary school. At Georgetown University, I saw world affairs as a contest between the West and communism. It is hard to image I would see the end of the Cold War in which the Soviet Union dissolved and Red China became our largest trading partner. Fascism vanished in Franco's Spain that I visited as a student and became a liberal democracy.

In my lifetime, there have been no wars between major countries on the European landmass. After the Vietnam war, peace returned to East Asia. Former Soviet bloc countries are becoming more integrated into Europe.

East Germany opened its borders and joyful students sledgehammered the Berlin War to smithereens. In Berlin, I stayed at a modern hotel next to the Check Point Charlie and visited the museum of martyrs who crossed those barbwire walls. The Iron Curtain fell, the Soviet Union dissolved and Russia emerged. Poland, Romania, Estonia and Ukraine were freed and became independent, democratic states and integrated into capitalist economic systems. I was present at these transitions from communism to free markets.

Proxy wars in Nicaragua and El Salvador and ethnic conflicts in the former Yugoslavia vanished. Dictators were replaced by democrats in the Philippines and Chile.

In the unstable Middle East, peace has lasted a generation between Israel and its Arab neighbors – Egypt, Jordan and Syria. After the Camp David Accords, I represented USAID in the Congressional hearings for the $2.5 billion annually given to Egypt and Israel to sustain the peace.

Yugoslavia broke up into seven republics, and after initial conflicts and genocide, are now the independent countries of Macedonia, Montenegro, Albania, Bosnia and Herzegovina where we supported entrepreneurs and struggling private companies and cooperatives.

In South Africa, apartheid was dismantled and where I helped disenfranchised Black farmers enter formerly closed markets.

While the sectarian conflict between North and South Sudan is mostly resolved, newly independent South Sudan has descended into ancient tribal warfare between Dinke and Nuer.

These events caught me by surprise. That I was able to promote democracy and free markets during in these transitions was unexpected. People-to-people programs bridged many Cold War barriers. They demonstrated that long-standing ideological differences can be overcome and understanding emerge among diverse peoples and cultures.

Today, the euphoria of the end of the Cold War has worn off. Many countries have reverted to more authoritarian governments, or collapsed entirely as failed states, no longer propped up by the great powers. Terrorism has replaced the nuclear arms standoff, yet Minuteman ICBMs remain a global threat to survival. They are relics of the Cold War. Nuclear modernization programs in Russia and U.S. are its echoes.

Every day the political and economic struggles and development challenges continue. There are more refugees today than when the Food for Furniture legislation sent food aid to millions in 1980. The two-state solution of Palestine and Israel remains stalemated over West Bank settlements.

Nation building has been a failure. In the post-Cold War period, we shifted our foreign policy focus from containment to political and ideological extension of US democratic and market views. Political transformation is up to the will of local actors who hold long-embedded habits and longstanding enmities or want to restore long-lost political traditions.

At an after-action 2002 conference held by the Rand corporation I attended, development professionals were sidelined in recovery efforts after the wars in Iraq and Afghanistan. Rather than take our advice to think small and provide assistance at the community levels, massive U.S. assistance corrupted these societies, and most resources were either squandered or stolen. These failures reinforced my view that people-to-people assistance to communities is more effective than government-to-government programs. I believe that projects that build independent sectors and grassroots leaders can build momentum to address corruption, crony capitalism and government reforms.

We cannot expect democracies as we know them to develop without setbacks and travails. Many countries are faux democracies with rigged elections, repression of a free press, and the shutting down of human rights and democratic NGOs.

Part of these state-building failures is the lack of democratic values that Americans take for granted. As Mónica Jimenez said, "Life in a democracy requires each person to understand his or her personal attributes and be aware of his or her rights and responsibilities." The fact that so many people in the US fail to vote, lack basic knowledge about our constitution and governance, and think the government is oppressive belies our own need for civic education.

Democracy is not only a system of government; it is a way of life. These values cannot be transplanted but must be internalized and built within societies. The best that we can do is to live up to our own democratic values and civic responsibilities. In the age of Trump, we have our work cut out for us to restore civic values, the value of government and our system of checks and balances.

The exporting of American values of free markets was mostlysuccessful. Capitalism does not explain how firms operate in an evolving market system. A more accurate perspective is to understand how resources are allocated throughout the economic system.

We taught budding groups of entrepreneurs that markets determine what to produce, how much was needed, when to produce it, and where to deliver it.   A company or a cooperative operates within this complex marketing system: prices, customer needs, competitors, regulation, and technological change. Technical assistance can help managers devise strategies to maximize value, profits, and investments.

In the former Soviet bloc countries, many citizens who resisted socialism embraced free enterprise. Projects and training in American practices of marketing, consumer relations, modern packaging, employee and management practices, and introduction of quality standards were rapidly adopted. Many of these enterprises prospered as they were integrated into European and international markets.

There were barriers to overcome: abrupt privatization of state companies, hyper-inflation, lack of trust in contracts and business relationships, pervasive bribes and red tape, lack of land tenure and an inability for farmers to get loans, large uneconomic and worn out factories and chambers of commerce that protected monopolies rather than support competition.

People-to-people assistance at the enterprise level generally worked. Broader economic reforms took longer and were only partly successful. People were motivated to launch, form, and build enterprises while reforms in government institutions were slow and difficult with entrenched bureaucracies. Many of the entrepreneurs we helped became leading business people in their newly market-based countries.

In developing countries, similar assistance efforts that we promoted in business development were not as successful as those in transition states. Some countries like Chile, Dominican Republic, and the Philippines made steady growth. Cooperatives and businesses prospered.

However, projects that I saw in Ethiopia, Haiti, Honduras, Malawi, Sudan, and Tanzania were less successful. They were hampered by stagnant economies where exporting American enterprise values had to overcome oligarchies, entrenched business elites, warlords, and tribalism.

Cooperatives faced unique challenges. In the former Soviet bloc, so-called cooperatives were part of Marxist ideologies that imposed top-down collectives rather than voluntary group businesses. Socialist practices and fragmented societies created inefficient state enterprises, and destroyed bonds of trust among entrepreneurs, critical to cooperation.

There are notable successes especially in Poland with its history of strong cooperatives before World War II. While formal cooperatives were difficult to form, cooperation took place, usually family-based or by like-minded business people who saw the advantages of working together. Excellent examples are two telecommunication cooperatives, the rapid growth of credit unions, dairy cooperatives and farm credit banks.

Many former Soviet bloc countries were slower to embrace free markets such as Romania, Russia and Ukraine because of entrenched oligarchs. While we helped form cooperatives in these countries, the lack of trust was sometimes crippling. Yet, Albania and Montenegro were exceptions where dairy and farm supply cooperatives took root.

In developing countries, cooperatives had to overcome an exploitative colonial legacy, mixed records of success, distrust among ethnic and tribal members, lack of supportive laws, over-regulation, donor financing rather than self-help and lack of member investment, among other problems

There are stunning successes: Cooperative insurance companies in Latin America reach the working poor. Cocoa cooperatives in Ecuador, the Dominican Republic, and Peru are growing with support from the global Fair Trade system. Pre-paid health insurance appears promising in Uganda. It is amazing that a rural electric cooperative survived in Yei, South Sudan.

It was a great honor to work with colleagues to promote democracy and free enterprise, especially cooperatives which contain both. There are universal values that can be adjusted and fit into different cultures, stages of economic development and shared on a people-to-people basis.

Each country I visited has a unique story and spirit:

Chileans are artistic and proudly show off their native art in their homes, not just for the tourist trade.

Haitians and Dominicans share the same island but are culturally distinct, hardworking and family oriented.

Guatemalans, Peruvians and Ecuadorians retain their pre-Spanish legacies in unique colorful native costumes, dances and music.

Estonians maintained a narrative in opposing communism that was passed down from mother to child, often through mythical stories.

Poles adopted rapid transformations benefiting from the only mass movement towards democracy -- accelerated by local elections and many American Polish investors.

Bulgarians had the easiest transition as one told me, "We tried communism, now we will try capitalism."

Russian women are extraordinary and drivers of change. They do everything: work, shop, and care of elders and are better educated than men.

Romanians were slower in adopting Western ways and struggle with corruption and poor governance. They flock to the outdoors every weekend, hiking mountains and hunting for wild mushrooms.

Palestinians are the most welcoming culture that I have ever experienced, inviting you to attend their weddings with a seat of honor.

In Malawi, I experienced a formal culture in which the family lined up and the husband went down the line to greet each child by age and finally his wife. At a general cooperative meeting, the "chief" greeted every member of the audience in which individuals stood up, said their names, and the chief acknowledged each one.

I was privileged to get to know many cultures and to witness and provide assistance in their transformations which was only possible through the encouragement, leadership and professional staff of the USAID who were willing to listen and approve projects I designed or evaluated.

As an advocate for people-to-people assistance programs, I lobbied for NGOs and cooperatives with central funding for over 20 years. These organizations have grown and matured into effective development agencies. They play a distinctive role in development as value-based and people-centered compared to purely financial support to governments. Unfortunately, some of these NGOs have become indistinguishable from large government contractors, a trend that I fought.

As a political appointee, member of USAID's Advisory Committee on Voluntary Foreign Aid, and leader of U.S. cooperatives, I am proud to have worked with six administrations, Republican and Democratic, that supported vital foreign assistance programs.

As a founder of the now powerful U.S. Global Leadership Coalition, I am optimist that smart power, engagement and development assistance will remain at the center of U.S. international values.

Sources

Preface

Davenport, Coral 2014, *Obama Builds Environmental Legacy with 1970 Law*, The New York Times, November 26, 2014.

Environmental Protection Agency 2011, *Detailed Summary: Clean Air Act Results*, EPA's peer-reviewed study, 2014

Hershey, Robert 1981, *Issue and Debate: Deregulation of Natural Gas*, The New York Times, May 16, 1981.

Introduction

James, Carol 1985. *Strengthening People-to-People Development into the 1990s: Clarifying the Vision*, U.S. Overseas Cooperative Development Committee, December 1985.

Weihe, Ted 2001. *A 20-Year Partnership*, International Outlook, Land O'Lakes International, 2001 Vol. 9, No 2, 2001.

Weihe, Ted. *Congressional Strategies for Development Cooperation Initiatives*, University of Michigan, 1988.

Weihe, Ted 1995. *Development Assistance and the Contract with America*, International Outlook, Land O'Lakes International, winter 1995.

Weihe, Ted 1997. *Models of Association Building: Land O'Lakes Experience*, November 1997.

Weihe, Ted. *Public Interest Lobbies in Emerging Democracies*, private papers, date uncertain.

Weihe, Ted. *The Art of Development: What We've Learned about How to do it Well*, private papers, date uncertain.

Weihe, Ted. *What Makes Good Technical Assistance*, private papers, date uncertain.

Chapter 1: Values Growing Up

Air Navigation Pioneer: Vernon Weihe Dies at 84. Obituary, The Washington Post, June 17, 1993.

Correspondence with Professor Jack Giles, July 24, 1964.

Craft, Kevin 2013. *When Metro Came to Town: How the fight for mass transit was won. And how its arrival left Arlington forever changed*, Arlington Magazine, November/December 2013.

Huntington, Samuel 1996. *The Clash of Civilizations and the Remaking of World Order*, Simon & Schuster, New York.

Quigley, Carroll 1961. *The Evolution of Civilizations: An Introduction to Historical Analysis*, Liberty Fund, Indianapolis, second edition, 1979.

Quigley, Carroll 1966. *Tragedy and Hope: A History of the World in Our Time*, Macmillan Company, 1966.

Shapiro, T. Rees, 2009. *A Local Life: Walter I. Giles, 89: GU professor served up a heady mix of rigor and enthusiasm*, The Washington Post, November 22, 2009.

Stokes, Bruce 1992. *How Carroll Quigley Made History*, National Journal, December 12, 1992.

The Link Flight Trainer, A Historic Mechanical Engineering Landmark, Roberson Museum and Science Center, Binghamton, New York, June 10, 2000.

Wcihe, Ted 2014. *Elizabeth Weihe: A Centennial Life*, available on www.lulu.com

Weihe, Ted 2016. *Vernon I. Weihe: Avionics Pioneer,* available on Amazon

Weihe, Ted 1974. *What Happens When Developers Plan a City?* Coalition on Optimum Growth, Inc.

Weihe, Vernon 1942. United States Patent Office, *Directional Antenna Controlled Craft Position Plotting Device*, Serial No. 451,645, renewed May 6, 1952

White, Frank 1993. Tribute to Vernon I. Weihe, Celebration of Life

Chapter 2: Life in the Air Force

Brewer, Lewis 2013. *The "Top Secret" Train Trip.* Personal correspondence but reflects my memoires of the trip.

Loory, Stuart, 1972. *Defeated: Inside America's Military Machine*, Random House (quoted my tie tack story).

Chapter 3: Moral Dilemma for a Missileer

Broad, William & David Sanger 2016. *Smaller Bombs Are Adding Fuel to Nuclear Fear*, The New York Times, January 12, 2016.

Burchard, Hank, 1972. *Emergency Attack Warning Proves to Be "Human Error"*. The Washington Post, February 21, 1972.

Cooper, Helene 2014. *Nuclear Corps, Sidelined in Terror Fight, Produces a Culture of Cheating*, New York Times, January 23, 2014.

Cooper, Helene 2014. *Reports of Cheating Prompt Review of U.S. Nuclear Launch Crews*, New York Times, January 28, 2014.

Cooper, Helene 2014. *92 Air Force Officers Suspended for Cheating on their Missile Exam*, New York Times, January 31, 2014.

Dumas, Lloyd 1980. *Human Fallibility and Weapons: as nuclear weapons systems become more sophisticated, technical and human errors may cause disasters*, The Bulletin of the Atomic Scientists, Vol 36, No 9, November 1980.

Ellsberg, Daniel 2017. *The Doomsday Machine: Confessions of a Nuclear War Planner*, Bloomsbury

Harkinson, Josh 2014. *Death Wears Bunny Slippers: Hanging out with disgruntled guys who babysit our aging nuclear missiles – and hate every second of it*, Mother Jones, November 10, 2014.

Hearings before Committee on Armed Services, United States Senate on S. 939, Part 2 of 5 Parts, pages 1662-1669.

McElroy, Robert, 1969. *Life with the Minuteman*, Newsweek, April 7, 1969.

Perry, William, 2016. *Why It's Safe to Scrap ICBMs*, New York Times, Sept. 29, 2016

Perry, William 2015. *My Journey at the Nuclear Brink*, Stanford University Press.

Pincus, Walter, 2007. *ICBM Crews' Work Largely Unchanged Since Cold War*, The Washington Post, November 23, 2007

Ripley, Anthony, 1972. *H-Bomb Duty: Alert for Armageddon*, The New York Times, April 4, 1972.

Robock, Alan & Owen Brian Toon, 2016. *Let's End the Peril of Nuclear Winter,* The New York Times, February 11, 2016.

Sagan, Scott 1995. *The Limits of Safety: Organizations, Accidents and Nuclear Weapons,* Princeton University Press.

Schlossser, Eric 2013. *Command and Control: Nuclear Weapons, the Damascus Accident, and the Illusion of Safety,* Penguin Books, New York.

Smith, Jeffrey 1997. *The General's Conscience: Why Nuclear Warrior George Lee Butler Changed His Mind*, The Washington Post Magazine, December 7, 1997.

Weihe, Ted, 1971. *Launch on the Count of Three. One…Two…Three,* The Washingtonian Magazine, May 1971.

Weihe, Ted, 1971. *When Armageddon Comes Will They Fire in the Hole*, Family, Army/Navy/Air Force/Times, November 17, 1971. Letters to the Editor, December 29, 1971, January 19, 1971.

Weihe, Ted, 1971. Private correspondence with Senators Symington, Miller and staff.

Chapter 4: An International Career

Craft, Kevin 2013, *When Metro Came to Town: How the fight for mass transit was won. And how its arrival left Arlington forever changed*, Arlington Magazine, November/December 2013.

Weihe, Ted, USAID Personnel files.

Chapter 5:   Undercover Trip to Haiti

Pear, Robert 1981, *Haitian Deportations Start; U.S. Orders Open Hearings*, New York Times, June 6, 1981

Chapter 6:   Saving a Million Lives

E-mail exchanges with Andy Maguire on the Food for Furniture Amendment.

Harley, Richard, 1980, *Congress ups food aid while toeing budget line,* July 9, 1980.

The source materials are in the author's files. The only public records are the Congressional Record, House Floor June 17, 1980, pages H 5103 to H 5109.

The reports on the boat crash are from *The Washington Post*, April 22, 1963 and April 24, 1963 without bylines.

Chapter 7: Palestine: The Seeds of Violence

Locy, Toni, 1997, *$4 million Tax Fraud Case goes to Trial*, Washington Post, January 29, 1997.

Locy, Toni, 1997, *Former Lobbyist's Day in Court Ends in Mixed Verdict*, Washington Post, March 11, 1997.

Kratka, Bruce, Gene Miller, David van Tijn. 1989. *Evaluation of West Bank/Gaza Cooperative Sector Projects,* TvT Associates, April 10, 1989.

Weihe, Ted 1986, *A Development Challenge: Strengthening West Bank and Gazan Cooperati*ves, U.S. Overseas Cooperative Development Council.

Weihe, Ted 1984, *Palestinian Cooperatives on the West Bank and Gaza: Findings from a study tour by U.S. cooperative Representatives,* U.S. Overseas Cooperative Development Council.

Weihe, Ted 1980, *Trip Report on CODEL McHugh to Near East – April 3-14, 1980.*

Weihe, Ted 1982, *Revitalized Advisory Committee on Overseas Cooperative Development*, NRECA newsletter.

West Bank: Accelerating Economic Growth in the West Bank, Quarterly report to USAID, July-September 2000.

West Bank: Accelerating Economic Growth in the West Bank, Final Report to USAID, February 2001.

Chapter 8: Mr. Cooperative

Goodwin, Lawrence 1978. *The Populist Movement: A Short History of the Agrarian Revolt in the America,* Oxford University Press, New York.

Hirschman, Albert 1984. *Getting Ahead Collectively: Grassroots Experiences in Latin America*, Pergamon Press, New York.

Cooperatives: Pathways to Economic, Democratic and Social Development in the Global Economy, 2007. U.S. Overseas Cooperative Development Council. (Available on line)

Weihe, Ted 2003. *Analysis of U.S. Cooperative Development Experience: Case Studies* (2003), U.S. Overseas Cooperative Development Council.

Weihe, Ted 1989. *A Guide to Debt for Development: Making the International Debt Crisis Work for Development*, U.S. Overseas Cooperative Development Council, September 1989

Weihe, Ted, 2002. *Co-op development: a tool to promote democracy, self-reliance.* Rural Cooperatives, USDA, March/April 2002

Weihe, Ted 1985, *Five Good Reasons for Cooperatives*, U.S. Overseas Cooperative Development Council

Weihe, Ted 1982. *Why Cooperative Development? Views of Some of the World's Leading Practitioners,* Cooperative Resources Committee.

Weihe, Ted 1984. *Why Cooperatives Succeed...and Fail: A Compendium of Views by International Cooperative Experts.* U.S. Overseas Cooperative Development Council.

Chapter 9: Advocate for Cooperatives

Congressional Records, April 13, 1999, September 19, 2000, October 3 & 17, 2000

Enabling Cooperative Development: Principles for Legal Reform (CLARITY – The Cooperative Law and Regulation Initiative), U.S. Overseas Cooperative Development Council, 2006.

Foreign Assistance Act of 1961 with revisions

New Directions brochure, 1979.

Report to Congress on the Implementation of the Support for Overseas Cooperative Development Act, USAID November 2001

Tribute dinner brochures hosted by U.S. Global Leadership Campaign and other materials.

Weihe, Ted 1987. *Achieving the Cooperative Promise: How to Do More with Less Foreign USAID*, U.S. Overseas Cooperative Development Council.

Weihe, Ted 1996. *Civil Discourse in a Democracy: Is it possible to disagree agreeably?*, The Voter, League of Women Voters of Minneapolis, *March 1996.*

Weihe, Ted 1988. *Congressional Strategies for Development Cooperation Initiatives*, University of Michigan, September 1988.

Weihe, Ted 1988. "With strong U.S. cooperative leadership: Congress will do more with less foreign USAID," OCDC press release

Chapter 10: Farmer to Farmer Volunteers

Correspondence with Doug Bereuter, October 26, 1990.

Land O'Lakes 2003. *Worldwide Farmer-to-Farmer Program, Final Report*, September 30, 1996 to September 29, 2003.

Truman, Harry 1980, *The* Autobiography *of Harry S. Truman*, University of Missouri Press, Columbia & London, 1980, 2002.

Weihe, Ted 2005. *A Personal History of the Farmer-to-Farmer Program*, available from author.

Chapter 11: Untold Story of Chile's Return to Democracy

Atwood, Brian 2015. *Correspondence with Ted Weihe.*

Barnes, Harry 1986-88. Various *correspondence with Ted Weihe.*

Barnes, Betsey, 2015. *About my Husband and the General.* American Diplomacy, March & April Issues.

Bereuter, Doug Hon 1986. *Democratic Society in Chile,* Congressional Record, Extension of Remarks, August 8, page E 2802

Boeninger, Edgardo, Pamela Constable, Arturo Valenzuela 1990. *Chile After Pinochet,* Journal of Democracy, Spring.

Campbell, Wallace J. 1990. *The History of Care: A Personal Account,* Praeger Press.

Chile Private Sector Cooperative Housing Guarantee Program: Interim Evaluation 1990. International Science and Technology Institute, May 1990.

Constable, Pamela, Arturo Valenzuela. 1993. *A Nation of Enemies: Chile under Pinochet.* W.W. Norton & Company.

The Democratic Revolution, 1989. Proceedings of a *Conference sponsored by the National Endowment for Democracy,* May 1 & 2.

Democracia en Chile, 1990. *Programa Oficial,* March 1990.

Jimenez, Jorge, 1990. *Correspondence with Breakdown of U.S. Child Assistance to Chile,* April 23.

Jiménez, Mónica 1995. *Participa "Lobbies" for Democracy.* Beyond Government, Extending the Public Policy Debate to Emerging Democracies, edited by Craufurd D. Goodwin and Michael Nacht, Westview Press.

Jimenez, Mónica 1989. *Mobilizing for Democracy in Chile: The Crusade for Citizen Participation and Beyond.* The Democratic Revolution, Struggles for Freedom and Pluralism in the Developing World, edited by Larry Diamond, Freedom House.

Jimenez, Mónica 2015. Correspondence especially about corrections in my draft about the General of the garrison on the night of the plebiscite.

Kennedy, Ted Hon. 1990. *Amendment on urgent care needs in Chile,* Senate S 5179, May 3.

Kennedy, Ted Hon. 1990. *Bill to further policy of the United States by providing support and assistance to the new democratic government in Chile.* S 2785, March 20.

Knickerbocker, Connie. 1990. *Pan Am's Santiago, Clipper Magazine.* Vol. 30, No.8.

La Segunda, March 13, 1990, page 17.

National Endowment for Democracy, 1989. *Presentation of Democracy Awards to Mónica Jimenez de Barros and Jacek Kuron,* May 2.

National Democratic Institute, 1988. *Chile's Transition to Democracy: The 1988 Presidential Plebiscite.*

National Security Archive, 2013. *National Security Archive Briefing Book No. 413, posted February 22, 2013,* edited by Peter Kornbluh.

Project Paper: USAID, 1990. *Private Sector Cooperative Housing II,* 513-HG-009.

Sigmund, Paul E. 1993. *The United States and Democracy in Chile,* The Johns Hopkins University Press.

Sommerhoff, Walter, 1988. *Correspondence on Housing Guarantee Ceremony, January 21.*

Summary of Truth and Reconciliation Commission Report, 1991. Chilean Human Rights Commission, Ministry of Foreign Affairs of Chile.

Weihe, Ted 1988. *Cooperatives as Agents of Democracy. Promoting Democracy: Opportunities and Issues,* edited by Ralph Goldman and William Douglas, Preager.

Weihe, Ted 1988. *Proposal to Support the Cruzada for La Participation Ciudadana: Nonpartisan Voter Education and Registration Program in Chile,* July.

Weihe, Ted 1989. *Proposal for Continuing the Voter Education Program in Chile,* March 1989.

Chapter 12: Micro-Insurance for the Poor

Co-operators General Insurance, Barbados website

HealthPartners *Uganda Health Cooperative Child Survival Annual Report* 2006-2007, October 2007.

International Cooperative and Mutual Insurance Federation/Americas website.

Sims, Jim 1989. *Hugo Log.* Excerpt from the log of Cat Ketch "Sea Fox," September 13-18, 1989.

Uganda Health Cooperative 2009. *Child Survival Annual Report,* October 25, 2009.

Osborn, Garth 2010. *HealthPartners Uganda Health Cooperative Child Survival Project, Bushenyi District, Final Evaluation Report, September 30, 2005 to September 29, 2010,* December 31, 2010.

Reinmuth, Dennis conversation; he reviewed and made corrections on my draft in the early formation of Barbados General Cooperative Insurance Company.

Weihe, Ted 2004. *Case Study: The Uganda Health Cooperative,* Land O'Lakes.

Weihe, Ted 2006. *Cooperatives: Pathways to Economic, Democratic and Social Development,* draft, May 2006.

Weihe, Ted with Patrick Roberts 1997. *Final Report Americas Association of Cooperative/Mutual Insurance Societies, April 1, 1994 – May 31, 1997.* August 8, 1997

Weihe, Ted with Karen Schwartz, and Nicole Dubois, 1997. *Impact of Group-Based Insurance Programs in Colombia, Bolivia and Guatemala.*

Weihe, Ted 1990. *Insuring Development through Popular-Based Insurance,* North American Association of International Cooperative Insurance Federation.

Weihe, Ted with Dennis Reinmuth 1992. *Mid-Term Evaluation of the International Program of the Americas Association of Cooperative/Mutual Insurance Societies,* August 1992

York, Michael 1989. *Deadly Hugo Slams Puerto Rico, Virgin Islands.* The Washington Post, September 19, 1989.

Chapter 13: Electricity for Peace & Prosperity

Harvey, Tom 1992. *Cold War's End Provided Impetus for Salvador Pact.* Sun-Sentinel, February 4, 1992.

Rowley, Storer 1989. *In El Salvador, New U.S. Approach: Local Input Part of Funded Projects,* Chicago Tribune, October 16, 1989.

Smyth, Frank 1992. *In El Salvador, Both Sides Say that New Year Pact Will End Long Civil War: Rebel leader cites importance of direct contact with U..S Ambassador,* Christian Science Monitor, January 6, 1992.

Weihe, Ted 1996. *A Final Evaluation of the El Salvador Rural Electrification Project, Bringing Light, Jobs and Peace to Rural Communities in El Salvador,* 1988-1996, March 8, 1996.

Weihe, Ted 2001. *Final Program Evaluation: Rehabilitation of Rural Electric Infrastructure Damaged by Hurricane Georges*, November 2001.

Weihe, Ted 2000. *NRECA/USDA "Electricity for Progress" Program Project Evaluation, Guatemala*, December 2000.

Chapter 14: Sudan & Yei Electric Coop

Jones, Jonathan Spencer, 2006. *Creating customers in southern Sudan*, Metering.com, East African Power and Mining Industry Convention, Dar es Salaam, Tanzania, August 24, 2006.

Sherwood, Thomas and Kirby Owen 2008. *Southern Sudan Rural Electrification Project,* Management Systems International, May 2008.

VOA News.com, Southern Sudanese Town Received Public Power Grid, October 31, 2009.

Weihe, Ted 2003. *Southern Sudan Trip Report*, U.S. Overseas Cooperative Development Council, November 24, 2003.

Chapter 15: Telephone Coops in Poland

Karski, Jan 2010. *My Report to the World: Story of a Secret State*, foreword by Madeleine Albright, revised book, original published in 1944.

Mellor, John 2009. *Measuring Cooperative Success: Poland: Cooperatives lead way to independent telecom systems better service*, U.S. Overseas Cooperative Development Council, page 22.

Mid-Term Evaluation of the Cooperative Development Program of the Office of Private and Voluntary Cooperation, Bureau for

Humanitarian Response, U.S. Agency for International Development, August 1996.

Piccini, Sara 2013. *Humanity's Hero: Jan Karski,* Georgetown Magazine.

Rok, Boleslaw & Iwona Kuraszko, 2007. *District Telephone Cooperative Tyczyn: Partnership for Local Economic Development,* UNDP.

Weihe, Ted 2003. *Cooperative Development Case Studies: WIST and Tyczn Telecommunication Cooperatives in Poland*, U.S. Overseas Cooperative Development Council.

Weihe, Ted 1992. *Mid-Term Evaluation of National Telephone Cooperative Association's Polish Telephone Cooperative Training Project*, USAID, October 1992.

Chapter 16: Market Reforms in Eastern Europe

ACVFA Recommendations on Monitoring and Evaluation, USAID, October 2, 2009.

Agricultural Cooperative/Business Development and Training for Central and Eastern Europe, Quarterly Report, Land O'Lakes, October 28, 1993.

Conversations with Jeton Starova, 2015 & two books by his uncle on national and ethnic identity in the Balkans. Luan Starova, *The Time of the Goats*, University of Wisconsin Press, 1997. Liam Starova, *My Father's Books*, University of Wisconsin Press, 2012

Freeh, La Vern "Vern", 2005. *Child of the Prairie Man of the World*, Germans from Russian Heritage Collection, North Dakota Universities Libraries, 2005.

Integrated NGO and Economic Development Project, Completion Report, March 31, 2003

Weihe, Ted, *A Twenty Year Partnership*, International Outlook, Land O'Lakes, Vol 9, No.2. 2001.

Weihe, Ted 1994. *Estonia – A Peaceful Laboratory*, Land O'Lakes International Outlook, Spring 1994.

Weihe, Ted, Lee Rosner, et al 1993. *Midpoint Evaluation of Agriculture Cooperative Development International Agribusiness Exchange Program for Central and Eastern Europe*, August 1993.

Weihe, Ted 1993. *Mid-Term Evaluation Land O'Lakes USAID-Funded Programs in Central and Eastern Europe*, Europe Bureau, September 1993.

Chapter 17: Seal of Quality in Macedonia

Enhanced competitiveness of the food production and processing industry, Seal of Quality, Land O'Lakes website, 2015.

Macedonia Agribusiness Marketing Activity, Final Report, Land O'Lakes, 2004.

MacKillop, John 2012. *Macedonia and Ukraine: Boasting Consumer Confidence in Domestic Quality,* Land O'Lakes International Outlook, Issue 1, 2012.

Unique recipes with Seal of Quality Products, Association of Meat and Dairy Processors in Macedonia, 2004.

Chapter 18: Dairy Farmers of Albania

An Assessment of the Competitiveness of the Dairy Food Chain in Albania, AgriPolicy document, European Commission, February 2009.

Albania Dairy Improvement Campaign, Final Report, 1995-2000, June 23, 2000.

Mertens, Richard, *The Cows come home in Albania Revolution*, Baltimore Sun, April 4, 1998.

Chapter 19: Cooperatives in Montenegro & Bosnia

Dairy Industry Restructuring Project in Montenegro, Final Report, Land O'Lakes, August 15, 2002.

Weihe, Ted, *Cooperatives in Conflict and Failed States*, U.S. Overseas Cooperative Development Council, June 2, 2004.

Chapter 20: Agricultural Reforms in Russia

Land O'Lakes, 1993. *Farmer-to-Farmer Special Initiative Program in the New Independent States of the Former Soviet Union*, U.S. Agency for International Development, January 28, 1993.

Land O' Lakes, 1999. *Farmer to Farmer in the NIS, September 1992-September 1999*, U.S. Agency for International Development, September 29, 1999.

Tri Valley Growers, 1994. *Farmer-to-Farmer Program, Annual Technical Progress Report, Year 2,* U.S. Agency for International Development, September 30, 1994.

Weihe, Ted 1995. *Final Evaluation, Tri Valley Growers Inc., Farmer to Farmer Program*, U.S. Agency for International Development, December 15, 1995

Weihe, Ted & Nelle Temple Brown 1992. *Grass-Roots Leaders in Russia Embrace Change*, The Christian Science Monitor, Friday, December 18, 1992

Weihe, Ted 1994. *Internal Evaluation and Implementation Workshop for Farmer-to-Farmer Program in Russia of Tri Valley Growers*, Inc. U.S. Agency for International Development, March 1994.

Chapter 21: Farming Reforms in Georgia

Weihe, Ted 1995. *Final Evaluation, Tri Valley Growers Inc., Farmer to Farmer Program*, U.S. Agency for International Development, December 15, 1995.

Chapter 22: Market Reforms in Ukraine

Communications Cooperative International 2010, *Project Profiles, Network of Business Internet Centers, Ukraine 2001-2005*.

Final Report 2003-2007. *Ukraine Agricultural Marketing Project,* Land O'Lakes & USAID, May 2007.

Ukraine Marketing Project (AMP) 2003-2007, Land O'Lakes website

Chapter 23: Sweet Retirement

Equal Exchange USAID Cooperative Agreement, AID-OAA-A-10-00024, Semi-Annual Technical Performance Report, July 2016 – December 31, 2016.

Trafford, Abigail 2004. *My Time: Sailing Home*, Washington Post, September 7, 2004

Surber, Kate 2005. *An Introduction to Fair Trade and Cooperatives: A Methodology* , U.S. Overseas Cooperative Development Council.

Weihe, Ted 2014. *Chocolate & Cooperative Equity: Reforming Small Farmer Co-ops So They Can Prosper*, e-book available on www.lulu.com

Weihe, Ted 2010. *Equal Exchange's USAID Cooperative Development Program with Small Scale Cocoa and Coffee Farmers*, U.S. Agency for International Development.

Weihe, Ted 2005. *Cooperative Fair Trade Coffee: The U.S. Experience* (Speech and Paper at COPAC in Berlin), U.S. Overseas Cooperative Development Council

Weihe, Ted 2010. *How Certifications Affect Cocoa Cooperatives*.

Weihe Ted 2012. *The Importance of Quality in Cocoa Cooperatives*.

Weihe, Ted 2014. *Two Year Enhancement, Equal Exchange's USAID Cooperative Development Program with Small Scale Cocoa and Coffee Farmers*, U.S. Agency for International Development.

Weihe, Ted 2015, *Saving Fine Chocolate: Equity, Productivity and Quality in Cocoa Co-ops*, www.lulu.com.

Weihe, Ted. *Why Member Equity is Critical to Successful Cocoa Cooperatives?* (World Cocoa Foundation, October 2013)

Conclusions

Friedman, Thomas 2016. *Impossible Missions*, The Washington Post, April 6, 2016.

Marketing and Agribusiness Management, Seminar Presentation by Partners in Economic Management Project & Sparks Companies, July 1992.

Photos: Practically all of the pictures in the book were taken by the author.

Acknowledgements

I have many colleagues with whom I worked in my successes and failures, and I am sure that I will fail to mention them all. Please forgive me.

First and foremost, I want to thank my special assistants who deserve much of the credit in my work with cooperatives: Joan Welsh, Pattie Bossany, Beth Haberstroh Leman, Beth Sheehy, Crystal Carr, Stella Kenyi, Gretchen Warner Hacquard and Lorena Shank. They did much of the OCDC work, freed me up to work overseas, and have gone on to successful careers of their own.

For Equal Exchange, I want to thank: Robert Flick (Ecuador/Peru), John Kehoe (TCHO/Guittard), Katie Gilmer (TCHO), Timothy Moley (Chocolove), Timothy Childs (TCHO), Brad Kintzer (TCHO), Barry Silver (NCB/Peru), Cristina Literati (Equal Exchange), Pat Burke, Dary Goodrich (Equal Exchange), Todd Caspersen (Equal Exchange), Aldo Reyes (Peru), Jaime Gómez (Dominican Republic), Julio Quiroz (Ecuador), Eustaquio Flores (Peru), Jose Luis Bardales (Peru), and Rob Everts (Equal Exchange). I thank the managers and staff of the cocoa coops that we worked with who made the projects successful.

For Chile, I must acknowledge the courageous leadership of Mónica Jiménez as well as Andrea Sanhueza, Walter Sommerhoff, Harry Barnes, and Lee Rosner (Chile & Romania).

I have enjoyed a special relationship with Land O'Lakes and its international staff and want to thank: Vern Freed, Vern Moore, Martha Cashman, Kristin Penn, Tom Verdoorn, Rob Nooter, Lori

Anderson, Helen Nelson, Judy Black, and Steve Krikava, among many others.

I had strong support from the National Rural Electric Cooperative Association which was my home office for 23 years: Bob Bergland, Sam Bunker, James Durnil, Vivek Talvadkar, Paul Clark, Jim Lay, Wally Rustad, and Venecia Lockhart.

In Eastern Europe and the former Soviet Union, the following chief of parties and project managers made my proposals successful: David Blood (Ukraine), Jeton Starova (Macedonia), Radosav Rosova (Montenegro), Roger Steinkamp (Montenegro), Will Bullock (Russia), Derek Brown (Russia/Bulgaria), Manuela Russeva (Bulgaria), Robert E. Lee (Ukraine), Andriy Yarmak (Ukraine), Debbie Wagner (Albania),John MacKillop (Macedonia & Bosnia), Kazimiera Jaworski (Poland),Tadeusz Slisz (Poland), Janusz Lato (Poland), and Josef Slisz (Poland).

In Palestine, I want to thank Peter Gubser (ANERA), Gordon Lindquist (CHF International), Adnan Obiedat, Wahib Tarazi, and David Davies. It was a wonderful experience getting to know the Palestinian staff on projects that I helped establish.

For rural electric projects, Myk Manon (Sudan & El Salvador) and David Kittelson (Guatemala), Jim Van Coevering (Bangladesh) and Hugo Arriago (Guatemala & Dominican Republic) as well as volunteers who work on these projects. For insurance projects, I want to thank Pat Roberts (Nationwide Insurance), Dennis Reinmuth (AAC/MIS), Carol James, Oriel Doyle (Barbados), and Karen Swartz (NCBA).

For Jamaica, I worked closely with Wes Moses.

I have been supported by outstanding USAID administrators who shared my vision for cooperatives: M. Peter McPherson, Doug

Bennett, Brian Atwood, and Andrew Natsios. I need to particularly thank Peter McPherson who introduced me to cooperatives.

The following USAID staff listened and helped me: Jean Lewis, Genta Hawkins Holmes, Kelly Kammerer, Tom Fox, Lou Stamberg, Bob Chase, Frank Mertens, Paul Bisek, John Grant, Jack Shaffer, Barbara Turner, Roger Winter, Brian D'Silva, Judy Gilmore, John Godden, Don Pressley, and Carol Lancaster. I want to especially thank Tom Carter – we have been soul mates in promoting and believing in cooperatives.

Congressmen who sponsored my legislation include: Doug Bereuter (R-NB), Floyd Fithian (D-IN), Joe Fisher (D-VA), Dante Fascell (D-FL), Ben Gilman (R-NY), Lee Hamilton (D-IN), Earl Hilliard (D-AL), Andy Maguire (D-NJ),Matt McHugh (D-NY), Dave Obey (D-WI), Senator Russ Feingold (D-WI),Senator Rod Grams (R-MN), Senator Chuck Hagel (R-NB), Senator Pat Leahy (D-VT), Senator Mac Mathias (D-MD), Senator Earl Pomeroy (D-ND), Senator John Melcher (D-MN), Senator Paul Wellstone (D-MN) and Senator Paul Simon (D-IL).

Important key Hill staff who helped me promote cooperatives: Nelle Temple Brown (House Banking), Mark Murray (House Appropriations), Terry Peel (House Appropriations), Will Painter (Senate Appropriations), Gary Bombardier (McHugh) Lewis Gulich (House Foreign Relations Committee) and Jerry Connolly (Senate Foreign Relations).

I have worked with many directors of the U.S. Overseas Cooperative Development Council and appreciate their support: Judith Hermanson (CHF International), Chris Baker and Paul Herbert (World Council of Credit Unions), Maria Kendro (Cooperative Communications International), Marlee Norton (National Telecommunications Cooperative Association), Mike Deegan (ACDI-VOCA), Paul Hazen, Morgan Williams, and Jim Cawley (National

485

Cooperative Business Associations), Don Cohen (VOCA), Susan Schram (ACDI-VOCA), and Don Thomas (ACDI).

Also, I thank cooperative development colleagues: Alex Serrano (NCBA), Don Crane (ACDI-VOCA), Antonio Gayoso (World Council of Credit Unions), Jim Phippard (ACDI-VOCA), and Judy Ziewacz (National Cooperative Business Association)

My colleagues on the USAID Advisory Committee on Voluntary Foreign Aid (ACVFA) who were special colleagues committed to a strong NGO-USAID partnership include: John Sullivan (Chamber of Commerce), Spencer King (International Executive Service Corps), William Reese (International Youth Foundation), Elise Fiber Smith (Winrock), Sam Worthington (InterAction), Noreen O'Meara (ACFVA staff), and Jocelyn Rowe (ACFVA staff).

For the floating crap game: Larry Minear (Lutheran World Relief) and Sheryl Morden (World Food Program). For Action in World Development and help with the Japanese cooperative project, I thank Frank Balance. Also, I want to thank Sharon Camp, Peter Gubser, William Douglas, Marianne Leach, Julia Taft, Sam Worthington and other colleagues in the development community.

For the creation of the U.S. Global Leadership Coalition, I appreciate the strong leadership by Liz Schrayer, Jason Gross, Craig Lasher (Population Crisis Committee), Jeff Colman (AIPAC), William Lane (Caterpillar), and George Ingram.

Mary Hynes inspired me to focus the memoirs on values that greately improved my story. I want to particularly thank Carol James who edited many of my documents and my memoir editors: Patricia Rockwood, Jan Wheeler and Judy Weihe. Judy did a masterful job in not only correcting spelling but clarifying content. She made it a better document. I would not have been able to spend so much time abroad and away from home, except for my loving and patient wife, Judy.

Made in the USA
Lexington, KY
09 January 2019